RESOLVING ORGANIZATIONAL CONFLICTS

A COURSE IN MEDIATION & SYSTEMS DESIGN

KENNETH CLOKE

JOAN GOLDSMITH

BOOKS BY KENNETH CLOKE AND JOAN GOLDSMITH

Thank God It's Monday: 14 Values We Need to Humanize the Way We Work, Irwin/McGraw Hill, 1997

Resolving Conflicts at Work: A Complete Guide for Everyone on the Job, Jossey Bass/Wiley Publishers Inc., 2000

Resolving Personal and Organizational Conflicts: Stories of Transformation and Forgiveness, Jossey Bass/Wiley Publishers Inc., 2000

The End of Management and the Rise of Organizational Democracy, Jossey Bass/Wiley Publishers Inc., 2002

The Art of Waking People Up: Cultivating Awareness and Authenticity at Work, Jossey Bass/Wiley Publishers Inc., 2003

Resolving Conflicts at Work: Eight Strategies for Everyone on the Job (Second Edition) Jossey Bass/Wiley Publishers Inc., 2005

Resolving Conflicts at Work: Ten Strategies for Everyone on the Job (Third Edition) Jossey Bass/Wiley Publishers Inc., 2011

Resolving Organizational Conflicts: A Course on Mediation and Systems Design, GoodMedia Press, 2021

Re-Designing the Way We Work: A Guide to Living with Pandemic, Climate Change, and Political Conflict, to be published 2022

BOOKS BY KENNETH CLOKE

Mediation: Revenge and the Magic of Forgiveness, Center for Dispute Resolution, Santa Monica, California, 1996

Mediating Dangerously: The Frontiers of Conflict Resolution, Jossey Bass/Wiley Publishers Inc., 2001

The Crossroads of Conflict: A Journey into the Heart of Dispute Resolution, Janis Publishers Inc., 2006

Conflict Revolution: Mediating Evil, War, Injustice and Terrorism, Janis Publishers Inc., 2008

The Dance of Opposites: Explorations in Mediation, Dialogue and Conflict Resolution Systems Design, GoodMedia Press, 2014

Conflict Revolution: Designing Preventative Systems for Chronic Social, Economic and Political Conflicts, (Second Edition) GoodMedia Press, 2015

Politics, Dialogue and the Evolution of Democracy: How to Discuss Race, Abortion, Immigration Gun Control, Climate Change, Same Sex Marriage and Other Hot Topics, GoodMedia Press, 2018

Words of Wisdom: Profound, Poignant and Provocative Quotes for Your Insight and Inspiration, GoodMedia Press, 2018

Ordinary Ecstasy: A Meditation Home Companion, Center for Dispute Resolution, 2018

The Crossroads of Conflict: A Journey into the Heart of Dispute Resolution, (Second Edition) GoodMedia Press, 2019

Mediation in a Time of Crisis: Pandemic, Prejudice, Police, and Political Polarization, GoodMedia Press, 2021

BOOKS BY JOAN GOLDSMITH

The Vietnam Curriculum (with Frinde Mayer, Adria Reich, Suzanne Thompson and Walter Popper) The New York Review of Books, 1972

Defining and Measuring Competence: New Direction for Experiential Learning, (with Paul S. Pottinger), Jossey-Bass, 1979

Picture This! Cameras and You, A Self-Developing Curriculum (with Beth Farb) Polaroid Corporation, 1984

Learning to Lead: A Workbook on Becoming a Leader, (Fourth Edition) (with Warren Bennis) Basic Books, 2010

Women Leaders at the Grassroots: 9 Stories and 9 Strategies, Joan Goldsmith, 2019

Searching for Daddy and Finding Myself, to be published by Joan Goldsmith, 2021

GoodMedia Press
An imprint of GoodMedia Communications, LLC
25 Highland Park Village, 100-810
Dallas, Texas 75205
www.goodmediapress.com

No part of this book may be reproduced or transmitted in any form or by any means, electronic or mechanical, including photocopying, recording or by any information storage and retrieval system, without written permission from the author, except for the inclusion of brief quotations in a review.

Copyright © 2021 Kenneth Cloke and Joan Goldsmith. All rights reserved.

Book cover and book layout design by GoodMedia Press.
The text in this book is set in Palatino.

Manufactured in USA

Publisher's Cataloging-in-Publication data

Names: Cloke, Kenneth, 1941-, author. | Goldsmith, Joan, author.
Title: Resolving organizational conflicts : a course in mediation & systems design / Kenneth Cloke ; Joan Goldsmith.
Description: Includes index. | Dallas, TX: GoodMedia Press, 2021.
Identifiers: LCCN: 2021950159 | ISBN: 978-1-7327046-9-5 (print) | 979-8-9852429-1-1 (ebook)
Subjects: LCSH Mediation--Handbooks, manuals, etc. | Dispute resolution (Law) Handbooks, manuals, etc. | Conflict management Handbooks, manuals, etc. | Negotiation--Handbooks, manuals, etc. | BISAC BUSINESS & ECONOMICS / Conflict Resolution & Mediation | LAW / Alternative Dispute Resolution | LAW / Arbitration, Negotiation, Mediation
Classification: LCC HM1126 .C56 2021 | DDC 303.6/9--dc23

I do not determine what is right and wrong by looking at the budget of my organization or by taking a Gallup poll of the majority opinion. Ultimately a genuine leader is not a searcher for consensus but a molder of consensus.

MARTIN LUTHER KING, JR.

The need is not really for more brains, the need is now for a gentler, a more tolerant people than those who won for us against the ice, the tiger and the bear. The hand that hefted the ax, out of some old blind allegiance to the past fondles the machine gun as lovingly. It is a habit man will have to break to survive, but the roots go very deep.

LOREN EISELEY

CONTENTS

Introduction	xi
1. Causes & Characteristics of Conflict in Organizations	1
Session 1 Lecture Slides	33
2. Systemic & Structural Sources of Chronic Organizational Conflict	53
Session 2 Lecture Slides	79
3. Leadership, Conflict & Organizational Change	93
Session 3 Lecture Slides	111
4. Organizational Culture & Conflict	129
Session 4 Lecture Slides	161
5. Mediating Organizational Conflicts	181
Session 5 Lecture Slides	207
6. Conflict Resolution Systems Design	227
Session 6 Lecture Slides	243
7. Using Dialogue, Mediation & Systems Design to Prevent and Resolve Political Conflicts	263
Session 7 Lecture Slides	287
Acknowledgments	315
About the Authors	316
Index	320

INTRODUCTION
COURSE SYLLABUS & OVERVIEW

This book is based on the lectures and accompanying materials for a course we designed and taught at Pepperdine University School of Law, Straus Institute for Dispute Resolution, in Malibu, California. The chapters consist of the lectures we gave that were videotaped, transcribed, and edited minimally for clarity and readability, but not significantly altered. Following the chapters are the slides we prepared and presented to the class in conformance with each chapter. The PowerPoint slides are available for download at www.GoodMediaPress.com/Bookstore. Use the code "ReaderGift" to access the slides at no cost. The chapters and slides follow the same outline, which is set forth in the Table of Contents, and both track the course syllabus, which is summarized and set forth in the section below. Readers are invited to use the lecture slides in their own teaching and to transfer these materials to their presentations in teaching their version of this course.

We designed this course to assist aspiring mediators and organizational leaders in developing skills in conflict resolution and systems design, and to aid those working in schools, community groups, small businesses, non-profits, corporations, labor unions, social justice organizations, government agencies, and political advocacy groups, as well as couples and families, in preventing and resolving conflicts, and reducing their costs.

These lectures and lecture slides are published together to enable you to access the course and subject matter, and provide you with a set of resources that may encourage you to share your skills and insights with others. You are welcome to use these materials however you wish; to modify, adapt, and improve them. As conflicts belong to everyone impacted by them, so also do the means of resolving, transforming, and preventing them. Each of these is a significant source of wisdom, and a common heritage for everyone. Please pass them on.

Overview and Purpose of the Course

Recently, as a result of the COVID 19 pandemic, increasing demands for greater diversity, and significant economic and political upheaval, organizations are experiencing rapid shifts and deep transformations in the nature and experience of work, and the expectations of employees, customers and society as a whole. These shifts are generating both new and systemic forms of conflict that present fresh challenges and opportunities for mediators, coaches, consultants and conflict resolvers everywhere.

Every organization and workplace generates *chronic* conflicts, and mediators are increasingly being asked to exercise skills in resolving organizational conflicts, provide conflict coaching, assist with organizational change, and analyze the systems, structures, relationships, processes, and "conflict cultures" that contribute to costly and intractable conflicts. To do so, we need to be able to show how organizational conflicts are created, escalated, and reinforced; facilitate paradoxical problem solving, consensus building, and strategic planning, sessions; develop leadership skills in responding to conflict; and design multi-layered, complex, self-correcting organizational systems that improve the capacity for conflict prevention, management, resolution, transformation and transcendence.

This course will provide practical frameworks for analyzing and mediating the emotional, interpersonal, and systemic sources of organizational conflict in public and private sector organizations, including corporations, government agencies, non-profits, work teams, and family businesses. It will assist participants in becoming organizational mediators and conflict coaches, and in developing and expanding their capacity to use facilitation, group dialogue, conflict resolution systems design, management theory, leadership and structural dynamics to resolve workplace conflicts. It will enable participants to identify preventative and transformational opportunities, and discover how to use conflicts to encourage systemic improvement, personal growth, organization learning, strategic change, emotional healing, forgiveness and transformation.

The course will deepen understanding about the origins, sources, and types of conflicts that arise within complex organizations, including corporations, partnerships, family businesses, non-profits, government institutions, schools and universities, and family and relational organizations. Course coverage will include mediating organizational conflicts, designing systems to resolve disputes and prevent them from occurring or escalating, and creating organizational cultures that encourage conflict resolution, collaboration, and creativity.

Students will participate in analyzing and creating models for responding to systemic organizational conflicts by designing preventative, interest-based conflict resolution and organizational systems. They will examine the relationship between conflict, leadership and organizational change, and the role of systems in couple and family businesses, as well as in non-profits, government institutions and social, economic and political conflicts.

Participants will learn to identify the sources of chronic conflict and the disruptions that accompany change and diversity. They will discover how facilitation, negotiation, dialogue, and similar alternative dispute resolution skills can be adapted to meet the needs of large-scale systemic change projects, as well as to common organizational conflicts. They will consider conflict as a system, the emotional and systemic sources of resistance to change, and methods for overcoming them. They will learn how to *be* the change they want to see in the world, and how to improve the way they seek to prevent, manage, resolve, transform and transcend the conflicts that impact their lives.

Course Objectives from the Syllabus

This course is designed to familiarize students with the theory and practice of conflict resolution and systems design for all organizations. Participants will learn to:

- Analyze and understand the chronic, systemic origins of organizational conflict
- Design organizational systems to prevent, ameliorate, and reduce the risks and costs of conflict
- Analyze the structures, systems, relationships, processes, and "conflict cultures" that contribute to workplace conflicts
- Develop and conduct conflict audits within their organizations
- Identify cultural obstacles to improving communication and relationships in a diverse organizational environment
- Examine leaders', managers' and employees' responses to conflict, as well as to resolution and organizational change, and apply strategies to prevent and resolve conflicts and overcome resistance to change
- Identify elements of organizational systems and structures that can optimize the prevention and resolution of conflicts and improve collaboration and creativity in the workplace
- Apply leadership theories, competencies, and styles to organizational conflicts and resolution techniques
- Understand and develop their competencies as "conflict leaders"
- Learn techniques to become more skillful in conflict coaching
- Design multi-layered, complex, self-correcting organizational systems that improve the capacity for conflict prevention, management, resolution, transformation and transcendence
- Improve their ability to mediate workplace and organizational conflict in public and private sector organizations, work teams, and family businesses

- Learn to design workplaces and organizations and identify transformational opportunities in conflict
- Discover how to use conflicts as opportunities for personal growth, organization learning, strategic change, emotional healing, forgiveness and transformation.
- Identify the conflicts that are likely to arise at each stage of a change process or systems design effort
- Improve skills in managing the stress and systemic failures typically associated with chronic conflict
- Develop skills in facilitating organizational systems design efforts through the use of consensus
- Learn methods for overcoming resistance to resolution and change, including social, economic and political change
- Design an organizational change initiative using diagnosis, strategic planning, implementation, collaborative negotiation, facilitation, coaching, conflict resolution systems design, evaluation and institutionalization

Class Outline

The course will cover the following topics, with readings specified in the next section. Homework consisted of 1-2 pages sent to everyone in the class the night before each class meeting responding to the topics listed below for each session:

Session 1: *The Causes and Characteristics of Conflict in Organizations:* the Components, Elements and Dimensions of Conflict, and Organizational Approaches to Resolution; Conflict and Organizational Evolution: Readings from *Mediating Dangerously*. *Homework*: List the most difficult and perplexing organizational conflicts you have encountered and their likely causes and common characteristics.

Session 2: *Organizational Systems, Structures, Processes and Relationships*: Systemic and Structural Sources of Chronic Conflict in Organizations: Readings from *The End of Management and the Rise of Organizational Democracy*. *Homework*: Review the systems and structures, processes and relationships in an organization with which you are familiar, identify how they contribute to conflicts, and suggest changes in them that could diminish the frequency or intensity of conflicts, or reduce their cost.

Session 3: *The Leader as Mediator and the Mediator as Leader;* Leaders and Managers; Relationship between Leadership and Conflict, Differences Between Managers and Leaders, What Can't Be Managed; Leadership, Conflict and Organizational Change: Readings from *Learning to Lead*.

Homework: Conduct a self-assessment of your competencies as a leader and a mediator, identify the leaders who have influenced your life and list five actions you will take to improve your leadership skills in preventing, managing and resolving conflict in your organization.

Session 4: *Organizational Culture and Conflict Stories*: Cross-Cultural Attitudes and Experiences of Conflict, Diversity, Race, Gender, Disability and Cultural Obstacles to Resolution and Improvement; The Narrative Structure of Conflict Stories: Readings from *The Dance of Opposites*.

Homework: Identify ways of shifting an organizational culture to support diversity, participation and strategies for conflict resolution.

Session 5: *Mediating Organizational Conflicts:* Mediating Organizational Conflicts, including Discipline and Discharge: Readings from *The Art of Waking People Up*. *Homework*: Design and outline an intervention or method that might be have been used in mediation to improve your organization's approach to a specific conflict.

Session 6: *Conflict Resolution Systems Design*: The Impact of Organizational Politics, Hierarchy and Bureaucracy on Organizational Conflicts; Strategic Planning, Team Building, Participatory Feedback, Performance Evaluation, Transformational Coaching, Strategic Mentoring, Paradoxical Problem Solving, and Designing Conflict Audits: Readings from *Resolving Conflicts at Work*. *Homework*: Outline the elements of a conflict resolution design for your organization that addresses one of the organizational systems addressed in this section.

Session 7: *Using Dialogue, Mediation and Systems Design to Prevent and Resolve Political and Social Conflicts*: Applying Interest-Based Skills, Techniques and Ideas to Resolving Social, Economic and Political Conflicts, the Neurophysiology of Conflict, the Language of Power, Rights and Interests, Bureaucracy, Political Culture and Communications, and the Uses of Dialogue. Readings from *Politics, Dialogue, and the Evolution of Democracy.*

Homework: Design a dialogue process, list questions for addressing a divisive issue that could be a source of conflict in an organization, and identify possible interventions.

Course Materials

The course is based on our research and writing in the following books. Each class will focus on readings from a different book.

1. Kenneth Cloke, *Mediating Dangerously: The Frontiers Of Conflict Resolution,* Jossey-Bass/Wiley (2001) ISBN: 0-7879-5356-3
2. Kenneth Cloke and Joan Goldsmith. *The End of Management and the Rise of Organizational Democracy,* John Wiley & Sons, Inc., (2002) ISBN: 0-7879-5912-X.
3. Joan Goldsmith and Warren Bennis . *Learning to Lead: A Workbook on Becoming a Leader,* 4th edition, Basic Books, (2010) ISBN: 978-0-465-01886-4.
4. Kenneth Cloke. *The Dance of Opposites: Explorations in Mediation, Dialogue and Conflict Resolution Systems Design,* GoodMedia Press (2013) ISBN: 978-0-9911148-0-1
5. Kenneth Cloke and Joan Goldsmith. *The Art of Waking People Up: Cultivating Awareness and Authenticity at Work,* John Wiley & Sons, Inc. (2003) ISBN: 0-7879-6380-1.
6. Kenneth Cloke and Joan Goldsmith. *Resolving Conflicts at Work: 10 Strategies for Everyone on the Job,* 3rd edition, John Wiley & Sons, Inc., (2011) ISBN: 978-0-470-92224-8.
7. Kenneth Cloke, *Politics, Dialogue and the Evolution of Democracy: How to Discuss Race, Abortion, Immigration, Gun*

Control, Climate Change, Same Sex Marriage and other Hot Topics, GoodMedia Press (2018) ISBN 978-1-7327046-0-2.

In addition, depending on the topic, the following optional books may also contain information that will be useful for the course, but are not required.

1. Kenneth Cloke and Joan Goldsmith. *Resolving Personal and Organizational Conflict: Stories Of Transformation & Forgiveness,* Jossey-Bass/Wiley (2000,) ISBN: 0-7879-5060-2
2. Kenneth Cloke, *Conflict Revolution: Designing Preventative Systems for Chronic Social, Economic and Political Conflicts* (Revised Second Edition) GoodMedia Press (2015) ISBN: 9780991114849
3. Kenneth Cloke, *The Crossroads of Conflict: A Journey Into the Heart of Dispute Resolution,* Janis Publications (2006) ISBN: 0-9734396-9-6
4. Joan Goldsmith, *Women Leaders at the Grassroots: 9 Stories and 9 Strategies,* Center for Dispute Resolution Publications, available from jgoldsm@aol.com.

Reading Assignments

We will discuss the course materials in more or less the following order:

- **Session 1:** *Mediating Dangerously,* Preface, Chapters 1, 2, 7, 8, 12, 14
- **Session 2:** *The End of Management and the Rise of Organizational Democracy,* Foreword, Introduction, Chapters 1-4, 9-15
- **Session 3:** *Learning to Lead,* Preface, Chapters 1, 2, 6, 7
- **Session 4:** *The Dance of Opposites,* Introduction, Chapters 1, 2, 8-10
- **Session 5:** *The Art of Waking People Up,* Chapters 1, 4-7, 9, 11, 12, 14

- **Session 6**: *Resolving Conflicts at Work*, Foreword, Introduction, Chapters 1-4, 7-10
- **Session 7:** *olitics, Dialogue and the Evolution of Democracy*, Chapters 1-3, 5, 8-10

Course Format

The course includes lectures, case studies, in-depth discussion, collaborative design and problem solving, teamwork, role plays, or dialogues related to the assigned topic.

Classes encourage questions and discussions. Students will be asked to reflect, analyze, and discuss topics with colleagues in the intervening times between asynchronous online lectures. They will be invited to bring issues, questions, concerns, and discussion topics to each class session. There is no final exam. Each student will write a final paper or project on a technique or aspect of conflict resolution, or a proposed systems design for an organization of his or her choosing.

Expectations

Students are expected to make "mistakes" and disagree with the professors and with each other. The focus is on learning through experimentation. Students will not be graded on their "successes" in conflict resolution, and will be expected to be open about their problems, mistakes, fears, and uncertainties, as well as their energy, passion, and creativity, their interest in learning, and willingness to offer their contributions and insights to others. Most importantly, we expect that the ideas and techniques in the course will be practiced, revised, and improved, rather than be regarded as static, eternal, or superior to experience.

A Final Word on the Scope of the Course

While the title of the course refers explicitly to organizations, much of the material in it can easily be applied to conflicts that occur in "minimal" or small-scale groups and organizations, like couples and families, as well as in "maximal" ones like communities, societies, and cultures.

Scale, of course, matters, and we are all impacted by the conflicts we experience and the relationships we form on every scale. Conflicts shape our lives as individuals, in groups and organizations, and as a *species*, and it is by facing our conflicts together that we discover their immense capacity to improve our lives, and transform our problems into solutions. We hope these volumes will guide and support you in the profound learning experience that comes from digging deeper, , and we wish you *great* conflicts!

CHAPTER 1

CAUSES & CHARACTERISTICS OF CONFLICT IN ORGANIZATIONS

The Causes and Characteristics of Conflict in Organizations (Ken)

Welcome to our course in resolving conflicts and designing preventative conflict resolution systems in organizations. This is our very first session, and we would like to welcome you and give you an overview of the causes and characteristics of conflict in organizations.

There is a lot of material in the slides, and all of the materials are designed to take you deeper into an understanding of where conflicts come from, because out of that understanding will come a series of techniques that lead to resolution, and to improving the nature and effectiveness of organizational systems that continuously generate chronic conflicts.

So let's begin with a fundamental idea, and the basic idea is that conflict exists in all organizations. You cannot go to work, you cannot produce goods or services, you cannot gather together in large groups without creating conflicts. But what exactly is an organization? We're going to be addressing this issue later in the session, but what we would like to introduce as a fundamental idea is that organizations exist on all scales.

The most fundamental and simplest level of any organization is the relationship between any two people who are connected to each other. So a couple is a kind of organization, a family is a kind of organization, and from there, we can graduate to corporations, nonprofits, and on to nation-states and even groups of nation-states.

So we would like to suggest that an organization is, in some ways, *scale-free* — that is, it is fractally organized and exists, in some form, on all scales. The question then becomes, if all these varieties of organization experience conflicts, why exactly is that? What are the sources of conflict within organizations? The very first one we want to look at comes from an understanding of the nature of organizations — that is, at a simple level, organizations are places where people work, where they engage in activity with each other.

And because they are acting in relationship to each other (without necessarily communicating what's important to them about that action, or what their role is, or what their goals are), they can come into conflict with each other. So every organization is an effort to *systematize* activity — that is, to organize work, and order people's actions and interactions, so as to reduce chaos, conflict, and waste, and produce effective outcomes.

But *how* we organize work, how we order that activity, can then becomes a source of conflict. Wendell Berry eloquently describes the alienation and ennui that characterize how many people feel about their work lives. He writes,

> More and more, we take for granted that work must be destitute of pleasure. More and more we assume that if we want to be pleased, we must wait until evening or the weekend or vacations or retirement. More and more, our farms and forests resemble our factories and offices, which in turn more and more resemble prisons — why else should we be so eager to escape them? We recognize defeated landscapes by the absence of pleasure from them. We are defeated at work because our work gives us no pleasure. Where else is our comfort but in the free, uninvolved, finally mysterious beauty

and grace of this world that we did not make that has no price? Whereas our sanity but there? Where is our pleasure but in working and resting kindly in the presence of this world?

As a result, we are confronted with two facts: first, that we take pleasure in work, in creating something that didn't exist before, in working together and collaborating, in producing something that is effective, in contributing and giving back to the world. And at the same time, we are eager to escape our workplaces at the end of the day and on the weekends, especially when we are working in conflict-ridden organizations. The question is why? What is it about the nature of our organizations and of work that deprives us of pleasure in the ways Wendell Berry describes? That is our project for this course: to figure out the sources of these conflicts, and discover through the identification of their sources the methods by which we can prevent and resolve conflicts and thereby improve our work lives.

Chronic Sources of Conflict (Ken)

Let's take a deep look at the sources of chronic and systemic conflict, and begin by saying that conflicts are of three fundamental varieties. First, there are conflicts that take place *inside* each of us; second, there are conflicts that take place *between* us; and third, there are *systemic* conflicts that arise not entirely just internally inside of us or between us, but as a result of the systems that we have created and adapted to our personal, relational, and organizational operations.

We can also think of conflicts in a separate way as having two characteristics. First, conflict can be one of a kind— that is, you face it once and it never occurs again. These conflicts are not particularly serious, and we all know how to deal with them. It is the second kind of conflict that we are mostly concerned with — those that occur over and over and over again, in other words, chronic and repeated conflicts.

Because they are occurring over and over again, the question we have to ask and look for answers to is: what is the source of the repetition? Here, we are drawn to an understanding of the nature of conflict as a *system* to understand what generates these *streams* of conflict.

Here are some important points. First, every conflict takes place not only internally and between individuals, but in a *context*; in a culture; in an environment surrounded by social, economic, and political forces; inside organizational systems, structures, technological settings; within families, nonprofits, and communities; among a diverse community of people; at a particular moment in time and history; on a stage; in a milieu, against a backdrop or setting.

Second, none of these elements is conflict-neutral. Each contributes, sometimes in veiled and unspoken yet profound ways, to the nature, intensity, duration, impact, and meaning of our conflicts. And it is the *meaning* of our conflicts that is most important to us in terms of conflict resolution, because out of that meaning emerges opportunities for transformation and transcendence.

Third, each of these chronic conflicts *profoundly* affects the quality of our work lives, our personal capacity for joy and compassion, and our ability to collaborate in solving problems. So that inside any organization, the systemic sources of conflict ripple outwards and have an impact throughout the workplace, not only with everyone in general, but with each person in particular, impacting each individual person in unique ways.

And like ripples in a pond, every conflict creates what I call a "mediation butterfly effect." The "butterfly effect" refers to the idea is that the weather is chaotic, meaning that it is "sensitively dependent on initial conditions." So much so, that a tiny little fluctuation that appears meaningless or unnoticeable can have a significant impact later on. We can therefore prove mathematically that the flapping of the wings of a butterfly in the Amazonian rainforest can give rise to a tornado in Texas months later. This is due to the innate sensitivity of chaotic systems.

Organizational systems can also become sensitive in this way, except that the object of organizational systems is to *desensitize* the organization to chaos, or eliminate it, in order to give people some sense of predictability about what's going to happen next. One of the goals of organizational systems is therefore to reduce sensitivity to the butterfly effect, and yet within conflict we discover that this arises in an interesting and important way, which we will discover more about as we proceed.

As a result, each of us can be seen as an "organizational citizen" who is responsible for creating and strengthening, encouraging and building conflict resolution capacity in our workplaces. Moreover, it isn't just up to the top leadership of the organization to address conflicts, it's up to each of us to bring a useful set of skills and an advanced set of techniques to all of our communications and interactions. But because conflict is organized as a system, a small intervention in one place can create a massive shift in another. *You* can be the butterfly in the Amazonian rainforest, or its' opposite— that is, you can cause or *prevent* that tornado in Texas several months later by how you respond to the conflicts that take place around you.

What are chronic conflicts? In our view, chronic conflicts are those that nations, societies, organizations, families, couples, or individuals have in *not* fully resolved, because if you fully resolve a conflict, it will disappear. Second, they are conflicts that we *need* to resolve in order to grow and evolve, because it is a source of pressure in the direction of growth and evolution and learning and change that creates the tension around conflict that gives it its chronic character.

Third, chronic conflicts are conflicts we are *capable* of resolving, because if we weren't capable of resolving them, we would simply give up and let them go. It is our *capacity* and the potential of resolution that create the tension that drives chronic conflicts onto center stage.

Fourth, they are conflicts that we can *only* resolve by abandoning old approaches and adopting new ones. In other words, we get into conflicts because we do the same things over and over, instead of adopting new attitudes, approaches, expectations, and intentions.

And finally, they are conflicts that we are *resistant* to resolving because we are frightened or dissatisfied or insecure or uncertain or angry, or simply unwilling to change. So we have, then, a combination of ingredients that create chronic conflicts, each which can be addressed at the level of technique.

The features of chronic conflict include repetition and low levels of resolution, they are commonly mistaken for miscommunications or personality clashes, and there is an incongruity between high levels of emotion and the apparent triviality of the issues over which people are fighting.

So in couples, for example, people often get into arguments over petty things, and there is a high level of emotion expressed in these arguments. Yet the reason for this seeming disparity between the high level of emotion and the low importance of the issue leads us to recognize that there is some other, deeper issue that is actually responsible for the high level of emotion, but which the couple has not addressed and is not discussing.

We can also notice in chronic conflicts a tolerance for disrespectful and adversarial behaviors, seeming irrationality, and accidental misunderstandings; yet, at the very bottom of these, an underlying similarity to all their conflicts. Here are four of what I think of as *meta*-sources of chronic conflict throughout thousands of years of human history: we can predict, for example, that there will be chronic conflicts whenever there is *social inequality*; whenever there is *economic inequity*; whenever there is *political autocracy*; and when there is *environmental degradation*.

People are trying to earn a living, for example, right now in East Africa, in Kenya, in Nigeria, in Somalia, in Sudan, yet global warming and climate change are producing a number of impacts on their ability to do so. There is a drought, which has lasted several years in many of these areas that is disrupting communities and creating chronic conflicts.

We operate in organizations in the United States, and most places around the world — in very different ways, of course — under the economic system of capitalism. And once we recognize that capitalism is a *system*, we will realize that, like all systems, it is the source of a number of chronic conflicts that are a part of its innermost nature. Here are a few of them: In capitalist systems, for example, there is intense competition for market dominance; unceasing efforts to maximize sales and profits; a primacy of the financial bottom line; constant innovation and technology; dependence of profits on costs of production, especially wages, rents, taxes, and raw materials; and an unequal distribution of profits.

We can then see that each of these sources of chronic dysfunction creates conflicts in society, economics, and politics; as well as in organizations, particularly economic organizations such as corporations that are in intense competition with each other, and these will have impacts within the organization.

In many organizations there are, for example, labor management conflicts, and these produce a number of chronic conflicts in labor management relations. For example, governments commonly pass legislation that does not reflect workplace realities; there is financing that is not within the parties' control; and political elections that periodically alter attitudes toward labor management relations; or there are assumptions that it is the primary responsibility of management to care for fiscal well-being, and of unions or labor to care for the well-being of workers, giving rise to adversarial styles of negotiation and problem-solving. We can see that each of these, again, becomes a source of chronic conflict within the workplace and in organizations.

We therefore need to improve our understanding of the relationship between the deeper nature of the organization, the environment in which it works, the processes it uses to operate, the relationships it generates inside of it, and as a result, the integrated whole these form that produces chronic sources of conflict, which in turn lead to classic conflict responses, such as avoidance, accommodation, aggression, and compromise.

But when we discover where these chronic conflicts come from, and what's useful about each of them, we can get to a place of higher order skills in our relationships with one another inside our organizations. And we can describe those higher order skills as collaboration.

Examples of Chronic Conflict (Joan)

Those of us working in conflict resolution, whether in families, large corporations, government agencies, or non-profit organizations, relate to people and power, and behave in different roles and styles. When we shift our behaviors towards conflict, and towards power, we become leaders who create environments that can shift dramatically, and help people feel more satisfied in their work, more comfortable in their families, and able to be creative and innovative, and make a true difference in their lives.

Conflict issues generated by people in power can trigger behaviors that are counterproductive. Ken and I were working with the director of one of the largest divisions of County government a while ago, and he was getting a lot of resistance from his twenty-five direct reports and hundreds of people working in the organization. He couldn't get his ideas across about strategies for deploying information systems throughout the County, and since this was his agenda, he felt stymied because the people who worked for him didn't understand what he was trying to accomplish.

We interviewed people in the organization, and showed him a list of behaviors everyone said he had engaged in. We then asked him to identify his own behaviors that he felt were counterproductive, or intimidating, or were causing conflicts with his direct reports and the staff that worked with them. To his credit, he wrote this memo to his direct reports:

> I request that you share my memo to you with the people who work for you: This is how I need you to communicate with me. I'm a technology person, I'm an IT tech guy, and I need you to give me lists of what you need and what you want. I need you to spell out the specifics. I need you to tell me what kind of commitments you need from me, and what you want to get from the people who work for

you. I want them to tell you the kind of commitments that they need from you in order to do their job.

He also indicated he wanted his direct reports to understand what dependencies they felt toward him, and how he could cut them loose to solve their own problems. He asked what he could say or do in his daily staff meetings with them, how he could empower them to be more creative, to take action, and to avoid seeing him or the people they worked with as the enemy.

He finalized it by saying *"I give you the opportunity to offer me options in writing, and then I will do the same for you."* His actions transformed not only his department within the IT division, but enabled them to empower the leaders of the other County Departments to be directly accessible to others in the County for answers, responses, and improved relations. That came out of this director of IT taking very seriously what he needed to do to change his behavior as a leader.

I want to give you one more example, because we worked with a man who was the CFO of a very large, well-known entertainment company. He was trying to organize his division into self-directed and self-managed teams because his boss, the head of the whole company, wanted the Finance Division to do so. He started organizing teams, and was told that in order for the teams to work, he was going to have to stop yelling at everyone. He frequently raised his voice, would stand up in meetings, point at participants, and complain that they were controlling — yet he was the one controlling their options, discovering their thumbscrews, and turning the screws.

We suggested that we act as mediators and facilitate a meeting between him and his direct reports, and the entire leadership team, who were all vice presidents of the Finance Division. We suggested videotaping the meeting and brought in a video technician to record the meeting and play it back to the participants for their review and feedback.

In the meeting, the CFO stood up and started yelling at the team members, shouting at them "I don't yell!" He was keeping people dependent on him, and attacking, or crushing them by yelling. When we replayed the video, he started crying in front of his direct reports. He shifted from being a toxic leader to being a real person, and said, "I see my father on this video. That's how my father was in our family. He was always yelling and controlling us."

I use this example because he did change his behavior, and instead of just saying, "my door is always open, you can come and talk to me anytime," he started walking around and visiting people where they worked, sitting down with them and asking them how he could help them, how he could behave differently. And this grew out of his seeing the toxic behavior he had learned from his father.

I'm not suggesting that you be a psychoanalyst, I'm suggesting that as you are coaching or consulting, you work with them to see where they learned their behaviors and why they adopted these behaviors, because we often bring behaviors we learned as children or young professionals into the workplace.

Another example concerns a man who left a position as head of product development at a large bank in Chicago, to work for an oil company in New England, where he was also head of product development. He had about 30 people on staff whom he hoped would be creative in developing new products, but they were so afraid of him that they were resistant, to creating products, and were failing in the market.

We suggested that he invite all the staff to have dinner with him. After dinner, we proposed that he honestly evaluate himself as a leader and ask them to give him equally honest feedback on how well he was doing. Well, that session went past midnight, and to his credit, he was willing to listen to the feedback he was getting and saw that the problem of keeping people frightened and dependent on him was blocking them from being creative.

They told him he was concealing his intentions, and he talked honestly and openly about how he felt he had failed at his last job, but had a big stake in their being creative, and hoped they'd challenge their limits, and step outside the "nine dots" of their expectations. He promised he would be open to hearing new ideas. That session completely shifted his attitude toward his staff and his behavior as a leader.

I want to share one more piece of information that comes from the work of Douglas McGregor, whose work some of you may know. Doug McGregor was part of a group of people who came to the Massachusetts Institute of Technology during and at the end of World War II. A wonderful historian who has since passed away, Tony Judt, wrote that we can trace much of what has been going on in the last 40 or 50 years, and what will be going to be going on in the next 20 or 30 years, to World War II and the postwar era.

During this time, a group of people came to MIT, to escape fascism in Germany, Italy, and other parts of the world. The group was brought together by a social scientist named Kurt Lewin, who recruited McGregor, Peter Drucker, and the philosopher Theodore Adorno and his wife Gretel to conduct significant studies of the Authoritarian Personality.

McGregor had been President of Antioch College and there was a myth at the college that McGregor invited faculty and students and staff to his living room and play the piano and sing with them and then invited them to form an administrative council to run the college. McGregor wrote:

> Out of all of this has come the first clear recognition of an inescapable fact. We cannot successfully force people to work for management's objectives. The ancient conception that people do the work of the world only if they're forced to do so by threats or intimidation or by the camouflaged authoritarian methods of "paternalism—" that is, I'm the papa or I'm the mama and I know what's best for you. You keep your mouth shut. That paternalism in organizations has been suffering from a lingering, fatal illness for a quarter of a century. I'd venture to guess it will be dead in another decade.

Well, McGregor was an optimist, and it's taken much longer, as paternalism and authoritarianism are alive and well. You may know of McGregor's work describing contrasting approaches to leadership. He defined *Theory X*, in which managers believe that people are not motivated by carrots, they're motivated by sticks — they've got to be threatened, they've got to be fearful, they've got to follow the rules.

He also identified *Theory Y*, which argues that people are motivated by feelings of self-worth, making their own decisions, and improving their circumstances; by their desire to contribute. McGregor's work and the work of other leaders at MIT gave us the foundations for mediation. Mediation is a way, a method, a tool for people to resolve their own conflicts, to come to their own understandings of what they need to do to be more successful at communicating, working as part of a team, resolving their conflicts, and supporting others in doing what they need to do.

Sometimes, when I am working with groups of mediators, I will say, "raise your hand if you settled a dispute last week," and almost every hand goes up. Then I say, "keep your hand up if you settled more than one dispute last month," and many hands go up. Then I say, "No, if you did your work as a mediator or as a leader, the kind of leader McGregor identified, the kind of leader we are advocating, you didn't settle anything. You enabled the people who were in conflict, or you enabled the employees, or the people that report to you to resolve their conflicts, or recognize their skills and talents, or be creative. So look at how willing are you to be a leader who enables others to find their own answers and create their own successes.

Ten Philosophical Propositions and Alternative Definitions of Conflict (Ken)

Our focus of this course is on conflict, so we need to begin by trying to understand what conflict actually is. In order to understand what it is, we first have to take a bit of a dive into philosophy, not on a deep level, but enough to understand what allows us to *think* about conflict, and some of the limits on whatever our ideas of conflict may be.

So here are a few philosophical propositions: Proposition 1: no two human beings are the same. Everyone is different. As a result of these differences, what conflict means, and what is going to work for one person, isn't necessarily going to be true or work for another.

Proposition 2: no single person is the same from one moment to the next. Therefore, whatever you decide to do that works at 10:05 is not necessarily going to work at 10:10. The individual human beings you're working with are constantly changing, and the nature of their conflict is also constantly changing. It's not fixed. It is a work in progress.

Proposition 3: all interactions and relationships between people are complex, multi-determined, subtle, and inherently unpredictable, and conflict is especially complex. By combining these three philosophical propositions, it is clear that we cannot completely define either conflict or conflict resolution. We can't know exactly, or in advance, what we're going to do in response to any particular conflict, because the people are constantly changing and different from one another, everybody is different from moment to moment, and their conflict is constantly changing,.

For this reason, conflict resolution is always an exploration. It's a discovery. It's an inquiry. It's not an answer. And as a result of these philosophical propositions, we can go a little further and recognize that I can't tell you how to resolve a conflict, and you can't tell me how to resolve a conflict. And whatever either of us does may work for one person and not work for someone else.

This means we have to discover what is going to work in each new conversation at each moment. We have to show up for that conversation, and interrogate the conflict through questions, in order to find out what is actually taking place right now beneath the surface.

Now, having mentioned these three philosophical propositions, I would like to mention three more that are their exact opposites. Counter-proposition number 1: yes, no two human beings are alike, yet on some level, we are all remarkably similar. Counter-proposition 2: yes, no single human being is the same from moment to moment, yet there is something continuous in our lives that makes us the same people today as we were two days ago, or 10 years ago. Counter-proposition 3: yes, conflict is complex and multi-determined. All our relationships and communications are complex, subtle, intricate, and unpredictable. And, at the same time, we can understand that there is something simple, clear, and predictable about these relationships and communications, and something about the nature of conflict that is continuous across all these lines.

So now we have two fundamental truths, the truth that nothing can be fixed or known in advance; that we don't have anything, really, to completely rely on, in terms of the work that we do with people in conflict. And secondly, the truth that we can accumulate experiences. We can develop skills. We can increase our knowledge and understanding of what is taking place beneath the surface. And this goes for virtually all of the philosophical propositions that are mentioned in the slides. Every one of them offers opportunities to evolve to higher levels of skill and awareness in how we respond to our opponents and our problems.

More profoundly, as a result, we can recognize that conflict is a rich source of improvement, learning, and wisdom. Conflict resolution is actually a *wisdom tradition*, both for individuals and for organizations and systems. What this means is that, instead of approaching conflict as a chaotic, dangerous, unpredictable battle in which things are scary and damaging, we can instead look at it as an adventure, in which, yes, painful things happen, *especially* if we do not learn or evolve and remain at the same level of skill and understanding that created the conflict to begin with.

But if we are prepared to learn from our conflicts, to learn from each other, to discover what inside of us, and what inside of the other person has led to this conflict, then we can turn it in a different direction. How do we do that? Here is the essential point: at the center of every conflict lies its "heart." That is, heart, meaning not only center, but a place of deep caring — about outcomes, about each other, about what we are doing, and about why we are doing it.

So there is not only a set of issues we need to address in order to resolve a conflict. Underneath this, the *meaning* of our conflict is important to each of us, and we need to develop the methodologies, the techniques, the processes that reveal their meanings, and the hidden drivers of our conflicts.

Let's think for a moment now about how we define conflict, and there are thousands of definitions that are possible. The dictionary definitions are probably the most trivial and least useful. What I would like to offer instead is a set of *alternative* definitions that represent the experience of working with conflict on a regular basis.

These alternative definitions are somewhat poetic. They are not designed to be precisely scientific or mathematical. But out of this poetry will come, hopefully, some insight into what is happening beneath the surface.

First, we can define conflict as representing a lack of awareness of the imminence of death or sudden catastrophe. What does this mean? It means that, if you are in conflict with someone and all of a sudden, \ you discover that you are about to die, or that they are, or that some catastrophe is about to take place, what will happen to your conflict? And the answer is, it will begin to disappear.

So what was your conflict to begin with? Well, here's another possible definition: it was a set of misplaced priorities. And if we can consider the human beings on both sides in first place, as a priority; if we can understand what is important to them and why it is important to them, we will be able to develop a set of skills that can reduce the intensity and seriousness and cost of that conflict.

Here is another alternative definition: conflict is a lack of acceptance of ourselves that we have projected onto others, a way of blaming someone else for what we perceive as the failures in our own lives and diverting attention from our mistakes. Do you know anyone who has done this? Have you ever done it yourself? It's very common to see this among children. But it's also very common to find it in the workplace. Conflict becomes a kind of camouflage, a smokescreen to divert attention from our mistakes.

Here is another definition: conflict represents a boundary violation, a failure to value or recognize our own integrity and, therefore, the personal space of others. So one element in conflict resolution is the creation of real, genuine, effective boundaries between people, together with an understanding of the permissions required to cross those boundaries.

Conflict can also be defined simply a lack of skill or experience at being able to handle a particular kind of behavior. There are some people who can handle nearly every kind of human behavior, or one kind or another, but not all kinds. And the ability to handle that behavior transforms conflict into a disagreement that can be resolved effectively, or into a problem that can be solved. But if we lack the skill or experience at being able to handle it, we will have a deep, emotional response to that behavior, or blame others for what happened, and that will trigger and continue the conflict.

Here is another definition: conflict is the continued pursuit of our own false expectations, the desire to hold on to our unrealistic fantasies. Everyone in the workplace has a set of expectations about how they are going to be treated. In every organization, there are expectations of the CEO, the COO, human resources, managers, coworkers, and of ourselves. And most of these expectations are not communicated. They exist beneath the surface, and emerge only when we discover that they aren't being satisfied. Yet we have never really have open conversations with each other about what those expectations are.

The same is true in families and couples. People have expectations of each other that they do not communicate. Why don't they communicate them? Because they're too important. Because they matter so much. Because we want them so badly. And here is another definition: conflict is a result of what is *not* communicated, of secrets, confusions, and cover-ups — sometimes about why we have these expectations.

Here is a useful definition, particularly for organizations: conflict is the *sound* made by the cracks in a system. Every system has cracks. And as songwriter Leonard Cohen, wrote, "there's a crack in everything, that's how the light gets in." And in systems, the cracks are an opening for improvement. That is, cracks appear when there is something that is not working inside an organization, something that could be fixed or made to work better, so *every* conflict is simply a way the organization can learn to operate better.

Here's another definition:. conflict is a place where there are two or more truths, where there is a paradox, an enigma, a contradiction, where two things are true simultaneously. And those two things can be contradictory, as in quantum mechanics, where an elementary particle can be both a particle and a wave at the same time, even though these are contradictory states.

We can then see another definition: that conflict is simply the voice of a new paradigm, a new way of operating, a call for change in a system that has outlived its usefulness.

Here I'm going to introduce an idea that we will come back to later. The idea is essentially this: in every system, there is a level of organization at which that system is operating. In order to evolve to a higher order of organization, the old system has to become disorganized. That is, it has to dissolve, in order to transition to a new, higher order system.

As a result, every advance, every step forward, every manifestation of progress is two things simultaneously. On the one hand, it is a step forward. But on the other hand, in order to take that step forward, it is necessary to leave the step you were on before. And the leaving of that step, the dissolving of that step, is often experienced as conflict.

So if we think of conflict as the voice of the new paradigm, we will begin searching in every conflict for what in the system most needs to change. What is it that has outlived its usefulness? What could we do better? Conflict, in this sense, is simply something that isn't working for someone that could work better.

Conflict can also be defined as an inability to say goodbye, a refusal to let go of something that is dead or dying. This can be a set of false expectations. It can be a dying relationship. It can be an attitude towards one's self. It can be a kind of security that we needed at a lower level of functioning, in preparation for the dangerous shift to going out and trying to function at a higher level.

We can also define conflict as a way of being negatively intimate when positive intimacy has become impossible. I think we have all seen this. People create conflicts in order to be in contact with each other, to be in relationship, to create a sense of intimacy with each other. What's better than negative intimacy, of course, is positive intimacy. But when positive intimacy becomes impossible, we would rather have negative intimacy than no intimacy at all. And every child on the planet knows that it is better to be yelled at than not to be noticed at all.

Conflict can also be defined as the antagonistic voice of half of a paradox, enigma, duality, polarity, or contradiction. It is taking something that has two correct answers and reducing them to one, then turning that one correct answer against the other correct answer in order to dominate or suppress it.

So what we need to do in conflict resolution is create paradoxical solutions for paradoxical problems. That is, solutions that have two or more correct answers. So, for example, if I ask you right now, what is the square root of 16? You're going to tell me that the answer is 4. But there's a second correct answer— minus 4. There are two correct answers to every square root in a quadratic equation, something that has an x squared in it. And if it is x cubed, a cubic equation, there are potentially three correct answers; x quartic, four correct answers; x quantic, five correct answers. How many correct answers there are to a question is an important element in turning conflict into a search for potentially viable solutions. And in organizations, it is commonplace to run into contradictions for which there are multiple correct answers.

Conflict can also be defined as a superficial interpretation of difference, diversity, and opposition. We have increasing diversity in the world, and what we need to do is to recognize that diversity as a gift and a challenge, and not as something that undermines our ability to succeed and solve problems, but in fact increases it.

For this reason, we can also define conflict as not just an opportunity, but a request — a request for authenticity, for emotional honesty, acknowledgment, intimacy, empathy, communication, understanding, growth, learning. In other words, a request for improved communication and a better relationship.

The Components of Conflict: Techniques for Each Location of Conflict (Ken)

Having taken a look at the importance of conflict in organizations, looked at some statistics and research on what happens at work, understood some of the practical sources of conflict for people working inside organizations, considered the philosophical propositions that determine how deep our understanding of conflict resolution can go, and looked at some alternative definitions of conflict, we now want to turn our focus inward to deepen our understanding of the elements of conflict, including the components, pieces, parts, and locations of conflict inside each of us, so we can have a better understanding of exactly how it gets triggered.

By isolating each component and location of conflict, we can identify a methodology or technique that will allow us to dismantle the conflict in that component or location. So let's ask a different kind of question to begin this process: Let's assume that we wanted to cook up a conflict on purpose. What is our recipe? What are the elementary ingredients that we would require in order to create a conflict?

If we think of it as a recipe, what are the very first things as ingredients that we would require in order to create a conflict, at its most basic level? And I think we would have to say that the most fundamental requirement for any conflict is that there be *two or more*. This can mean two or more individual people, or two or more sides of the same person.

The reason is quite simple: without two, there is no conflict. But the implication is profound. We all understand the phrase, "It takes two to tango." What we don't realize is that there is a hidden corollary: *it takes one to stop the tango*. And that one could be you.

So now we can ask the question, what is a methodology that we can use for turning two into one? Well, if we imagine a conflict between two kids on a school playground, if you were present, and saw two kids having a conflict, what is the very first thing that you would want to do? Probably your answer is to separate them. Separation is a technique or, if you will, an *operation* that we perform on a conflict that takes two and separates them so that there's only one. And without the second, it is quite difficult to hold onto the conflict or escalate it. The kids begin to calm down because they haven't got someone *outside* them stoking the conflict *inside* them.

Also, if there are two or more, there are going to be diverse interests, and with them, the possibility of misunderstanding, disagreement, distrust, and competition. What then is needed? Nearly always, it is communication, openness, collaboration, and mutual recognition of common interests, values or goals. But here is the difficulty: If two kids are fighting on a playground, separating them will help them stop fighting and de-escalate, but separation won't improve their communication. It's just going to calm them down and prevent renewed escalation of the conflict, which will make it possible for them to come together and communicate constructively.

Caucusing, in conflict resolution, is the same as separating the kids on the playground. All it does is stop the fighting and potentially de-escalate it, and that's about the best they are going to get, because it can't take them any further, because they are separated.

In order for the resolution of the conflict to proceed to a higher level, a new component and a new set of techniques are needed. Here is the transition question that gets us to this new element in our recipe: Can you have two or more people and not have a conflict? The answer is yes, and therefore, there must be another ingredient in the recipe. We haven't cooked up a conflict just by having two. We have to have something else. What is the second ingredient? It is the answer to a follow-up question: What do the two or more have to *do* to create a conflict? What has to happen between them in order for a conflict to arise? The answer is, they have to disagree, perhaps over the content of some issue, or a process, or relationship, or outcomes, whatever it might be.

We can consider the first component, two or more people, to be a *physical* description of the conflict, and the act of separating the kids on the playground to be a physical intervention. This means approaching the conflict in its physical location, in a physical dimension, using physical techniques. But a disagreement is not physical. It's *mental*. It has to do with some issue, some unresolved difference, perhaps over facts, or competing issues, or solutions that are personal to one person, but not the other.

So if there is a physical location for the conflict, which we experience inside our bodies physically, are there other physical things that we might do to impact the conflict? The answer is, yes, we can shift the physical space, including the amount of distance between us. We can soften our tone of voice and speak more slowly. We can use touch. We can do a variety of physical things, including using body language, to communicate to the other person how we feel.

And now, if we look at conflict in its mental location, what is missing? What's needed? What is wanted? The answer, I believe, is some kind of communication and engagement between the parties, which moves from separating the kids on the playground to doing is the exact opposite and bringing them together.

The purpose of separating the kids is to calm them down enough so that the physical part of the conflict is not predominant or controlling, which then allows them to move on to discuss their disagreement over the issues that are in conflict. How do they do that? They can, for example, analyze the issues logically. They can seek advice or other perspectives on the problem. They can discuss their common interests, or use brainstorming, collaborative negotiation, creative problem solving, and dialogue. They can identify criteria and possible solutions, or adopt a number of techniques that would have been useless when they were separated.

If the likely outcome of the physical component, or physical intervention, is stopping the fighting and de-escalation, the likely outcome of the mental component, or mental intervention, is settling the issues. We can then return to our basic, operative question: Can you have two or more people and a disagreement and *not* have a conflict? Again, the answer is yes, which means there must be a third element in order to cook up a conflict.

We have a physical element, and we have a mental one, so what's left? The answer is that there must be an *emotional* component that turns a disagreement into a conflict. In other words, *every* conflict, without exception, that is more than just a disagreement, has an emotional component.

So how good are we at understanding and responding to intense negative emotions? Fear, anger jealousy shame, guilt, grief, these are some of the feelings that can arise between people who have a disagreement, that then solidify or are reinforced, turning their disagreement into a conflict.

This can happen as a result of unexpressed or hostile emotions, incomplete or inadequate compassion, or an inability to let go. What we need is some kind of emotional closure, typically through introspection, acknowledgment, venting, or empathy. What mediators do with intense negative emotions is first to acknowledge and help people process them. The question is: what do you get if you successfully process emotions and help people work their way through them? The answer is: you *resolve* the underlying reasons that gave rise to the conflict, that will continue to generate new conflicts until it's resolved.

Consider, for example, a sibling conflict, in which the first sibling says, "she got more than I did" of a piece of cake, you can settle that conflict by taking smaller slivers off the larger slice of cake and adjusting the portions until everyone feels they are equal. But as soon as you've settled that issue, they are going to move on to another conflict because the underlying emotional issues between them have not been addressed or resolved. Sibling rivalry will generate fresh disputes *chronically*, simply because the siblings have not had an opportunity to talk to each other at a deep, emotionally satisfying level.

With this third component, we can say that we now have enough to cook up a conflict. If there are two or more people with a disagreement experiencing negative emotions, there is enough to create a conflict. But let's take a look at what happens in the workplace with each of these ingredients.

Separating people in the workplace is very common. It is usually the first step most managers take when responding to conflict. Separate Mary and Fred, by putting Mary over here, and Fred over there, and tell them to just not talk to each other. That's a common managerial solution, but it won't get them to level two.

Assuming there is enlightened leadership, or that mediation has come into the workplace, a manager may be able to create a conversation between Mary and Fred that addresses their issues and comes up with a solution. But what is the attitude of most organizations towards intense negative emotions? How are they handled? What is the level of skill at being able to handle them?

The answer is that the level of skill is nearly zero. And if you ask, what advice is given to people who are experiencing intense negative emotions at work, the answer is commonly to just shut them down, take your emotions somewhere else, don't express them, suppress them. But what happens to *you* if someone tells you to shut down your emotions, or just suppress them?

The answer is that your emotions don't go away, but if anything, intensify because you've now added a new element of disrespect, disregard, not caring, and possibly fear and anger over the way you've been treated. As a result, what will happen is that the emotion and the conflict will remain unresolved, because most managers don't know how to initiate or facilitate an emotionally intelligent conversation.

Some managers do. But managers as a *class*, as a group, are not often trained in how to work with emotional issues. Increasingly, management schools are recognizing the importance of emotional intelligence in leadership and management skills. But we still have a long way to go before it is practiced in the workplace in a widespread and skillful way.

As a result, what organizations require is a group of people who *have* these skills. These are sometimes Human Resources (HR), and sometimes they are in-house peer, or outside professional mediators. But the difficulty with using HR in these conversations is that they are part of the hierarchy of the organization, and there are limited possibilities for them to engage in emotional acknowledgment, venting, caucusing, etc. — partly because of confidentiality, and partly because they are simultaneously responsible for representing the organization and protecting it.

Back to our recipe. While the first three ingredients give us enough to start a conflict, there are three more, and these additional three levels, or components of conflict, are essential to understanding the range of methodologies that are applicable in organizations.

So we now have physical, mental, and emotional components —.what's left? I think the answer is *spiritual*, and here, we have to redefine "spiritual," which ordinarily implies "religious," but that is not what we mean. Instead, we are referring to the *quality of life energy* you invest in your conflicts. Or, I can put it in slightly different terms, it is the *memory* of what happened to you and the inability to *let go* of that memory. It is a spirit of antagonism, a lack of sensitivity to others, even to parts of ourselves. It is a kind of intolerance.

If we think of it as the memory of what happened to us, we take a long time to forget, and holding on to those memories has serious consequences in terms of our life energy, because we dedicate part of our life energy to something that is *over*, and give it to someone who no longer deserves it. So if we are holding on to a conflict, we want to find out how to let go of it. Forgiveness is in fact a methodology for letting go, which we will discuss later in more detail.

Here is the next difficulty. You can experience a conflict, stop the fighting, settle the issues, resolve the underlying emotional issues, and forgive someone, yet every time you see them, a little knife goes right through your heart. Or, to put it differently, in couples, you can forgive your partner, yet your heart remains closed to them.

Indeed, the very first thing that happens when we experience conflict with another person, defensively, inside of us, is that a little gate comes down to protect our hearts. And the last thing we do in conflict is re-open our hearts to the other person. But how exactly do we do that? And what do we call the outcome? We call it reconciliation, which happens when we care about the other person and are no longer stuck in the conflict.

Children do this routinely. It becomes harder when we get older, and is very difficult in organizations. Our methodologies for separating people are quite good. Our methodologies for settling the issues are pretty effective, but not adequate. But when we get to the emotional, spiritual, and heart locations where conflict is organized, we have a far more difficult task, and our level of skill is correspondingly lower. We are less likely to face those issues, but at the same time, they are present in miniature in every conflict.

Even at a level of children on a playground, there is still a closed-heartedness between them that somehow needs to be addressed. And it can be addressed between children relatively easily, and they can become best friends by opening their hearts to each other after fighting. With adults it's more difficult, yet we are going to be looking at how to do this inside organizations.

There is a final element or component of conflict. After we have stopped the fighting, settled the issues, resolved the underlying reasons that gave rise to the issue, reached forgiveness, achieved reconciliation, and opened our heart again to the other person, what's left? The answer is that we have missed something incredibly important, which is this: Every conflict takes place within a *context*, a culture, an environment, a system. And we need to transform that system to prevent the system from routinely producing *chronic* conflicts that we have mistakenly personalized and treated as personality issues when, in fact, they were systemic all along.

And what are these systemic issues inside organizations? They are the adversarial, bureaucratic, hierarchical, antagonistic, competitive systems that treat others as the enemy. These systems arise out of the ways we organize, the context of our work, and the culture and environment in which we act. So we need to look for ways of improving the environment and culture of work, or "working conditions," if you will, and we do this using the preventative methodology of conflict resolution systems design.

The Crossroads of Conflict: Dimensions and Styles (Ken)

Now that we have described the components of conflict and the locations of conflict, let's take a deeper look at what is taking place beneath the surface, and the *meaning* of conflict to each of us.

I think of this as *the crossroads of conflict*. I'd like to describe it this way: There are two groups of people who do *not* experience conflicts. First, there are no three-year-olds who experience conflicts over romantic love. Why? Because they are not ready yet. It's not a problem for them. They don't experience it as a conflict that is personal to them. Second, there are no 60-year-olds who experience conflicts over curfew with their parents (we hope). Why? Because they should already have solved this problem.

So who, then, gets conflicts? I believe that the answer is defined by a *crossroads* that is created, on the one hand, by a problem we are now required to solve; and, on the other, by the fact that we do not yet have all the skills we need in order to solve it.

In other words, throughout our lives, there is an *evolution* in the conflicts we experience. We begin experiencing conflicts as babies, over whether our needs are going to get met. But, for example, if we take two babies and place them side-by-side, and give them a toy, they will engage in what is called "parallel play." They will play side by side, but not with each other. If one baby takes the toy, the other baby hardly notices. There is little or no conflict in parallel play over the removal of the toy.

But at a certain point, the babies will notice each other and want to begin playing with each other, at which point they will begin to experience relational play, play with each other, or "collaborative play." And all the conflicts that take place between them will take place in the transition between these stages, as they acquire skills in being able to handle their differences and build a relationship.

So if one baby takes the other baby's toy, what do they do about it? Do they bite? Scream? Kick? Punch? What did you do? Well, what we have to do is learn a new set of skills that consist of asking the other baby to pass the toy back, and that way they will be able to play with each other.

All the conflicts we experience in life begin at lower levels of skill, as ways of helping us transition to higher levels of skill, that consist, essentially, of conflict resolution techniques — techniques in how to communicate, how to negotiate for what we want. And therefore, every one of our conflicts simply reflects a lack of skill in connection with a problem that we are now required to solve. When we see this, we start to look at our conflicts differently.

The same is true for organizations. Organizations also have crossroads of conflict. Here are some crossroads we face in conflict. Initially, as individuals, but we can also think of them as having an organizational reflection. First, whether to engage in the conflict and behave badly, or calm down and try to talk about it. That's a very common crossroads we face, but as we grow older, we get better and better at not behaving badly in our conflicts. Second, whether to acknowledge the other person's truth or deny it, remain rooted in our own story, and slip into biased or delusional thinking. Third, whether to experience negative, intense emotions and feelings, or repress and sublimate them, let them come out somewhere else, someplace that makes you look crazy. And as we become better at experiencing and responding to negative emotions and develop emotional intelligence, these conflicts move into the past. It's not so much that we resolve them; instead, we never experience them again, because we have learned how to handle them skillfully.

A fourth crossroads is whether to experience our opponent as an equal human being who is entitled to respect, or demonize him or her and victimize ourselves. A fifth is whether to aggressively assert and hold tight to our position, or search for solutions that satisfy both sets of interests. A sixth is whether to forgive, reconcile, and reintegrate with our opponent, or remain isolated and wounded deep inside. A seventh is whether to open our hearts to the other person again.

If we look at organizations, we can consider conflict in terms of the skills that are required in connection with power, because organizations are places where power is concentrated. But there is a relationship between power, forms of justice, and forms of decision-making. So we may have power against, power over, power through, or power with. And these correspond to different forms of decision making. If it's power against, decision-making is likely to take the form of an announcement of the decision. It will take the form of dictation. But as we proceed in a more collaborative direction, it requires more time and energy in order to get there, and will produce a greater level of unity.

Notice also that there is a shift in the kind of *justice* that we perceive as emanating from different forms of power. We think of this as a third *dimension*, moving from a revengeful or retributive forms of justice, to reparative and restorative forms of justice.

So we can think about conflict from the point of view of dimensionality. A dimension is defined in mathematics and physics in two ways. First, it is the number of bits of information we require in order to describe where something is located: in zero dimensions, we don't need any information to know where it is. It's just right there. If we need one piece of information, it's located along a line; two dimensions, it's located on a plane; three, in a cube, *et cetera*.

The second definition of a dimension is that it is "a degree of freedom." And this is the definition that I like best for our purposes. If we think of the dimensions of conflict as degrees of freedom, both individually and organizationally, we can see that there is a transition from lower to higher dimensions, which are potentially infinite.

If we are at zero dimensions, we don't need any information, and believe there's nothing we can do to resolve the conflict, there's no place to go, no information required, we're just at impasse, and there's chaos and anarchy. One dimension is a way of escaping chaos and anarchy through dictatorship or authoritarianism — meaning we only need one piece of information, or ask one person's permission. The boss controls what is going to happen, or the parents. It will be dad's solution or mom's solution, or my solution. One piece of information is all we need. It's very factually informed, and what we get as an outcome is obedience.

Moving to two dimensions means that there is a negotiation that is going to take place because one dimension represents what one person wants, and the second dimension represents what somebody else wants. This is what we call a "rights-based" form of decision-making that is adversarial, and generally ends up in compromise. Anything dad wants and the teenager doesn't, or anything the teenager wants that dad doesn't, is going to end up on the x- or y-axis of a two dimensional plane, and everything in the middle will be a compromise. It is legally informed, as people talk about their rights in connection with one another, and what we get fundamentally, as an outcome, is acceptance.

When we move to three dimensions, we introduce depth, by acknowledging emotions, or by surfacing and satisfying interests, which could be a separate fourth dimension. Interests are not *what* we want, but the reasons *why* we want it. Interests are not win/lose, but win/win, and therefore *inherently* collaborative. In three dimensions,, communications are emotionally informed, and what it is possible for us to get as an outcome is emotional completion and consensus-based decisions.

We can also move to four or five dimensions, where we have conversations, for example, that are heart-based, caring, and relationally informed. And it is possible for us then to get to open-heartedness and unanimity as a form of decision-making.

We can see, for example, how this works in connection with teenage/ parent conflicts over curfew. Zero dimensions is equivalent to impasse, with people are shouting accusations at each other, like "You're irresponsible." "You're bossy."

One dimension is equivalent to the "command" approach, which is where the parent says, "you're going to be home by 10:00 PM, period." That means the teenager is either going to obey or be punished. And that's going to work for a period of time, but if you try that with a 16-year-old, it's not going to work.

With two dimensions, you get a 16-year-old and a negotiation, because the parent says "10:00 PM" and the teenager says "2:00 AM." And the outcome will be a compromise, perhaps because the teenager said "2:00 AM" because he or she actually wants to arrive home at midnight.

There is a third, emotional dimension in which people talk about how they feel, ad a fourth dimension that takes the form of a dialogue over interests. What is the interest of the parent? Perhaps it is safety. What's the interest of the teenager? Perhaps it is freedom. Now we discover, if we ask which of those is correct and which is not, the answer is that they're both correct, because you can't have safety without some degree of freedom, and you can't have freedom without some degree of safety. So we have to come up with a solution that is two-sided, that values both safety and freedom, and acknowledges both of them.

At five dimensions, we come to a deeper, heartfelt issue, which arises out of the fact that the parent/teenager relationship is about to end. This is the death of the family, as they have known it, and the possible emergence of some new form of family.

Throughout this process, their conflict *defines* them and gives their lives energy and meaning. It ennobles their misery, safeguards their personal space, generates negative intimacy, powerfully communicates what they feel, gets results, and prompts change.

At various points in our lives, we have to look at the questions: What do we do with what's been done to us? What will our approach be to the conflicts that we experience at home and in the workplace? There are four constructive ways of responding to what has happened to us and to our conflicts. First, we can accept it, that is, not deny it or push it onto others, but accept that it happened. Second, we can own it, and claim responsibility for it — not 50 percent, but 100 percent, and something that is ours. Third, we can shape it, and by shaping it, turn it in the direction of learning and growth, problem solving and helping others and ourselves. Fourth, we can figure out how to let it go, move on, and continue evolving.

This is the great unspoken promise of conflict resolution, and of the organizations in which we work, and it is the aim of this course to move us a little closer to realizing this promise.

SESSION 1 LECTURE SLIDES

Out of all this has come the first clear recognition of an inescapable fact: we cannot successfully force people to work for management's objectives. The ancient conception that people do the work of the world only if they are forced to do so by threats or intimidation, or by the camouflaged authoritarian methods of paternalism, has been suffering from lingering fatal illness for a quarter of a century. I venture to guess that it will be dead in another decade.

DOUGLAS MCGREGOR

𝕮𝖍𝖊 𝕹𝖊𝖜 𝖄𝖔𝖗𝖐 𝕮𝖎𝖒𝖊𝖘𝕮𝖍𝖊 𝕹𝖊𝖜 𝖄𝖔𝖗𝖐 𝕮𝖎𝖒𝖊𝖘

White-Collar Salt Mine

A 2013 survey of 12,115 workers worldwide found that many lacked a fulfilling workplace. MAY 31, 2014

DO NOT HAVE THIS AT WORK		DO HAVE THIS
70%	Regular time for creative or strategic thinking	18%
66	Ability to focus on one thing at a time	21
60	Opportunities to do what is most enjoyed	33
50	Level of meaning and significance	36
50	Connection to your company's mission	25
49	A sense of community	35
48	Opportunities for learning and growth	38
47	Opportunities to do what you do best	36
46	Ability to prioritize your tasks	36
45	Overall positive energy	36
43	Understanding of how to be successful	40
40	Ability to balance work and home life	37
40	Ability to disengage from work	42
40	Comfort in truly being yourself	45

Source: The Energy Project

94 percent of those surveyed were in white-collar jobs; 6 percent were in blue-collar jobs.

14

Surveys on Workplace Conflict (1)

A global report authored by the business psychology firm OPP and the Chartered Institute of Personnel and Development (CIPD) found:

- A majority of employees (85%) have to deal with conflict and 29% do so 'always' or 'frequently'. In Germany this figure jumps to 56%, while employees in Ireland (37%) and the US (36%) also spend a significant amount of time managing disputes.
- The level at which most conflict is observed is between entry-level and front-line roles (34%), but conflict also exists at the most senior levels: one in eight employees (12%) say that disagreements among their senior team are frequent or continual.
- The primary causes of workplace conflict are seen as personality clashes and warring egos (49%), followed by stress (34%) and heavy workloads (33%).
- Culture also plays a part in the perception of causes: as Brazilian workers are more likely to see a clash of values as a major cause of conflict (24%). In France, 36% of employees saw a lack of honesty as a key factor, compared with a global average of 26%.
- The average employee spends 2.1 hours a week dealing with conflict. For the UK alone, that translates to 370 million working days lost every year as a result of conflict in the workplace. One in six (16%) say a recent dispute escalated in duration and/or intensity, only 11% of those surveyed have never experienced a disagreement that escalated.
- 27% of employees have seen conflict lead to personal attacks, and 25% have seen it result in sickness or absence. 9% even saw it lead to project failure.

© Kenneth Cloke and Joan Goldsmith

15

Surveys on Workplace Conflict (2)

- 70% of employees see managing conflict as a 'very' or 'critically' important leadership skill, while 54% think managers could better handle disputes by addressing underlying tensions before things go wrong.
- 31% of managers think they handle disagreements well, but only 22% of non-managers agree. Nearly half of non-managers (43%) think their bosses don't deal with conflict as well as they should, compared to 23% of managers who agree.
- Less than half (44%) of all those questioned have received training in how to manage workplace conflict. This figure rises to 60% in Brazil and 57% in the US. 72% of Belgian workers and 73% of those in France have had none.
- Over 95% of people receiving training as part of leadership development or on formal external courses say that it helped them in some way. A quarter (27%) say it made them more comfortable and confident in managing disputes and 58% of those who have been trained say they now look for win–win outcomes from conflict. 85% change the way they approach conflict over the course of their working lives; they become more proactive and take it less personally as a result of experience.
- Among all employees, 76% have seen conflict lead to a positive outcome, such as better understanding of others (41%) or a better solution to a workplace problem (29%). This figure rises to 84% and 81% in Brazil and the US, countries where training is most common. Belgium and France, where employees experience the least training, also have the lowest incidence of positive outcomes.
- The number of self-employed US workers could triple by 2020 to 42 million, and 97% of those who freelance say they're not interested in returning to traditional work — up from 10% in 2016. © Kenneth Cloke and Joan Goldsmith

More Surveys on Workplace Conflict

- A 2013 study by Gallup of employees in 142 countries found that just 30% of employees feel engaged at work in the US, globally it is just 13%.
- In a 2012 meta-analysis of 263 research studies across 192 companies, Gallup found that the top 25% of companies with engaged employees, compared with the bottom 25%, had 22% greater profitability, 10% higher customer ratings, 28% less theft, and % fewer safety incidents.
- Employees who take a break every 90 minutes report a 30% higher level of focus than those who take no breaks or just one during the day. They also report a nearly 50% greater capacity to think creatively and a 46% higher level of health and well-being.
- The more hours people work beyond 40 and the more continuously they work the worse they feel and the less engaged they become.
- Feeling encouraged by one's supervisor to take breaks increases nearly 100% people staying with a company and doubles their sense of health and well-being. Employees who have supportive supervisors are 67% more engaged.
- Only 20% of those surveyed said they were able to focus on one task at a time at work, but those who could were 50% more engaged. Only one-third were able to effectively prioritize their tasks, but those who did were 1.6 times more able to focus.
- Employees who found meaning and significance in their work were three times more likely to stay with the organization and had 1.7 times higher job satisfaction.
- When leaders modeled these approaches, employees were 55% more engaged, 53% more focused and more likely to stay at the company.

[Source: Tony Schwartz and Christine Porath, "Why You Hate Work," NY Times, June 1, 2014.]

The Systemic Nature of Conflict

- Every conflict takes place not only between individuals, but within a *context*, culture, and environment; surrounded by social, economic, and political forces; inside organizational systems, structures, and technological settings; among a diverse community of people; at a particular moment in time and history; on a stage, milieu, or backdrop.
- None of these elements is conflict-neutral. Each contributes – sometimes in veiled and unspoken, yet profound ways to the nature, intensity, duration, impact, and *meaning* of our conflicts.
- Each profoundly affects the quality of our work lives, our personal capacity for joy and compassion, and our ability to collaborate in solving our problems.
- Like ripples in a pond, every conflict and every resolution in the workplace extends outward, impacting others and creating a "mediation butterfly effect."
- As a result, we are each responsible as organizational citizens for building conflict resolution capacity in our workplaces.

© Kenneth Cloke and Joan Goldsmith

What are Chronic Conflicts?

Chronic conflicts are those that nations, societies, organizations or individuals

- Have not fully resolved

- Need to resolve in order to grow and evolve

- Are capable of resolving

- Can only resolve by abandoning old approaches and adopting new ones

- Are resistant to resolving because they are frightened, dissatisfied, insecure, uncertain, angry, or unwilling to change

© Kenneth Cloke and Joan Goldsmith

Features of Chronic Conflict

Chronic conflicts can often be distinguished by their:
- Repetition
- Low levels of resolution
- Incongruity between high level of emotion and apparent triviality of the issues over which people are fighting
- Being commonly mistaken for miscommunications or personality clashes
- Tolerance of disrespectful and adversarial behaviors,
- Seeming irrationality
- Accidental misunderstandings
- Apparent idiosyncratic causes and circumstances
- Underlying similarities

4 Meta-Sources of Chronic Conflict

- Social Inequality

- Economic Inequity

- Political Autocracy

- Environmental Degradation

12 Sources of Chronic Conflict in Capitalism

1. Intense competition for market dominance
2. Unceasing efforts to maximize sales and profits
3. Primacy of the financial bottom line
4. Constant innovation in technology
5. Dependence of profits on costs of production, especially wages, rents, taxes, and raw materials
6. Unequal distribution of profits
7. Hierarchical control over investments, wages, and management
8. Separation and division of labor
9. Centralized organization of work processes
10. Increasing dependence on employee motivation and participation in decision-making
11. Unending search for inexpensive raw materials, cheap labor, and markets for finished products
12. Race for the bottom in globalization of production and distribution

© Kenneth Cloke and Joan Goldsmith

10 Meta-Sources of Labor-Management Conflict

1. Legislation that does not reflect workplace realities
2. Financing that is not within the parties control
3. Political elections that periodically alter attitudes toward labor management relations
4. Primary responsibility of management for fiscal well-being
5. Primary responsibility of unions for the well-being of workers
6. Adversarial styles of negotiation and problem-solving
7. Power and rights based systems, relationships and processes in labor and management relations
8. Inability or unwillingness to discuss or negotiate non-mandatory subjects
9. Unilateral and non-collaborative approaches to decisions
10. Conflict avoidance, accommodation, aggression and compromise

© Kenneth Cloke and Joan Goldsmith

The 48 Laws of Power and Toxic Leaders

Among the recommendations in *The 48 Laws of Power* by Robert Greene are the following toxic, power-based ideas, each of which generates chronic conflicts:

- Conceal your intentions
- Court attention at all costs
- Get others to do the work for you, but always take the credit
- Learn to keep people dependent on you
- Use selective honesty and generosity to disarm your victim
- Pose as a friend, work as a spy
- Crush your enemy totally
- Keep others in suspended terror: cultivate an air of unpredictability
- Do not commit to anyone
- Play a sucker to catch a sucker – seem dumber than your mark
- Play the perfect courtier
- Play on people's need to believe to create a cult like following
- Control the options: get others to play with the cards you deal
- Discover each man's thumbscrew
- Be royal in your own fashion: act like a king to be treated like one
- Create compelling spectacles
- Think as you like but behave like others
- Despise the free lunch
- Strike the shepherd and the sheep will scatter
- Preach the need for change, but never reform too much at once

"More and more, we take for granted that work must be destitute of pleasure. More and more, we assume that if we want to be pleased we must wait until evening, or the weekend, or vacations, or retirement. More and more, our farms and forests resemble our factories and offices, which in turn more and more resemble prisons - why else should we be so eager to escape them? We recognize defeated landscapes by the absence of pleasure from them. We are defeated at work because our work gives us no pleasure... Where is our comfort but in the free, uninvolved, finally mysterious beauty and grace of this world that we did not make, that has no price? Where is our sanity but there? Where is our pleasure but in working and resting kindly in the presence of this world?"

Wendell Berry

Ten Philosophical Propositions (1)

1. *No two human beings are the same.* Everyone is different, and while we share certain characteristics, at a given level of nuance or subtlety, nothing that occurs between two people is more than grossly predictable. Therefore, no conflict resolution technique, however evolved or skillfully executed, will succeed with everyone.
2. *No single human being is the same from one moment to the next.* Not only is it impossible to step into the same river twice because it continues flowing, we also are continually flowing, and different from one moment to the next. Therefore, no matter how stuck anyone is, they can become unstuck at any moment.
3. *The interactions and relationships between human beings are complex, multi-determined, subtle, and unpredictable,* if only because they involve two or more different, changing individuals. Therefore, while it makes sense for conflict resolvers to plan and strategize, it also makes sense to improvise, and let neither plans nor strategies stand in our way.
4. *Conflicts are even more complex, multi-determined, subtle, and unpredictable* because they involve intense emotions, negative behaviors, miscommunications, contrasting cultural norms, jumbled intentions, false expectations, and dysfunctional systems, any of which can easily increase the level of opposition. Therefore, linear, scientific, logically rigorous approaches to conflict and resolution need to be softened and combined with holistic, artistic, creative, non-logical approaches.
5. *Most conflicts take place below the surface,* underneath the superficial topics over which people fight, and hidden from their conscious awareness. Therefore, every conflict leads to the center of the issues in dispute, and the hearts and minds of those who are stuck.

© Kenneth Cloke

Ten Philosophical Propositions (2)

6. *Chronic conflicts are systemic,* and all systems, be they personal, familial, organizational, social, environmental, economic, or political, defend themselves against change, even when it is essential for their survival. Therefore, the greater the need for change and the deeper the potential transformation, the greater the resistance, and the more difficult it is to imagine how the conflict might end, or let it go.
7. *Every conflict is holographic,* so that each part both contains and recapitulates the whole. Therefore, every issue, no matter how trifling or insignificant, allows conflict resolvers to alter the whole by transforming any of its parts.
8. *Every conflict reveals an internal crossroads,* and is polarized because each path leads in a radically different direction. Therefore, every conflict allows us to move backward toward impasse, enmity, and adversarial relationships, or forward toward evolution, learning, and transcendence.
9. *Every conflict offers opportunities to evolve* to higher levels of skill and awareness in how we respond to our opponents and problems. Therefore, every conflict is a rich source of improvement, learning, and wisdom, both for individuals but systems.
10. *At the center of every conflict lies its heart,* and a potential for resolution, transformation, and transcendence. Therefore, every conflict has a capacity to ensnare and entrap, or liberate and transform us, along with the relationships and systems that created it. By opening peoples' hearts in conflict, we *automatically* initiate their evolution to higher orders of conflict.

© Kenneth Cloke

Alternative Definitions of Conflict (1)

1. Conflict represents a lack of awareness of the immanence of death or sudden catastrophe.
2. Conflict arises wherever there is a failure of collaboration or community.
3. Conflict reflects an ignorance of our essential inter-connectedness, of the beauty of the human spirit.
4. Conflict is a lack of acceptance of ourselves that we have projected onto others, a way of blaming someone else for what we perceive as failures in our own lives, of diverting attention from our mistakes.
5. Conflict represents a boundary violation, a failure to value or recognize our own integrity, and therefore the personal space of others.
6. Conflict reflects a need to support or maintain a false image of who we are.
7. Conflict is a way of obtaining the acknowledgment, sympathy or support we need by casting ourselves as the victim of some evil doer.
8. Conflict is a lack of skill or experience at being able to handle a particular kind of behavior.
9. Conflict is the continued pursuit of our own false expectations, the desire to hold on to our unrealistic fantasies.
10. Conflict is a lack of appreciation of subtlety in what someone else is saying.
11. Conflict is a result of what is *not* communicated, of secrets, confusions and cover-ups.

© Kenneth Cloke

Alternative Definitions of Conflict (2)

12. Conflict represents a lack of effectiveness or clarity in communicating what we feel, think or want.
13. Conflict is a way of opposing someone who represents the parent with whom we have not yet resolved our relationship.
14. Conflict is the sound made by the cracks in a system, the manifestation of contradictory forces coexisting in a single space.
15. Conflict is the voice of the new paradigm, a call for change in a system that has outlived its usefulness.
16. Conflict reflects an inability to say good-bye, a refusal to let go of something that is dead or dying.
17. Conflict is a way of being negatively intimate when positive intimacy has become impossible.
18. Conflict is the antagonistic voice of *half* of a paradox, enigma, duality, polarity or contradiction.
19. Conflict is a superficial interpretation of difference, diversity and opposition, one that ignores their essential role in creating balance and symbiosis.
20. Conflict is an opportunity and a *request* for authenticity, emotional honesty, acknowledgment, intimacy, empathy, communication, understanding, growth, or learning; in other words, for a better relationship.

© Kenneth Cloke

Components of Conflict

Indispensable Component of Conflict	Likely Results of Component	What is Needed, Wanted or Missing	Possible Strategies for Intervention
1. Two or More People (or internal parts of the same person)	Diverse Interests, Isolation, Distrust, Competitive Relationships	Communication, Openness, Positive Intent, Common Goals	Ground Rules, Listening, Story Telling, Empathy, Common Interests, Caucusing
2. Disagreement over Content, Process, Relationship, or Outcomes	Unresolved Issues, Differences over Facts, Competing Issues, Personal Solutions	Engagement, Logical Analysis, Neutral Identification and Discussion of Common Interests	Brainstorming, Collaborative Negotiation, Creative Problem-Solving, Dialogue
3. "Negative" Emotion, i.e., Anger, Fear, Jealousy, Shame, Guilt, or Grief	Unexpressed or Hostile Emotions, Incomplete or Inadequate Compassion and Letting Go	Emotional Closure, Introspection, Venting, Empathy, Acknowledgment, Self-Esteem, Rituals, Completion	Venting, Acknowledgement, Caucusing, Emotional Processing, Rituals of Closure
4. Lack of Awareness of Self or Others, Antagonistic Spirit, Intention, or Energy, Intolerant or Unforgiving Aim, Attachment, Embittered Life Force, Soul or Chi	Chronic Conflict, Illness, Injury, Blindness to Self And Others, Confusion, Spiritual Imbalance, Feeling Stuck, Incessant Suffering	Forgiveness, Mindfulness, Expanded Awareness, Compassion, Authenticity, Acceptance, Release, Letting Go	Honesty, Empathy, Introspection, Centering, Meditation, Ritual, Shift from Negative to Positive Energy
5. Closed-Hearted Attitude, Hostile, Self-Centered, or Withholding Outlook or Relationships	Dysfunctional Relationships, Depression, Self-Centeredness, Broken Heart	Reconciliation, Compassion, Positive Attitude, Heart-to-Heart Dialogue	Open Hearted Communication, Confession, Learning, Acceptance of Self and Other
6. Adversarial, Bureaucratic, or Highly Competitive System, Contest, Culture, or Environment	Inimical Social Conditions, and/or Structure or System; i.e., Inequity, Hierarchical, Bureaucratic and Autocratic Relations	Systemic Change, Collaborative Relationship, Cultural Sensitivity, Increased Equity, Equality, and Democracy	Transform System, Alter or Adapt to Environment, Balance Power, Build Participation, Consensus, and Ownership

© Kenneth Cloke

Conflict Resolution by Location (1)

1. Physical Techniques:
- Moving out from behind our desks into an open circle of chairs
- Modulating our voices
- Arranging our bodies to subtly mirror the parties' postures
- Lowering our height to appear less threatening
- Making eye contact with our "non-dominant" eye
- Nodding to encourage trust
- Using hand gestures to communicate calm
- Moving closer to communicate sensitive information
- Using body language to counteract aggressive or defensive postures
- Using touch to "anchor" negative feelings in one physical location and positive feelings in another
- Indirectly embracing the space around the parties with our arms
- Lightly touching someone to soothe their wounded feelings
- Leaning forward to interrupt fruitless exchanges, or backwards to open a space for direct communication
- Holding up our hands to stop a combative communication or block an aggressive party from becoming violent
- Closely observing body movements to monitor shifting states of mind, emotion, and attitude
- Expanding body awareness by asking questions about how someone is physically sensing themselves, others, or the conflict

© Kenneth Cloke

Conflict Resolution by Location (2)

2. *Mental Techniques:*
   - Clarifying and explaining the parameters of the resolution process
   - Establishing clear ground rules
   - Listening to facts and explanations
   - Identifying the issues requiring settlement
   - Defining the issues
   - Analyzing the issues
   - Setting an agenda listing issues for discussion
   - Contracting and agreeing to work toward solutions
   - Caucusing to explore hidden agendas
   - Brainstorming options
   - Clarifying interests
   - Accumulating points of consensus
   - Using law, research, and expert opinion to resolve differences
   - Evaluating arguments and proposed outcomes
   - Facilitating negotiations
   - Urging settlement for objective and subjective reasons
   - Making recommendations and evaluations to promote settlement
   - Drafting agreements
   - Reviewing and solidifying commitments

© Kenneth Cloke

Conflict Resolution by Location (3)

3. *Emotional Techniques*:
   - Listening to and naming the emotions parties express
   - Acknowledging and accepting emotional declarations
   - Normalizing and validating emotional concerns
   - Mirroring emotional affect
   - Releasing hidden emotions by asking probing questions
   - Reframing to raise or lower emotional intensity
   - Searching for emotional triggering mechanisms
   - Connecting emotions to vulnerability and internal issues
   - Revealing the benefits gained from intense emotion
   - Empowering people to tell others how they feel and set limits
   - Eliciting and surfacing repressed emotions
   - Reducing emotional resistance and ego defenses
   - Redirecting emotion from people to problems
   - Separating intentions from effects
   - Shifting focus from emotions to behaviors
   - Agreeing to change behaviors in the future
   - Connecting emotions with underlying interests
   - Modeling appropriate emotional responses
   - Acknowledging and apologizing for negative, disrespectful, or counter-productive communications

© Kenneth Cloke

Conflict Resolution by Location (4)

4. *Spiritual Techniques*:
   - Centering, relaxing, and balancing internally
   - Releasing past recollections, emotions, and judgments
   - Releasing future expectations, goals, plans, and desires
   - Expanding present awareness
   - Clarifying and concentrating energy, spirit, intention, or *chi*
   - Setting the physical stage for intimate conversation
   - Opening with an appeal to the parties highest intentions
   - Sitting in silence and slowing the pace of conversation
   - Watching the energy flowing within, around, and between the parties
   - Using compassion to understand for the parties' deepest intentions, motivations, and desires
   - Asking questions that clarify people's deepest intentions
   - Using silence, pacing, body language, tone of voice, and emotional vulnerability to communicate sincerity and positive intentions
   - Asking questions that encourage responsibility for intentions, attitudes, and choices
   - Encouraging forgiveness, acceptance, and letting go
   - Identifying all the reasons for *not* forgiving, what is wrong with those reasons, and the price for not forgiving
   - Designing rituals of release, completion, and closure

34
© Kenneth Cloke

Conflict Resolution by Location (5)

5. *Heart Techniques*:
   - Welcoming people with an open heart
   - Opening with a question, invocation, or invitation directly to the heart
   - Asking people to tell each other why they want to resolve the conflict, or what kind or relationship they would like to have with each othert
   - Eliciting the heart-meaning of conflict stories
   - Opening our hearts and searching for questions that invite the parties to speak and listen from theirs
   - Asking direct, honest questions that encourage integrity and trust
   - Being vulnerable and encouraging vulnerability in others
   - Honestly communicating heartfelt insights, preferably in the form of questions
   - Encouraging them to ask heart-felt questions and answer openly and honestly
   - Focusing attention and awareness on what is taking place at the center, core, or heart of the dispute
   - Bringing humor and play into the conversation
   - Encouraging participation in activities likely to result in positive, collaborative, open-hearted experiences
   - Asking each person what they learned for themselves from the conflict
   - Identifying what each person is willing to do differently as a result
   - Encouraging complete reconciliation
   - Jointly designing new consensual relationships
   - Ending with heart-felt acknowledgements and appreciations

35
© Kenneth Cloke

Conflict Resolution by Location (6)

6. *Systems Design Techniques*:
   - Conducting a "conflict audit" to identify the chronic sources of conflict
   - Analyzing and targeting chronic sources of conflict, and systems, structures, culture, communications, strategies, change, values, morale, motivation, styles, and staffing
   - Viewing conflicts not as isolated events, but as part of a stream of disputes
   - Identifying existing cultural ideas, approaches, and mechanisms for resolving conflict
   - Supplementing with alternatives that emphasize prevention and early intervention
   - Approaching conflict resolution in multiple, diverse ways with different methods
   - Emphasizing integrated conflict resolution systems over discrete procedures
   - Focusing on interest-, rather than rights- or power-based solutions
   - Expanding the number and kind of alternatives available internally and externally
   - Arranging these procedures from low to high cost
   - Encourage early informal problem solving
   - Including a full range of options from process changes to binding arbitration
   - Providing low-cost rights and power back-ups
   - Creating "loopbacks" to informal problem solving and negotiation
   - Encouraging consultation before, facilitation during, and evaluation afterwards
   - Supporting inclusion, empowerment, equity, dialogue, collaboration, and consensus,
   - Develop training programs in conflict resolution
   - Simplifying policies and procedures and encouraging use of resolution procedures
   - Increasing motivation, skills, support, and resources to make these interventions work
   - Continually evaluating why these succeed or fail, and improving the design

© Kenneth Cloke

12 Arenas/Sets of Approaches of Conflict

1. *Physical* (i.e., trigger points/proximities/stresses)
2. *Intellectual* (i.e., paradigms/theories or ideas/linguistics)
3. *Emotional* (i.e., affective styles/reactivity/attitudes)
4. *Spiritual* (i.e., energy, attachment, awareness or mindfulness)
5. *Heart* (i.e., degree of kindness, level of caring, open-heartedness)
6. *Relational* (i.e., style or form of communication/intimacy/intention)
7. *Systemic* (i.e., familial/organizational/social-economic-political)
8. *Procedural* (i.e., rules and formalities/patterns/rituals)
9. *Substantive* (i.e., content of issues/analysis/objective criteria)
10. *Temporal* (i.e., timing/past histories/evolutionary opportunities)
11. *Cultural* (i.e., stories or narratives/biases/socially assigned meanings)
12. *Environmental* (i.e., ecologies, contexts, interdependencies)

© Kenneth Cloke

Native American Medicine Wheel

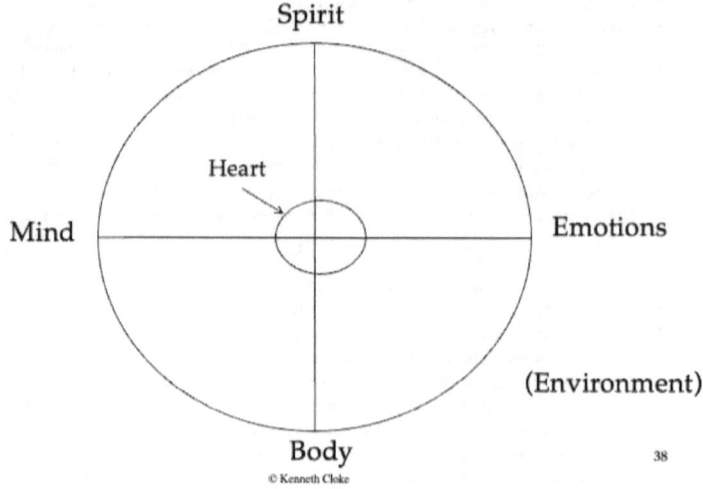

The Crossroads of Conflict

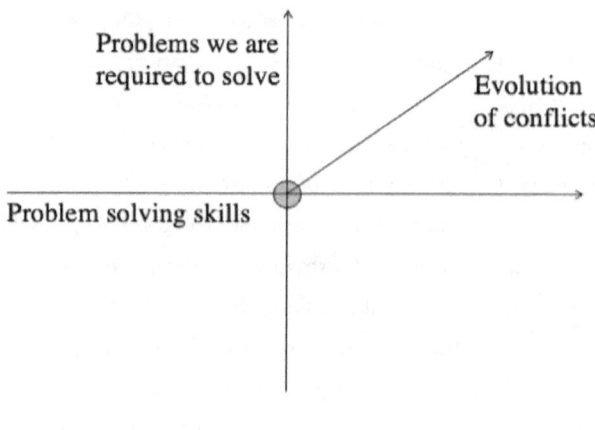

Some Crossroads in Conflict

- Whether to engage in the conflict and behave badly, or calm down and try to discuss it.
- Whether to acknowledge the other person's truth or deny it, remain rooted in one's own story, and slip into biased or delusional thinking.
- Whether to experience intense negative emotions and feelings, or to repress and sublimate them.
- Whether to experience one's opponent as an equal human being entitled to respect, or to demonize him or her and victimize oneself.
- Whether to aggressively assert and hold tight to one's position, or to search for solutions that satisfy both sets of interests.
- Whether to acknowledge and grieve one's losses and then let them go, or hold on to one's pain as something precious and continue reliving them.
- Whether to learn from one's opponent and the conflict so as to transcend it, or hold on to one's grievances and being right, and leave it bottle it up inside.
- Whether to forgive, reconcile and re-integrate with one's opponent, or remain isolated and wounded deep inside.

© Kenneth Cloke

Power, Justice and Decision Making

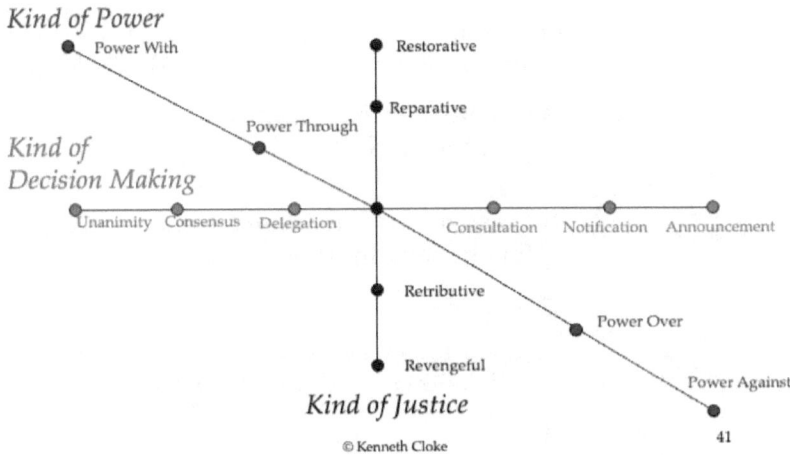

© Kenneth Cloke

6 Levels of Conflict Resolution

1. Cease Fire/Stopping the Fighting/De-Escalation

2. Settlement of the Issues

3. Resolution of the Underlying Emotional Issues and Satisfaction of Interests

4. Forgiveness and Self-Forgiveness

5. Reconciliation, Restoration of Relationship and a Return to Open-Heartedness

6. Prevention and Systems Design

Dimensions of Conflict Resolution

- = 0 Dimensions = Impasse, Chaos, Anarchy

- = 1 Dimension = *Power*-Based, Dictatorial, My Solution, Factually Informed, *Obedience*

- = 2 Dimensions = *Rights*-Based, Adversarial, Compromise, Legally Informed, *Acceptance*

- = 3 Dimensions = *Interest*-Based, Collaborative, Emotionally Informed, *Consensus*

- = 4 Dimensions = *Heart*-Based, Caring, Relationally Informed, *Unanimity*

Dimensions in Teenage-Parent Conflicts

#	Form	Focus	Parent	Teenager
0.	Impasse	*Accusations, Insults*	"Irresponsible."	"Bossy."
1.	Command	*Position*	10 PM	Obedience or Punishment
2.	Negotiation	*Compromise*	10 PM	2 AM
3.	Emotional Exchange	*Empathy, Dialogue*	Anger, Fear	Resentment, Shame
4.	Discussion of Interests	*Negotiation*	Safety	Freedom
5.	Spiritual Awareness	*Learning, Forgiveness*	Death of Family	Loss of Security/Support
6.	Heartfelt Desire	*Relational Intimacy*	Love, Acceptance	Love, Trust
7.	Family System	*Change, Transcendence*	Prevention, Change	Supportive Relationship

© Kenneth Cloke

Conflict Styles

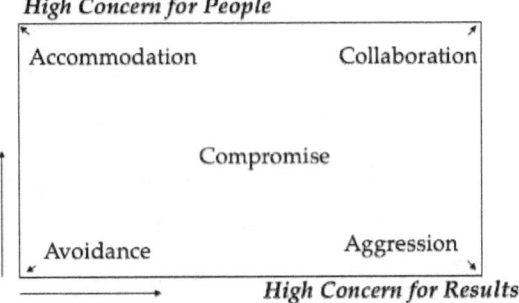

[Thomas-Kilman Model]

© Kenneth Cloke

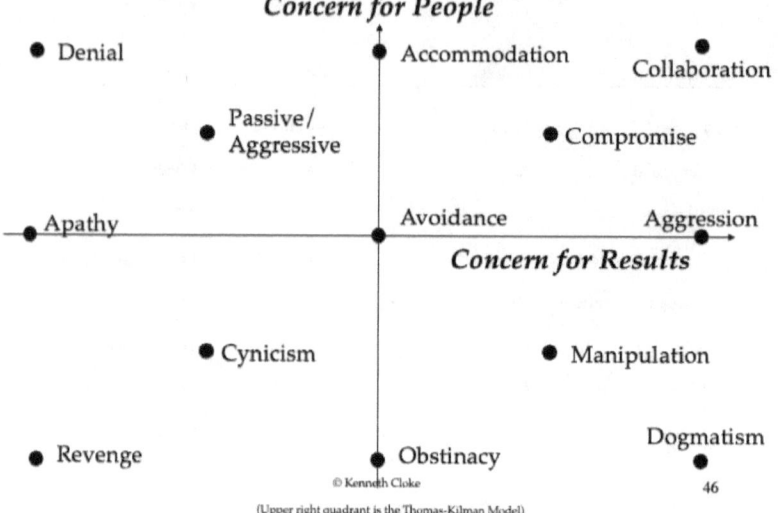

Seven Paradoxes in Conflict

1. Competition vs. Cooperation
2. Optimism vs. Realism
3. Avoidance vs. Engagement
4. Principle vs. Compromise
5. Emotions vs. Logic
6. Neutrality vs. Advocacy
7. Community vs. Autonomy

[Bernard Mayer, *The Conflict Paradox: Seven Dilemmas at the Core of Disputes*, ABA/Jossey-Bass 2015.]

What to Do with What's Been Done to You

1. **Accept it:** Don't deny it or push it on to others, but accept that it happened.

2. **Own it:** Because you accept it, you can claim it entirely – not 20% or 50% but 100%.

3. **Shape it:** Because you own it, you can convert it into something positive, redirect it toward learning, growth, problem solving and helping others.

4. **Drop it:** Because you have shaped it, you can let it go, move on and continue evolving.

CHAPTER 2

SYSTEMIC & STRUCTURAL SOURCES OF CHRONIC ORGANIZATIONAL CONFLICT

What Is an Organization? (Ken)

The topic for this session is what is an organization, and we're going to look at organizations from a variety of different points of view.

The first idea we would like to introduce is by Douglas McGregor, who wrote: "Management's insistence that the individual is the unit of organization is as limiting as an engineer's insistence that the atom is the unit of physical systems." In other words, an organization is a *relationship*, and not just an isolated entity. McGregor goes on to describe how relationships give rise to various properties that can't be predicted basis on our knowledge of the properties of atoms alone.

In a similar way, organizations represent what in science are called "emergent phenomena," which emerge to create higher orders from lower levels that can't be imagined until they arise, in exactly the way that a drop of water doesn't offer us much that is useful in describing a waterfall or a rainbow.

We can therefore think of organizations as complex and emergent. And some of the properties we want to describe in organizations are important in understanding the sources of conflict and the sources of resolution. So what exactly *is* an organization?

At a very trivial level, an organization is a place where people work. Or if we're thinking about families or couples or communities or teams, they can be described as places where people act and interact with each other, and the ways their actions impact one another.

As soon as we say that an organization is a place where people work, we then begin to think about *how* they work, *who* defines how they work, *why* they work, and is it possible to reimagine the way they work from the perspective of conflict resolution?

We can also describe an organization as a diverse group of people committed to a common goal, and it's clear from many research studies that diversity is an important element in problem solving. The more uniform a group is, the less capacity it has to imagine innovative solutions, and the more diverse a group is, the more variety and creativity there is in finding solutions.

We are living in a world in which diversity is increasing, and it is important to see that diversity is not something we *ought* to do for legal reasons, or even for moral or social or interpersonal reasons, but simply as the gift of a slightly different perspective, or set of experiences, or pair of eyes, looking at the same problem.

Diversity is the first part and the second is commonality. If you have diversity without commonality, everybody goes off in different directions and nothing gets achieved. If you have commonality without diversity, everyone may agree on a single proposal, idea, perspective, or way forward, but it may not be a very creative one, and may not stand up in a complex, difficult or rapidly changing environment. So what we want is to create a combination of diversity and commonality, and that's what an organization *is*, essentially, what it's trying to achieve.

Another way of defining an organization is that it is a *system*. What is a system? Our answer to that it is anything that turns in a circle, that replicates, repeats, or reinforces. It is common to think of a system simply as a cycle created by a set of inputs, work that is done in connection with those inputs, an output, and a feedback loop.

Here's a simple idea of a system that many of you will be familiar with. A system can be defined as a two-year-old plus a coffee table with expensive things on it that matter to the parents. That is a system, and it's going to turn in a circle. And it isn't anybody's fault. That's the nature of the system. You have combined a curious being who doesn't understand financial or economic or other forms of value in connection with possessions, plus a low table with those expensive things on it that the parents care about. So what we want to do with systems thinking is apply these understandings to organizations.

A fourth way of defining an organization is that it is an organism; that is, a living thing, something that is evolving, moving, adapting, and changing; that is alive on some level. And because we think of it as being alive and adapting and evolving, we can understand that conflicts represent a failure or glitch or setback in the evolutionary process, an evolution that has begun but hasn't been completed; an evolution that people are only beginning to be aware of, but don't yet really understand exactly what it means or what its consequences are.

An organization can also be thought of as a variety of interlocking activities and processes that are coordinated with one another, that support and reinforce one another, as opposed to canceling or contradicting one another. An organization can also be defined as a set of relationships and processes. And we'll come back to this idea later.

More interestingly, we can think of an organization as a group of conversations. Everyone at work engages in conversations, and these conversations are very different in marketing, production, sales, human resources, legal, *et cetera*. So we want to think about organizations not just as a thing, but a relationship, a process, and a set of conversations. Doing so will allow us to design conversations that make organizations more successful and effective.

An organization can also be thought of as a culture, a mindset, an attitude, a set of expectations. And if we think of organizations as cultures, we can impact the organization by shifting the way people inside it think about it, the way they *imagine* it.

An organization can also be seen as a method for diffusing responsibility. Certainly, corporations were legally defined to make sure that investors and entrepreneurs would not be held personally liable for corporate mistakes; but inside organizations, responsibility is also diffused, spread out, and it sometimes becomes difficult to figure out exactly where the buck stops. This can also be a source of conflict.

An organization can be thought of as a compact, an agreement, a contract, a set of unspoken understandings about how people will be treated, what will happen if someone does something that is inconsistent with what people imagined, and what will and will not happen as a result. Sometimes the contract takes the form of an unspoken set of assumptions, based on idealizations or generalizations, or on what someone in leadership is rumored to have said.

An organization can also be thought of as a mix of unspoken expectations and desires. Everyone comes into workplaces and organizations with unspoken expectations, and it's important for those expectations to be clarified, discussed, spoken about, and negotiated.

An organization is also an evolving set of values and purposes, including ethics, morality; the many different ways organizations "true" themselves to their purposes; declare themselves as standing for something; how they achieve those values, and how they act in relation to them.

Here, we can identify three *orders* of values. First, there is the particular value that someone may have — the value of education, or the value of empathy or caring, or the value of conversation, or conflict resolution. The second order of value, and a higher order of values, is the value of *having values*, which may take any number of different forms. It could be the value of education, or the value of respect and dignity, but whatever it may be, the value of having values is a higher form of value. The third order of values is *becoming* the value.

That is, instead of listening being a value and something you are striving for, you just listen. You become the value yourself, at which point it ceases being anything that is external to you, and becomes a way of being.

Possibly the most important element in defining what an organization is that an organization is also a mechanism for resolving conflicts. It is a *mediation* between its diverse parts. It is a way of processing, managing, or handling conflicts. So if we imagine that an organization is a diverse group of people who are committed to a common purpose, the conflict between diversity and commonality is likely to be expressed in multiple ways, and an organization can be thought of as the total of those different ways of resolving conflicts, and an ongoing mediation designed to create unity out of diversity.

An organization can therefore be regarded as a method of group learning, based on assessment and feedback and evaluation; or as a series of methodologies for adapting and learning from mistakes. Peter Senge has written a useful book called *The Fifth Discipline* about the idea of organizational learning. And organizations need most importantly to learn from their conflicts, from the things that go wrong, from their failures, as well as their successes.

Finally, organizations are figments of our imagination. They don't actually exist. General Motors does not exist. There is a physical plant. There are office buildings and human beings. But General Motors is an imaginary construct. It is a fantasy. It is a short-hand or heuristic we have created in order to summarize quickly and simply in an image what we mean when we refer to it as a whole.

The same goes for the United States of America, which is not just a set of borders and a particular landscape. It is an imaginary creation. And because of the fact that it is something that occurs in the imagination, we can imagine it *differently*. And that gives us great power and great responsibility in our role as organizational conflict resolvers. It becomes possible for us, on the basis of these definitions, to imagine organizations in fundamentally different ways.

There are other definitions we can offer, but these are a good place to start, because they are designed to free up our thinking so we can approach organizational conflict from a variety of different points of view, each of which can increase our ability to resolve them.

Here is another idea that helps in defining an organization. Right now, I'm holding a pen. This pen was created by a group of people who got together in an organization of some kind and manufactured it. And while they were manufacturing the pen, they were concerned and focused primarily on its *content*, or on the pen. But while they were manufacturing the pen, invisibly, they were also manufacturing the *process* of making pens. And between the pen and the process of making pens, which is the more powerful? Which is more lasting? Which is more fundamental? Which determines what will happen most directly and powerfully? The answer, of course, is the process. Yet far more attention is paid to the pen than is paid to the process of making pens.

In addition to the pen and the process of making pens, a third thing is happening, also invisibly, and that is that *relationships* are being created between all of the people who are making the pens, the people who are making the pens and the customers of the pens, between them and the raw materials that go into making the pen, and also with future generations who will have to think about how this pen bio-degrades and what is going to happen to all of the left-over pens.

So between the pen, the process of making pens, and all of the relationships formed around the making of the pen, which is more fundamental? Which is more lasting? Which is deeper? Which has the strongest impact on what will happen? And the answer is the relationships, of course, yet the least amount of attention is paid in organizations to relationship.

In addition to these, we are also, in making pens, manufacturing organizational culture, social status, economic disparities and equalities, political systems, philosophies, ecological and environmental consequences, and a range of other elements, all of which are in the background.

So what we are proposing in relation to conflict resolution is that instead of focusing simply and purely on the presenting issues, the topics that divide people, or that people disagree about, let us also pay at least equal attention, if not more, to the process whereby they came into disagreement, the process being used to resolve their disagreement, the relationships between them, their expectations regarding those relationships, how they have managed them, their culture and environment, what they really want from each other, and why.

Fundamentally, we need all these. If you focus only on content, you will produce a pen, but if the process is flawed, it may be the last pen you're going to produce. And if the relationships are destructive or dysfunctional, again it may be the last pen you produce. You can also pay attention to relationship and not pay attention to content, in which case you will never get around to producing a pen, so we need to pay attention to all these elements.

So this is a complex description of the nature of organizational life that requires input to understand what is happening. And particularly in conflict, we require a great deal of attention paid to process and relationships, culture and environment, in addition to the content or issues in dispute.

The 7S Model (Joan)

I would like to introduce a very special model that is a tool for analyzing organizations, discovering conflicts, and resolving them. This is called the 7S model because each element of the organization described by the model begins with the letter S.

The apocryphal story about the creation of this model is that it was developed by four very famous, excellent management consultants, Tom Peters, Bob Waterman, Tony Athos, and Richard Pascale, who were working with a very large and complex organization, and trying to come up with a clever way of talking about organizational elements. Supposedly, as they told me the story, they were staying at a hotel together and stayed up all night coming up with elements of the organization that begin with an "S" so it would be easy to remember and had a good sound. These guys wanted to make a difference in organizational change, and also wanted to sell their books.

The 7S model became a model for looking at organizations, and we have adapted it to reflect the sources of organizational conflict, and have used it in many different organizations to resolve conflicts, from large government structures to public high schools where teachers unions and administration were in conflict. We've used it in very large, complex international corporations, banks, and non-profits.

First of all, if you look at the model, you will notice that at the center of the organization, at the heart of it, are *shared values*, and we have added shared mission to the shared vision. We ask: What is shared among all members of the organization? And to articulate that, to develop it, everyone needs to be involved.

Many people thinking about organizations look at what are called the "hard S's." That is the *structures, strategies*, and *systems*. These are the S's that most organizations think about when they think about themselves, and most organizational consultants, and sometimes mediators, only look at the hard S's.

What is the structure? Are people organized in teams? Or is it a hierarchy? What is the strategy? Is it mostly a competitive strategy, or is the strategy to carve out some part of the market and own that? And what are the systems? Are the systems mostly technology systems? Are there systems for interpersonal communication? For team building?

Tony Athos and Richard Pascale came up with the soft S's, the three S's that are often ignored. The styles of people: How do they operate with each other? Is there an informal style? Is there a dress down Friday where people can wear whatever they want? In all organizations, there is a style element.

Staff: Who are the staff members? Does everybody — every manager have an HR person? A secretary? A technology person? Or are these roles lumped together? Is there a secretarial pool and can anybody have access to the secretarial pool? Or do staff members in the technology unit serve everybody in the organization?

And skills: What skills are needed? Are people invited to the organization and tested on their ability to think creatively, to be innovative, to resolve conflicts? These elements of an organization need to be included. When you work in any organization, company, government agency, or school, ask them to identify and describe their 7S's, and what the reality is.

As an illustration, the shared values can be commitments that everybody knows about and feels committed to, and people really work with each other to uphold them — or not. Is one of the values teamwork? For example, we worked with an organization on team building, and the team wanted to meet with the Chief Information Officer to question a decision she had made. So they invited her to a meeting, provided the refreshments, secured the flip charts, and created the agenda. They determined who was going to speak first, how were they going to interact with her, how were they going to summarize her interests and at the same time question her decision. They worked together based on a shared value of teamwork.

The staff "S" focuses on relationships, including acknowledgments. How are people acknowledged for the work they did? Are they given bonuses, or celebrations where parents, children, and spouses are invited to a picnic? Are they acknowledged publicly for the achievements their team has made?

The skills and behaviors are very important, and mediation is one of the skills that can be developed in every part of the organization. For example, we worked with a large Fortune 100 manufacturing organization where everybody on the assembly line was trained as a peer mediator. So if I'm making widgets on the assembly line, and I get into a conflict with Harriet, who's next to me, but is not sending the widget fast enough for me to do my job, we can ask Alice, who's on the other side of the assembly line, has been trained as a mediator, to come over and work with us to mediate the conflict.

Regarding styles, what is the culture and level of authenticity at work? How are people treated when they're having difficulty? When there's been a death in their family? When they're troubled or when they've been out of work or ill? Are they treated with authentic respect? Are they invited to take the time they need to recover?

And in relation to the structure of the organization, are people invited to participate in making decisions? If one of the shared values is teamwork, then participation should be included in the structure, and you've got to have a structure that encourages teams to develop. Or in relation to strategy, what is the strategy of the organization in encouraging mediation and dialogue, or inviting people to meet and engage in dialogue over the issues that are troubling them?

We have also used the 7S model with community conflicts. We worked with a city in California where there was a big conflict because the nonprofit agency that worked with homeless people who were mentally ill, rehabilitated them psychologically, enabled them to get jobs, and placed them in apartments, mostly in areas where there were stores, or shops, or factories. This agency received a $6 million loan from the city to buy four apartments in an up-scale community neighborhood, and the neighbors said, "We don't want these people in our backyard."

We started working with people in the neighborhood, in city government, and in the rehabilitation clinic to discuss "What are the values we share in this community?" They said, "democracy" and "caring for people." Afterwards, city and nonprofit staff were willing to come into the community and work in the apartments, be available for any conflicts that might arise, and mediate them. We trained the members of the community in mediation, and helped them develop meditative processes and systems.

One woman who lived in the community had a brother who had been diagnosed as schizophrenic. She took care of him and took on the role of creating a neighborhood watch system and being captain of the Neighborhood Watch, and the structure invited everybody to participate in coming up with a plan that would welcome these people into their community.

So the shared mission, vision, values can be described in terms of mediation, and be made explicit through a commitment to resolve our conflicts, listen to each other, and create dialogue around any issues that arise. If that can be stated explicitly in the shared values, then it can permeate the organization so that the strategy and the overall direction of the organization is one where conflicts, when they arise, are dealt with directly and not swept under the rug.

In another example, we were asked to work in a university engineering department, where the dean acknowledged that, as the middle child in his family of origin, he had learned to sweep conflicts under the rug and not deal with them. That was his strategy whenever anyone came to him with sexual abuse or discrimination allegations, or with conflicts over who was going to get to use the Xerox machine. He would try to avoid them, often making them worse. So we recommend a strategy of inviting people to raise conflicts, and dealing with them immediately, collaboratively, and constructively.

There need to be organizational systems for conflict resolution, and we are going to talk about that later when we discuss system design. But with structure, there need to be not just HR as an option, or even mediation, or an ombudsperson responsible for resolving conflicts, but multiple structures that can improve everyone's skills in every kind of conflict and communication.

The styles, skills and culture of conflict resolution need to be described and developed. Here is an example that was very powerful for us. There is an international bank that has offices in Europe and New York that was using an information technology strategy to transform how they did their investing in the market, and handling stocks and bonds and investments for clients of the bank.

They created an information technology process, and had managing directors earning about $500,000 a year or more, and each of them had four or five vice presidents reporting to them, who were earning about $250,000 a year. There was little communication between the managing directors and the vice presidents, even though they worked next to each other in an investment banking office. So they asked us to train the managing directors in coaching skills, on how to coach the vice presidents to understand the information technology strategy, how to use it, and how to pass it down the line to the people who were working the systems and technology, how to get it to staff.

So we agreed to conduct trainings for the managing directors in New York and London, with people coming from around the world. We made one stipulation: that the vice-presidents be included, because they needed to understand the style and culture of communication they were now going to be responsible for implementing. How were these managing directors supposed to communicate with them and how were they to behave? What was the role of the vice-presidents in communicating with the staff who reported to them? And what skills did they need to strengthen and communicate?

The training included a number of role-plays and lots of practicing skills and mediation techniques to enable the managing directors and vice-presidents to communicate with each other, empathize, and listen — a critically important skill.

The structure of the bank didn't change. They still worked in a hierarchy. But within it we introduced non-hierarchical systems for communication, including weekly team meetings, cross-organizational conferences, and created, in the architecture of the building, rooms where people could mediate and confer off-line, and systems that encouraged them to communicate non-hierarchically, and talk to each other privately. So if I had a problem with my managing director and I needed to tell him or her that I wasn't getting it, or that I didn't understand what the IT strategy was, I could now call a meeting, using a system that was non-hierarchical. This worked partly because they had a shared value, mission, and vision of being a place where leadership teams felt comfortable, knowledgeable, and able to do the work that needed to be done.

We knew we had been successful when the human resource professionals inside the company, based in Moscow, London, New York, and Berlin, took the training and began training people beyond the managing directors and vice-presidents, so everybody down the line began learning the strategy of information systems and the skills of communicating and resolving conflicts.

Organizational Hierarchy and Organizational Evolution: The Dimensions of Conflict (Ken)

Let's now take a closer look at the structure of organizations, and how their structure impacts conflict, by looking at hierarchy, bureaucracy, and the ways organizations evolve.

To begin, let's consider a traditional organizational hierarchy, which is ordinarily pyramidal, with a small number of people at the top and a large number at the bottom. The people at the top are usually the owners, directors, and majority shareholders who set policy; then come the leaders, including the CEOs and top officers, who lead and plan and think; next come the managers and supervisors who check and manage; and last (and usually least) come the staff and employees, who largely do and obey. Outside the organization are members of the public, consumers, and society, along with the environment.

In this typical hierarchical model, it is easy to see that power and compensation, along with status, motivation, and ownership, increase as you move up the pyramid; and that dependence, blame, disrespect, and negative feedback increase as you move down the pyramid.

As soon as we have described any organization in these terms, we can predict many of the chronic conflicts that people inside the organization are likely to confront. To make this clear, imagine how communication will necessarily take place inside an organization that is structured in this way. Imagine what will happen, for example, to any communication that wants to get from the apex of the pyramid down to the base.

And now imagine that the pyramid is subdivided internally not only into horizontal layers, but vertically into various departments or "silos." There is production, sales, marketing, legal, human resources, et cetera, with many different departments. Each department will predictably interpret any communication from the top differently, and those at the top will use different styles of communication, and understand different meanings than those at the bottom.

We can easily understand, just by familiarity with the classic communication game of telephone, that if you say one thing to someone who whispers it to another person, sooner or later, the message is going to get distorted. And we can easily see how there are multiple forms of distortion that arise in siloed, hierarchical organizations.

Imagine what will happen to any of the countless communications that want to get from the bottom of the pyramid up to the top. The answer, of course, is that any communication that criticizes managers who stand between the people who are working under them and those who are leading it above them is going to get altered — not only because the manager who is being criticized wants to make it into the upper ranks and believes it won't happen if he or she is made to look bad, but because there are simply way too many messages at the bottom and not all of them can make it to the top.

So can we predict which messages are actually going to make it to the top? One of those that will is, "I have a lawyer," or "There is criminal fraud in this organization," or sexual harassment, or any number of key words that will produce an immediate response.

Imagine also how conflict is likely to be handled in an organization like this, how people will respond to differences between them; and recognize that each of these layers and each of these silos inside an internally divided hierarchy is going to have its own unique culture, its own language, its own ways of interpreting everything that happens. So we can see that there are chronic sources of conflict that emanate *specifically* from hierarchy. And every form of structure has its own particular chronic conflicts that emanate from it.

Here is another source of conflict. Where do most of the problems that have to be solved in a hierarchical organization get confronted? The answer is at the base of the pyramid. And where is the problem solving authority concentrated? And the answer is at the top or apex of the pyramid.

So again, we can predict a number of the conflicts that will transpire in an organization where this is the form of organization. All you have to do is increase the number of levels in the hierarchy, increase the number of silos, and you will add exponentially to the level of misunderstanding that is possible in that kind of organization. As a result, a lot of work is being done today on flattening organizational hierarchies.

Let's look at this problem now in a slightly different way. I'd like to go back to the dimensions of conflict, but look at it now from the standpoint of organizational systems and structures, policies and procedures, rules and regulations. We can then say, for example, that zero dimensions represent impasse, chaos, anarchy. One dimension, we can say, is power-based and represents hierarchy. Two dimensions is rights-based, and can be thought of as representing bureaucracy. But when we get to three dimensions, we have what we can call a *heterarchy*, which is a multi-dimensional structure in which you can move in at least three different ways. And in four dimensions, we have what we can call "organizational democracies."

Now let's hold this idea for a moment and look at these four dimensions from a different perspective. If we consider just three dimensions, with time as the fourth dimension, we can see that there is height, width, and depth inside an organization. The height can be charted from staff to the CEO, width from individuals to the organization as a whole, and depth can be thought of in terms of organizational change that can reinforce the status quo or produce a transformational outcome.

Here, we can see that conflict has the capacity to touch multiple dimensions, multiple areas inside the organization, particularly when it moves in a transformational direction, and that can impact individuals and organizations simultaneously — teams, departments, *et cetera* across the organization.

In order to understand the impact of organizational structure on conflict, we have to ask a different question. For the most part, what we have in the United States today can be thought of as *managerial* organizations, in which the idea is that there is a middle group of managers who translate from those at the top of the organization to those bottom, and *vice versa*, based on the assumption that those who perform the work need managers standing over them supervising what they do and how they do it.

But problems arise when we ask the question: "What can't be managed?" And the answer is: trust, attitude, caring, dedication, creativity, leadership, curiosity, honesty, insight, courage, synergy, empathy, integrity, compassion, consensus, understanding, *et cetera*, down to collaboration and follow through.

When we say these can't be managed, what we mean is that you can't stand over someone's shoulder and tell them to do these things. They have to be chosen and implemented by the person who's doing them. So you can't order someone to trust. Whether they actually trust is a choice on their part, their attitude is a choice.

So there is a fundamental flaw in the managerial organization and its assumptions, because these are the most important elements in organizational life. They are the things that make the organization successful or unsuccessful, and if they can't be managed, what do you do about them?

The answer is that you can *lead* in attitude, dedication, honesty, courage, empathy, insight or understanding, but you can't stand over someone's shoulder and order them to do it, or manage the way they do it. These things require *leadership* in place of management, and the assumption that you can manage them is going to predictably produce chronic conflicts. So what these chronic conflicts represent is a drive toward organizational evolution.

We can create a diagram that displays the form of the organization on the vertical y-axis, along with the degree of collaboration, the style of leadership, the complexity of the problem that you are able to solve, the use of planning, and the level of participation that goes into each of these areas; while the x-axis horizontally is simply a time frame, and the place where the y-axis meets the x-axis is the present moment.

If we look into the past, at the very the lowest form of organization we can have, this is the moment of *catastrophe*, , and what is the form of organization that arises in that moment? The answer is: there isn't any. Meaning there is no "archy" at all, no governance or organization. The method of operation is simply survival. That is the single thing that determines people's activity, and the level of their participation is simply surrender to the catastrophe.

The first step out of catastrophe is *crisis management*. What kind of organization manages crisis best? The answer is a hierarchy, because hierarchy operates by command. And the level of participation it gets in response is obedience. So if there is an earthquake, someone is going to step forward and say, "Quick, go over here and do this." And you will then go over there and do that. But if someone else says to do something different, it's not going to work. People accept dictatorial forms of power in moments of crisis because they see it as a step out of anarchy. Even though it doesn't represent exactly what they want, it is better than nothing. And who knows? Perhaps this person knows best what to do, and the most important thing then is to act together.

So hierarchy works when we are facing a crisis. And for this reason, military police, and similar organizations that face crises are organized hierarchically, because there isn't time to sit down and strategically plan how we're going to handle the crisis in the moment it is happening.

Notice that both catastrophe and crisis management are concerned with the past. The first step into the future occurs when we move into *administration*. What kind of organization handles administration best? Bureaucracy. The method of operation of bureaucracy is not command, it is control, and the level of participation is not obedience, it is compliance.

So now what we have are *command and control* styles of organization that operate primarily either from the past or the present, as the goal of the bureaucracy is to prevent the present from slipping back into crisis, just as the role of crisis management is to prevent a crisis from slipping back into catastrophe. So they are each oriented in some way to the past, based on the idea that if you can somehow command and control everything, you will be safe.

The first real step into the future happens when organizations operate using *management by goals* or objectives. This is Peter Drucker's idea, which describes typical managerial organizations. The method of operation is supervision, and the level of participation is involvement, because there are goals or objectives that individual employees have to be involved in meeting. A manager can tell you what your goals are and direct you in meeting those goals, but there has to be some involvement of the employee or the organization will simply revert back to the level of bureaucracy and administration, or worse.

The next level is *strategic planning,* because a strategy is different from a goal and requires a longer-range vision. What is then required is *matrixed* organizations — that is, ones in which employees have a hierarchy they report to, but a lot of the work is done in teams. Here, organizations operate in two different ways simultaneously: through visionary leadership and teamwork. These work synchronously to create higher levels of independent, creative activity on the part of employees, which for the first time represents real participation, because for a strategic plan to work, people have to participate and cooperate over time.

The highest level, we believe, is *strategic integration,* and with strategic integration, we create, for the first time, what we call *organizational democracy.* Here, everyone participates in making strategic decisions across both horizontal lines that separate upper from lower management, supervisors from employees; and across vertical lines that separate silos or departments. That is why we call it *integration,* because the goal is to act in an integrated and strategic way across the organization.

For this, organizations require *ubiquitous* leadership, meaning everybody acts a leader with regard to something. And what we get as a level of participation is *ownership*, genuine ownership of all the activity inside the organization. Needless to say, the level of effectiveness and efficiency at this level of organization is far higher than in any of the earlier levels, and the time and effort needed to create it is also greater.

In all of these evolutionary stages, organizations face the problem of what we call the "dialectic of direction." In responding to any organizational problem, there is likely to be a division of responses that range between order and anarchy, or between centralization and decentralization. Order and centralization, in turn, subdivide, so if you simply focus on order and that is all you do, you are going to create two outcomes: one is obedience, and the other is rebellion. These will lead to a *non-transformational* synthesis or combination, in which what we create is "public compliance and private defiance."

On the other hand, if we focus exclusively on anarchy and decentralization, you are going to create two outcomes: one is freedom, and the other is isolation, because groups and individuals can move in different directions and become too far apart. There is nothing to hold them together. This will also lead to a non-transformational synthesis consisting of "private liberty and public chaos." A *transformational* synthesis only takes place when we create "ordered anarchy," and "centralized decentralization," each of which requires a creative combination of leadership and self-directed or self-managing teams.

It is possible to use the same kind of analysis regarding any of the conflicting, paradoxical forces in organizational life. There is a conflict or paradox in every organization, for example, between transparency and the need to know, or between intuition and planning, individualism and teamwork, security and risk, uniformity and diversity, emotion and logic, closure and continuity, *et cetera*, and each of these can give rise to different conflicts that become chronic and systemic as a result.

The essential point here is this: conflict resolution suggests that instead of treating these as "either/or" propositions, we treat them as "both/and," and search for the transformational syntheses that allow us to combine these opposites in creative and fundamentally new and transformational ways. That is the essence of conflict resolution, and it applies to all the conflicts we encounter.

Organizational Bureaucracy (Ken)

Just as hierarchy is a source of chronic conflict in organizations, so is bureaucracy, which is very common in organizations, and another source of chronic conflict. There are many alternative definitions of bureaucracy by various writers that describe its complex elements. What is most important is, first, to recognize that bureaucracy is a human invention. It does not exist in nature. There are no forms to be filled out in triplicate in nature. In fact, if anything, nature is hostile to bureaucracy, because it requires energy, and the primary goal of nature is to reduce the expenditure of unnecessary energy.

Fundamentally, bureaucracy is an effort to prevent change and control complexity through simplification. Yet, as Albert Einstein advised, "Make everything as simple as possible, but no simpler." And the great defect of bureaucracy is that it makes things simpler than they actually are.

The goal of bureaucracy is also to prevent us, as we indicated before, from slipping into crisis or catastrophe through the mechanism of control. Its' theory is that if you control enough things, fear will surrender and you will begin to feel comfortable that whatever has happened in the past is going to happen in the future. So the implicit goal of bureaucracy, is to manage the way change happens in order to prevent it from becoming transformational, substantive, structural, or systemic.

Bureaucracy is therefore a means by which hierarchies and elites retain power and preserve the status quo, by placing procedural obstacles in the way of change. There are too many hoops you have to jump through, too many preconditions, and the goal is to create as many obstacles as possible so people may perhaps have time to calm down emotionally before proceeding with the change, in part to determine how strong the desire for change is, and in part to control the change process so as to make it safe for the existing system.

As a result, any change that seeks to fundamentally transform a system will be resisted, and one of the many and varied forms of its resistance will be bureaucracy. Bureaucracy can therefore be seen as an effort to institutionalize or freeze the present; as a defense against the fear of what might happen in the future. Balzac described it as "a giant set in motion by dwarfs." He wrote a novel called *The Bureaucracy*, in which he described "the report" as one of the greatest obstacles to change ever invented.

Bureaucracy is essentially "rule-driven values," as opposed to "value-driven rules.," In other words, first there is the rule, and then there is the value. But in authentic, democratic, non-hierarchical, non-bureaucratic, collaborative, meditative organizations, the value comes first and the rule comes second, and flows from the value.

Often, bureaucracy is simply the legal face of bribery, graft, and corruption. And in many countries around the world, we can see this directly. The bureaucracy is the organizing *center* of bribery, graft, and corruption in many countries. It is also a defense against empathy and compassion, against connection with others. Karl Marx described bureaucracy as the "deification of authority," and Hannah Arendt memorably called it "the dictatorship of nobody." A beautiful phrase suggesting a Kafkaesque maze that ends nowhere, yet systematically favors subordination and blind obedience. It is a universal form of counter-revolution; a retreat to passive-aggression, disguised as security.

Max Weber, the brilliant German sociologist, wrote a book about bureaucracy containing deep insights into its nature. Some of the characteristics of bureaucracy he mentioned include its use of precise, formal separations that make communications problematic. And if we look at the hierarchical, bureaucratic, pyramidal structure of modern corporations, you can see how communications become problematic as a result of separations that divide it vertically and horizontally, and prevent it from having depth. Bureaucracies do so by generating distinct jurisdictional areas defined by regulations that interrupt the natural flow of work. There is also an over-centralization of functions, leading to inflexibility, waste, and reduced innovation and motivation. There are impersonal hierarchies of titles, offices, powers, and privileges that reinforce relationships based on superior and inferior status, and we can see this in many bureaucracies today. The fundamental goal of these different titles and positions is to create hierarchies of status.

There are also fixed rules and consequences that reduce creativity, authenticity, and individuality. Government positions and job titles are seen as the private property of individuals, while goals, processes, rules, and policies are determined by others. There is a separation of official from unofficial truth, resulting in rumors and gossip to fill in the blanks. There is loyalty to regulations and positions, rather than ideas or people. Structures, systems, and rules are regarded as superior to values, processes, and relationships. There is personalized blame and impersonalized responsibility. Secrecy and the need to know are used to withhold information and augment personal status and power; and avoidance, aggression, and accommodation are given precedence over listening, dialogue, and collaboration.

What we need to do to address the chronic conflicts that are routinely created as a result of these characteristics is find ways of shifting out of bureaucratic ways of thinking into greater authenticity, integrity, responsibility, connection, and collaboration. In order to do this, we have to find ways of circumventing bureaucracy, and turning it in the direction of honest and empathetic communication, collaborative problem solving and consensus based forms of conflict resolution. The bureaucratic approach to conflict is one that requires those who have conflicts to, for example, first talk to their manager, then to HR, then to file a complaint within a set of time constraints. In a unionized environment, there are fixed steps in the grievance process. But what everyone wants to do in conflict is to have a respectful, constructive conversation with the person we have difficulty with. How can that happen? Through skillful conflict resolution, it is possible to skip all these steps and go straight to the conversation.

Finally, bureaucracy is a way of sabotaging organizational effectiveness. In 1944, the OSS, Office of Strategic Services, predecessor of the CIA, issued a sabotage field manual for use in Europe that recommended ways people could disarm hostile organizations and demoralize the enemy. Here is a direct quote from its manual:

> Insist on doing everything through channels. Make speeches. Talk as frequently as possible and at great length. Refer all matters to committees. Bring up irrelevant issues as frequently as possible. Haggle over precise wording of communications. Refer back to matters already decided upon, and attempt to question the advisability of that decision. Advocate caution and urge your fellow conferees to avoid haste that might result in embarrassments or difficulties later on. And be worried about the propriety of any decision.

This is like a handbook on how to be a bureaucrat. What gets triggered as a result is the sabotage of organizational effectiveness, and what we have to figure out is how to design collaborative systems that encourage people to enter into authentic conversations about the issues that matter to them, and then bypass and dismantle fear-based bureaucracies.

Organizational Democracy (Joan)

I hope you're not feeling overwhelmed with all the conflicts generated by the bureaucracies we face every day in our lives. Even if they are simplified bureaucracies, they try to control our behavior, place limitations on us, and encourage us to confirm.

In viewing yourself as a consultant, coach and conflict resolver, please consider as an alternative what we call "organizational democracy." In this session we are offering a brief summary of the ideas we developed in our book, *The End of Management and The Rise of Organizational Democracy*. We are not saying that managers ought to be completely eliminated. We need managers to maintain *parts* of our organizations. But managers can operate democratically, in which case, they won't generate as many chronic debilitating conflicts. How do we do so?

First, we "shape a *context* of values, ethics, and integrity," so that everybody in the organization can participate in defining and specifying their values, and the ethics and integrity they want to live by. When we advocate integrity, we are talking about being *integrated*, being whole, being complete. A democratic organization is a complete form of organization, it has integrity and is integrated.

Second, we "form living, evolving webs of association." This means, instead of living in silos, people live in their interconnections and webs of association, in which they relate to each other informally, rather than in rigid structures.

When we talk about webs of association, I think about Ann, who was in charge of environmental responsibility for a county government in the Western part of the U.S.. Her role extended across every department in the county. So she met with every staff person and talked with them about ways they could become more responsible for the environment. She worked with them to identify specific actions they could take, and connected them with other departments where individuals were taking similar actions, so the whole county government became interconnected through a web of association, and more responsible environmentally. And when the economic downturn happened in 2008 and many county governments were firing people to meet their budgets, because this county government had connected and energized their staff, not one person was fired. When we refer to organizational democracy, we're not talking about a vague fantasy, but about real actions that were able to improve — not only the environment, but the lives of the people who worked in the organization.

Third, we develop what we call "ubiquitous linking leadership." This means leadership is everywhere, not only at the CEO level, but at the level of the person who cleans the restrooms, or works in the cafeteria, who may notice problems – like someone using drugs in the office, and can report a need to human resources for drug education or medical care or counseling.

Fourth, we "build innovative self-managing teams." What self-managing teams often bring is an expanded capacity for innovation and improvement. Teams ask questions like: How can we do this better? How can we achieve more? What's a more creative way of solving this problem? These teams manage themselves, come up with fresh ideas, share their ideas through webs of association, and look for innovative ways of implementing change.

Fifth, we "implement streamlined, open, collaborative processes." This means not forcing people to go through formal bureaucratic steps, but streamlining and encouraging the use of informal processes. When processes become open and collaborative, there is less conflict. People feel they can move at their own pace. They feel they can streamline their work. They feel they can get their work done on their own, and they don't have to meet pointless requests or go through the motions. They can work collaboratively to improve processes.

Sixth, we "create complex self-correcting systems" that are looked at continually and self-corrected. There need to be ways built into every system that allows it to be evaluated and corrected without having to get permission from the top of the hierarchy to make needed changes. This is about organic healing and self-correction, based on the idea that an organization is an organism, and organic processes are self-correcting.

Seventh, we "integrate strategically and change the way we change." Many organizations have time-honored change processes. For example, once a year in many organizations, every employee is evaluated by their boss, and that is the primary way they figure out how to change. But if we integrate the change process into every day, every work process, it becomes more strategic, and flows from the basic strategy, vision, and mission of the organization, including improving the way we change.

These are the primary steps, in our experience, in creating an organizational democracy. We have seen them work in many organizations, from public schools to large-scale corporations, neighborhoods and communities. We've seen webs of association in communities where people in the neighborhoods look out for each other, or take care of each other, and do it spontaneously, feeling they are part of a team.

We've seen it in the neighborhood where we live, where there are a number of families with young children located near a community college and a middle school. As a result, we were inundated with traffic every morning, and a young family organized a way for the community to act as a self-managing team, and support the shared values of keeping kids and the elderly safe from traffic. We created streamline processes through meetings with city police, school hierarchies, and campus police. We came up with traffic plans and now have four new stop signs, and everybody feels much safer walking across the street. We also changed the way we change, so instead of having big adversarial meetings, we spoke informally, personally, and collaboratively with each other in small groups and distributed written surveys.

We invite you to look at your organization, your neighborhood, your family, and ask: are there ways we can become more democratic, get more people involved who feel touched by the issues, reduce conflict, and change the way we change?

SESSION 2 LECTURE SLIDES

Management's insistence that the individual is the unit of organization is as limiting as an engineer's insistence that the atom is the unit of physical systems. The limitations of a physical technology based at one level alone would be great indeed. A molecule is an assembly of atoms, to be sure, but certain relationships among the atoms result in molecules with given properties, whereas other relationships result in entirely different properties. These properties of molecules cannot be predicted solely on the basis of knowledge of the properties of atoms.

DOUGLAS MCGREGOR

What is an Organization?

- A place where people work
- A diverse group of people committed to a common goal
- A system
- An organism
- A variety of interlocking activities and processes
- A set of relationships and processes
- A group of conversations
- A culture or mind-set
- A way of diffusing responsibility
- A compact, agreement, or contract
- A mix of unspoken expectations and desires
- An evolving set of values and purposes
- A way of resolving conflicts, a mediation between its diverse parts
- A method of group learning based on assessment and feedback
- A figment of our imaginations

Content, Process, Relationship, Culture

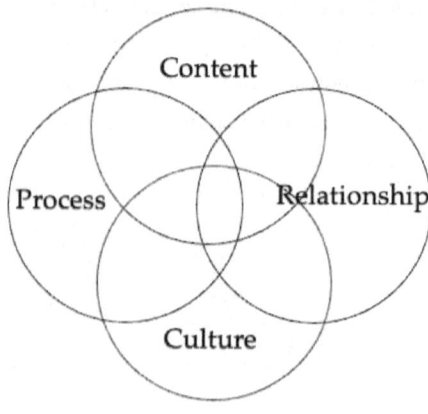

The Organization as an Organism

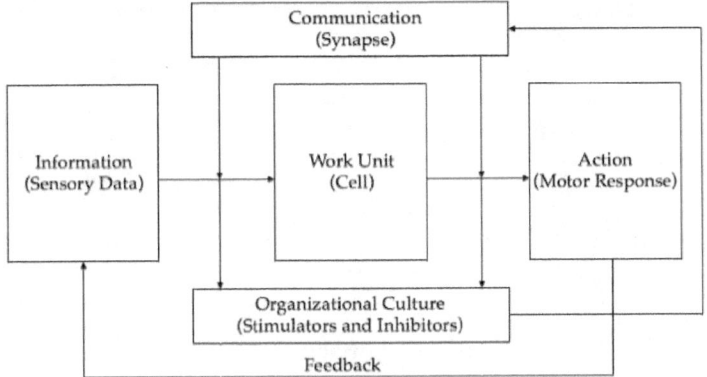

[Based on work by Heinz von Foerster]
© Kenneth Cloke and Joan Goldsmith

Ecological Systems

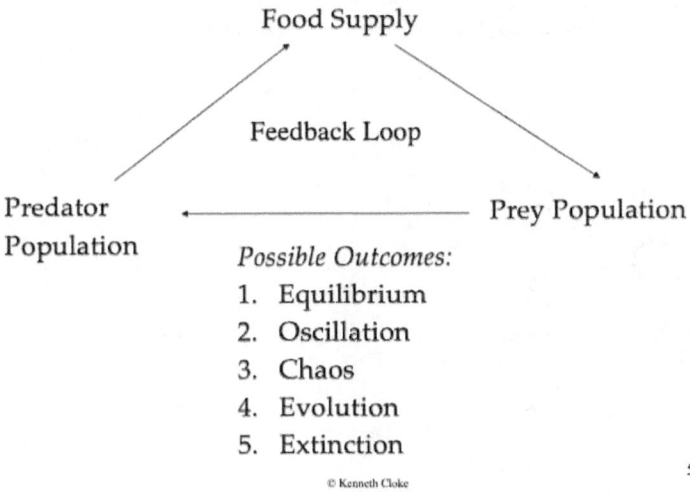

Possible Outcomes:
1. Equilibrium
2. Oscillation
3. Chaos
4. Evolution
5. Extinction

© Kenneth Cloke

2 Kinds of Organizational Systems

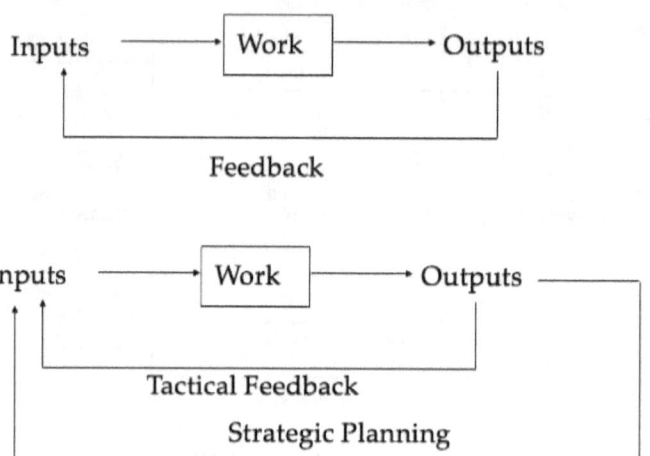

The Organization as a System

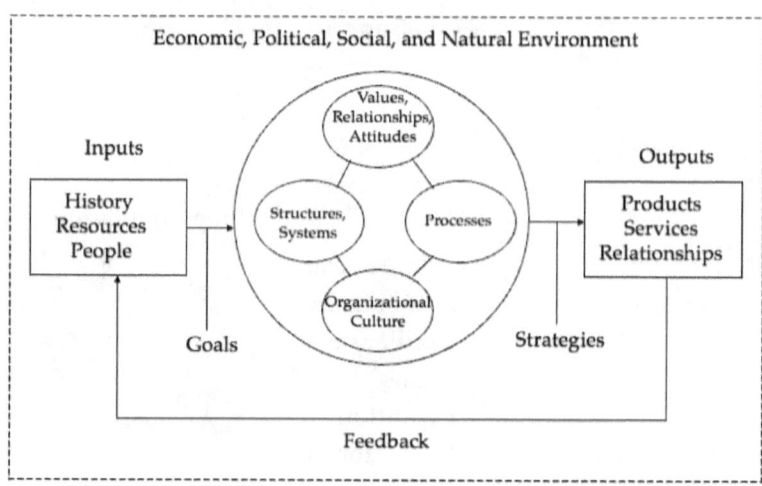

Aspects of Organizational Systems

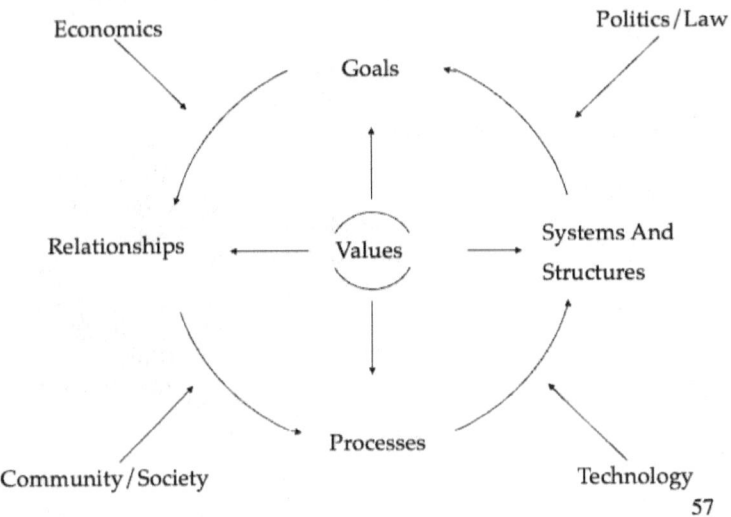

The "7 S" Model of Organization

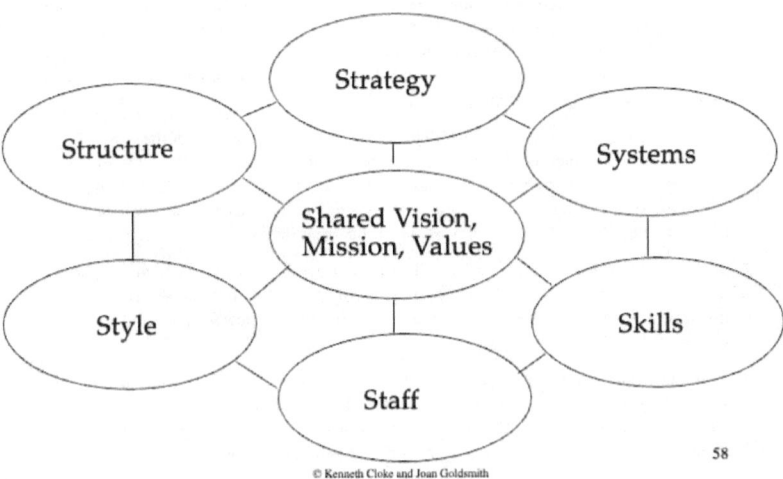

The "7 S" Model Expanded

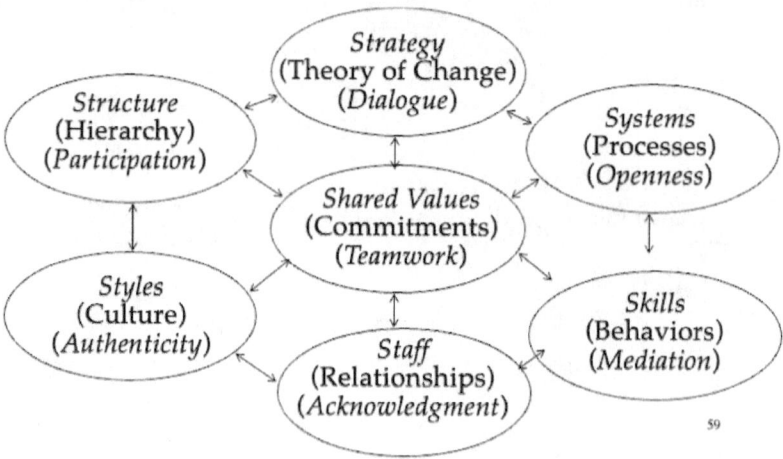

[Based partly on work by Tony Athos and Richard Pascale]

Elements in the Seven "S" Model (1)

The "7S Model" provides an organizational framework useful in planning or assessing the impact of a proposed change. The following model, with several revisions, was first developed by Tony Athos and Richard Pascale in *The Art of Japanese Management*. It asks change agents to consider the impact of seven organizational elements, as well as the interactions between them.

Shared Vision, Mission, or Values: The vision, mission, or values of the organization. The elements of vision, mission, or shared values are usually few in number, but are very powerful influencers of behavior, and often go unspoken. Changes, to be lasting, must be consistent with the vision, mission, and values and these must be shared by those who work in the organization.

Strategy: Plans for the future overall direction of the organization, which may be invented and announced by senior management or developed by consensus within the organization as a whole. Strategy usually includes the *how* for realizing shared values.

Systems: The methods or procedures, both hard and soft, by which the internal and external business of the organization is conducted, including business processes. Organizations often substitute systems for solutions. Most reengineering projects begin with an analysis of systems in order to streamline business processes.

© Kenneth Cloke and Joan Goldsmith

Elements in the Seven "S" Model (2)

Structure: The organizational chart, the arrangement of the work and management of the organization. Customarily organizations have both formal and informal structures, which may or may not closely resemble one another. Changes in these structures enable new systems to flourish and should reflect shared values in their design.

Skills: These are both interpersonal & technical. Derivative of staff, these skills comprise the human resource currently available to the company. The skill profile of staff must change in order to successfully implement a new organizational plan.

Staff: The type of personnel who are employed by the organization, whose skills and resources have been acquired gradually over time. Currently staffing patterns are being changed through downsizing, outsourcing and reskilling programs..

Style (or Culture): Although every organization has particular cultural qualities that differentiate it from other organizations, this element refers to leadership and management styles and other cultural aspects. These can be callous or caring, people-centered or punishing, bottom-up or top-down. If the style is inconsistent with the planned change, it will be considerably more difficult to carry out.

© Kenneth Cloke and Joan Goldsmith   61

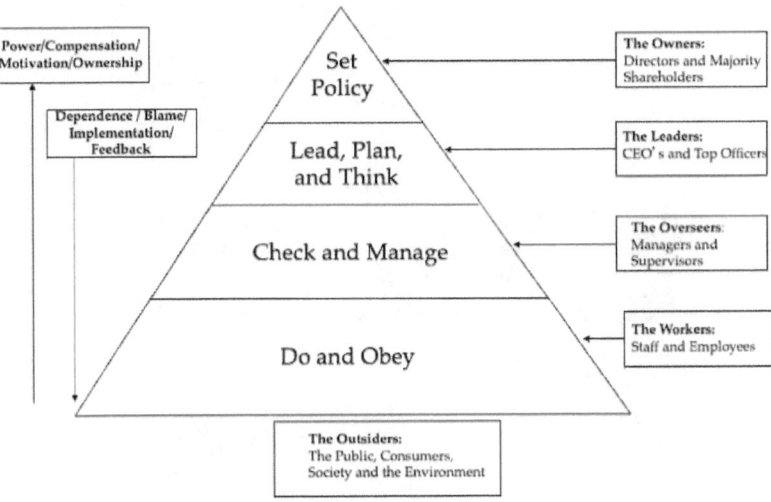

Hierarchies and Communication

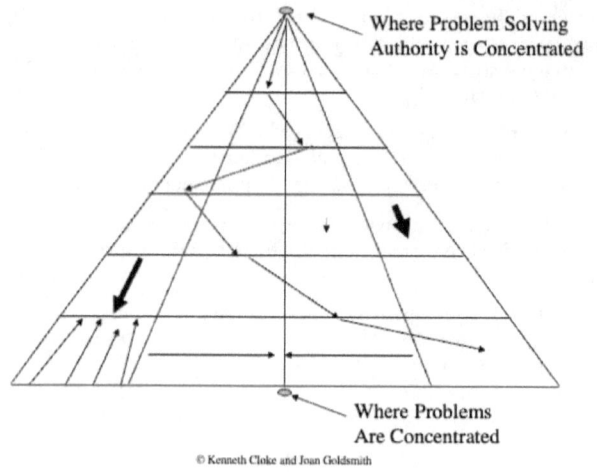

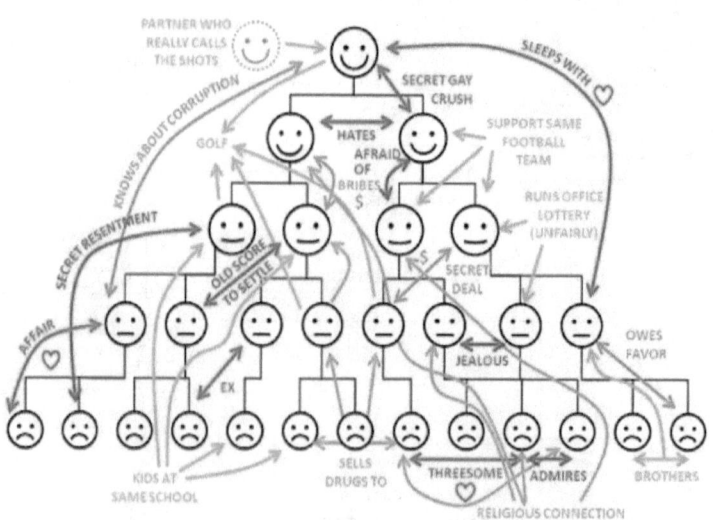

4 Dimensions of Organization (1)

○   = 0 Dimensions = Impasse, Chaos, Anarchy

| = 1 Dimension = Power-Based, *Hierarchies*, Dictatorial, My Solution, Fact Informed, *Obedience and Orders*

□   = 2 Dimensions = Rights-Based, *Bureaucracies*, Adversarial, Compromise, Legally Informed, *Compliance and Voting*

▢   = 3 Dimensions = Interest-Based, *Heterarchies*, Collaborative, Emotionally Informed, *Participation and Consensus*

✦   = 4 Dimensions = Heart-Based, *Democracies*, Caring, Relationally Informed, *Ownership and Unanimity*

© Kenneth Cloke

4 Dimensions of Organizations (2)

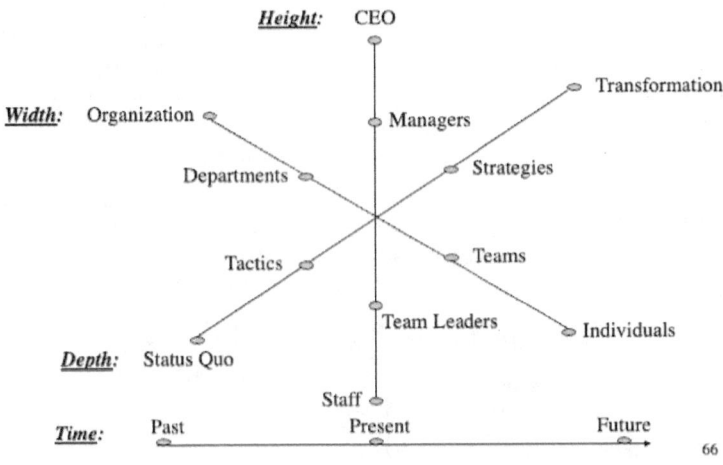

© Kenneth Cloke and Joan Goldsmith

What Can't Be Managed

Trust	Attitude
Caring	Dedication
Creativity	Leadership
Curiosity	Honesty
Insight	Courage
Synergy	Empathy
Integrity	Compassion
Consensus	Understanding
Craftsmanship	Wisdom
Values	Passion
Perseverance	Forgiveness
Initiative	Unity
Flow	Fortitude
Collaboration	Follow-through

© Kenneth Cloke and Joan Goldsmith

Organizational Evolution

Form of Organization Degree of Collaboration/ Style of Leadership/ Complexity of Problem/ Use of Planning/ Level of Participation

○ Strategic Integration
(Organizational Democracy/ Ubiquitous Leadership/Ownership)

○ Strategic Planning
(Matrixed Organization/Teams/ Visionary Leadership/ Participation)

○ Management by Goals or Objectives
(Managerial Organization/Supervision/Involvement)

○ Administration *(Bureaucracy/Control/Compliance)*

Time Frame

○ Crisis Management
(Hierarchy/Command/Obedience)

○ Catastrophe/*(Anarchy/Survival/Surrender)*

© Kenneth Cloke and Joan Goldsmith

The Dialectic of Direction

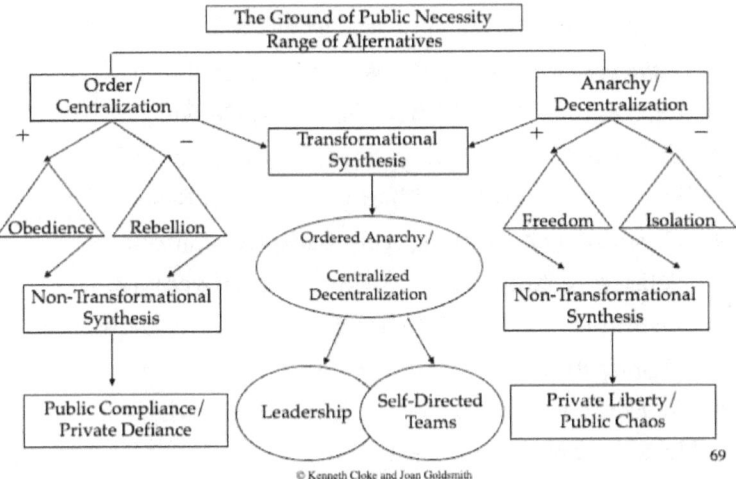

Creativity vs. Control

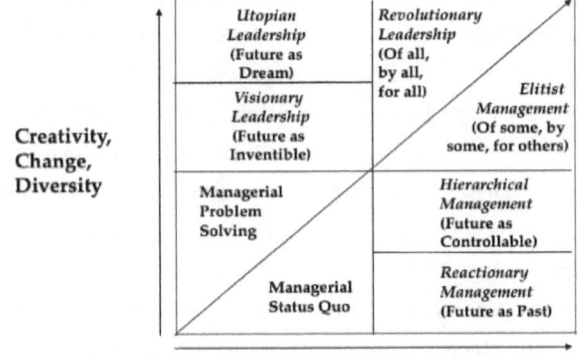

6 Stages of Organizational Development

1. *Start-Up:* Design, Vision, Invention, Innovation, Recruitment
2. *Achievement:* Define Roles and Responsibilities, Operations, Projects, Boards, Goals, Delivery
3. *Consolidation:* Create Systems, Mission Control, Integration, Strategic Planning, Conflict Resolution
4. *Organizational Learning:* Feedback, Evaluation, Self-Correction, Quality Control, Improvement
5. *Institutionalization:* Policies, Structures, Strategies for Sustainability
6. *Renewal*: Return to Design, Vision, Re-Invention, Innovation, Recruitment

Conflicting Forces in Organizational Life

Centralization vs. Decentralization
Competition vs. Collaboration
Change vs. Consolidation
Center vs. Periphery
Individuation vs. Integration
Creativity vs. Control
Destructive vs. Generative Conflicts
Uniformity vs. Diversity
Individualism vs. Team-Work
Specialization vs. Generalization
Integrity vs. Advantage
Security vs. Risk
Emotional vs. Logical

Anarchy vs. Order
Complexity vs. Creativity
Movements vs. Institutions
Global vs. Local
Spontaneity vs. Strategy
Democracy vs. Autocracy
Transparency vs. Need to Know
Positions vs. Interests
Responsiveness vs. Planning
Short-Term vs. Long-Term
Artistic vs. Scientific
Tradition vs. Transformation
Closure vs. Continuity

Bureaucracy and Innovation

[T]he latest and most formidable form of ... domination [is] bureaucracy ... which could be properly called rule by Nobody. If, in accord with traditional political thought, we identify tyranny as government that is not held to give account of itself, rule by Nobody is clearly the most tyrannical of all, since there is no one left who would even be asked to answer for what is being done.

HANNAH ARENDT

[The bureaucracy] was permanently organized under the constitutional government, which was, inevitably, the friend of all mediocrities, the lover of authentic documents and accounts, and as meddlesome as a petit bourgeois. Delighted to see the various ministers constantly at odds with four hundred petty minds, with their ten or twelve ambitious and dishonest leaders, the various government offices hastened to make themselves indispensable by substituting real work for written work. Thus they created a power of inertia named "the Report."

HONORE DE BALZAC

The bureaucracy is a circle from which no one can escape. Its hierarchy is a hierarchy of knowledge. The highest point entrusts the understanding of particulars to the lower echelons, whereas these, on the other hand, credit the highest with an understanding in regard to the universal; and thus they deceive one another.

KARL MARX

[T]he latest and most formidable form of ... domination [is] bureaucracy ... which could be properly called rule by Nobody. If, in accord with traditional political thought, we identify tyranny as government that is not held to give account of itself, rule by Nobody is clearly the most tyrannical of all, since there is no one left who would even be asked to answer for what is being done.

HANNAH ARENDT

CHAPTER 3

LEADERSHIP, CONFLICT & ORGANIZATIONAL CHANGE

The Leader as Mediator and the Mediator as Leader (Joan)

The topic of leadership challenges all of us to improve our ability to lead in the direction of dialogue and resolution, rather than hostility and impasse. This suggests two basic ways of thinking about leadership. First, we want to consider *the leader as a mediator*. Those of us who are mediators, or have mediation skills, have a responsibility to train organizational leaders to become better at mediation – to train them, coach them, and be models for them.

Second, we want to consider *mediators as leaders*. This requires each of us who has skills or has been trained in mediating with families, couples, organizations, or anyone in conflict, to think of ourselves as leaders. This starts with being leaders *in our own lives*, leaders who work to create more humane and democratic relationships, communities, and organizations.

The model I personally have for someone who lived this role is Eleanor Roosevelt, who, as you know, was First Lady of the United States during World War II when her husband, Franklin Delano Roosevelt, was President. When he was in the White House and while he was living, she acted as his advisor and advocated that the

U.S. welcome people escaping from the European Holocaust and help them find new homes in the U.S..

During the Great Depression, many farmers and workers who were unemployed camped in protest near the White House to demand economic support, and Mrs. Roosevelt walked among those families, asking what they needed, how she could help, and how the government could support them. She then worked to provide aid to them. Partly as a result of her work, the New Deal created jobs, medical care, and support for destitute people. In those days Eleanor Roosevelt wrote,

> One's philosophy is not best expressed in words, it's expressed in the choices one makes. In the long run, we shape our lives and we shape ourselves. The process never ends until we die. And the choices we make are ultimately our responsibility.

Her challenge to us, as mediators and as leaders, is to make choices, to create ourselves as leaders, and to be contributors to democracy, by helping to resolve social conflicts, and enabling others to do the same.

Eleanor Roosevelt was both a leader and a mediator. After her husband died, she invited ambassadors from the countries that had been enemies during World War II to meet in her apartment in New York. She also invited leaders of the world's major religions to join this gathering. She led and encouraged them in reaching agreement on what became the Universal Declaration of Human Rights. Representatives from countries that had been at war came up with the foundation document for the United Nations. In this way, Eleanor Roosevelt became one of the founders of the United Nations, and we look to her today for inspiration and leadership in building peace and democracy.

In thinking about leadership, it is helpful to return to the writings of Douglas McGregor, who created "Theory X and Theory Y," as examples of how managers thought about the people with whom they worked, and how they motivated them. Those who subscribe to

Theory X believe that people are naturally lazy and prefer to do nothing. They work mostly for money and status, and the main force keeping them productive is their fear of being demoted or fired.

Those who subscribe to Theory believe that people are naturally active, like to set their own goals, and enjoy striving to achieve change They seek satisfaction in work, including pride of achievement, enjoyment of processes, sense of contribution, pleasure of association, and the stimulation of new challenges. As they meet these challenges, the main force keeping them productive is their desire to achieve personal and social goals.

Traditional managers and heads of bureaucracies who believe in Theory X maintain control through fear and threats. McGregor was coming out of World War II, and was working the idea that people could be treated as if they are mature, and could be independent and self-fulfilled. Because they are close to the problems, they can see and feel what is needed. They understand and care about what they're doing, and they need to feel respected and capable of assuming responsibility for self-correcting. Theory Y is an expression of the underpinnings of mediation in organizations. In mediation, we give people responsibility for correcting themselves. They crave respect, and mediation treats them respectfully.

Hierarchy of Needs and Webs of Association (Ken)

If we think of leadership as a *relationship* between leaders and those who agree to follow, then we can see that the needs and definitions of leadership will vary as the problems people confront vary. It's important to see that leadership is not a single thing, and may take different shapes and assume different forms based on the needs people have.

One of the ways of looking at this is through what Abraham Maslow called the "hierarchy of needs," and I think most of you are probably familiar with this idea. Maslow developed a really interesting way of describing the *evolutionary* process that begins with a set of basic fundamental needs and graduates to higher-order needs. As it does so, the nature of leadership, along with the nature of organization and the conflicts we face, also shift as we move through these diverse needs.

When we are facing basic physiological needs, including survival needs that have to do with hunger and thirst, for example— we need a kind of leadership that is very results-oriented and doesn't pay a lot of attention to process or relationship, but is going to be concentrated on creating a single, clear outcome. The conflicts that are faced in meeting physiological needs are fundamentally different from those that are faced at other points in the evolutionary process, and the forms of organization we create, and the ways we group together will also be different.

So, typically, when people are facing physiological needs or safety needs, they group together in gangs, which are fundamentally different from teams. And the conflicts they face are very different from the conflicts we confront when we have social needs or esteem needs, and especially self-actualization needs.

What is interesting about the period in which we are living is that we are creating a number of mechanisms for addressing these higher-order needs, really, for the first time in history. And what we have discovered as a result of tremendous developments in technology, including smartphones and computers, and other advanced means of communication and transportation, is that we are being propelled into areas of need that we had not imagined before. And as a result, we require different attitudes toward leadership, ones that look to *ourselves* as leaders in our own lives, and alter the form of our organizations. For example, we create "webs of association" – as described in our book, *The End of Management and the Rise of Organizational Democracy*, and if you contrast webs of association with a typical organizational hierarchy or pyramidal structure— not just in relation to Maslow, but to the hierarchies of power and decision-making that exist in most workplace organizations — there is a fundamental difference in how they operate.

Webs of association operate through nodes, and the connections that are made between nodes, are meridians that connect people, primarily through *interest-based* democratic processes, rather than through *rights-based* bureaucracies or *power-based* autocracies. And webs and interest-based democracies are more natural, and more *human* forms of organization. If we take a look at how people connect over the internet, it looks like webs of association, and the same is true for how diseases spread, or technology and understanding spread, and how communication works between equal groups of people.

What we discover as a consequence of this understanding is that we need more natural and human forms of organization that reflect multiple, diverse and varying populations. A particular web of association may last for some period of time for a particular group of people, but it doesn't pretend to be permanent or universal— unlike hierarchies, bureaucracies, and pyramids, which seek permanence in order to consolidate an unequal distribution of power, and hold it in an unequal pattern.

Instead, in democracies, power is encouraged to follow the problem, and to grow and evolve as interest in solving the problem grows and evolves. So what we see in webs of association is not merely a different form of organization, but a different form of leadership, of problem solving, and of conflict resolution.

In webs of association, there are small clusters, and at the center of each cluster are people who are connecting with others in that cluster, and these places of connection can be regarded as places where conflicts are identified and successfully overcome on some level, in order for people to connect in this way. If the conflict is not successfully overcome, people will split off and form a different node in the web, and old connections will be lost, but may grow again in some new place. We often find this in civil society organizations — particularly nonprofits, community organizations, and networks that are not well established. There is a very rapid evolution and adaptation that takes place as a result of conflicts in these organizations.

What is interesting here is that the nature of the leadership also changes as a result of the form of organization and interaction. You can't really have an effective manager in webs of association, because there is no mechanism of control. The purpose of the pyramid is to clearly identify a semi-permanent, universal chain of command, so that it is clear who is in control and who is not, whose voice needs to be listened to and whose does not. In webs, we need to listen to a variety of voices and find ways of connecting and synthesizing them.

So, in the hierarchical model, there are a series of problems in leadership that occur simply as a result of the hierarchy, particularly with the use of primitive, simplistic, hierarchical command and bureaucratic control methods, that need to evolve in order to achieve higher order results and solve more complex problems.

For example, if we imagine that the leader or head of the hierarchy gives an order, the most common responses always include blind *obedience*, and with it, a surrender of organizational responsibility, resulting in a loss of energy, initiative, awareness, creativity, and active collaboration. Clearly, this will have an impact on the organization and its effectiveness.

A second common response will be a passive-aggressive *acquiescence*, or what we referred to earlier as "public compliance and private defiance." This will result in hypocrisy, silence, deceit, subtle forms of sabotage, suppressed rage, cynical obedience, and a seemingly endless cycle of unresolved conflicts. Notice that there will be fewer conflicts in this case than with orders and silent obedience, but there will still be a significant organizational cost.

A third option is active *rebellion* and refusal to comply, which will result in discipline or termination at work, adversarial communications, a hardening of positions on both sides, and a loss of synergy and even the possibility of collaboration, and a high opportunity cost that can be reduced only through cooperative efforts to tackle problems.

Finally, there is a fourth option, which is *strategic engagement*, which encourages people to commit to participate, both within themselves and in collaboration with others, resulting in personal ownership, conflict transformation, team involvement, and organizational learning.

Notice that this option is transitional to higher forms of organization, and is really more appropriate to webs of association than to hierarchy or bureaucracy, and can be seen as a process of moving out of and away from hierarchy and bureaucracy, and the beginning of the creation of a new, higher form of organizational order based on voluntary collaboration and consensus.

As we described earlier, at any given level of order, in order to evolve to a higher level of order, we need to pass through a period of disorder. And in this period of disorder, it becomes possible to create strategic engagement, increase commitment to participation, and to personal leadership as a part of that participation. These in turn become essential parts of the transition to higher forms of leadership, higher forms of organization, and higher forms of conflict and resolution.

Competencies of Leadership (Joan)

When we consider the competencies of organizational leaders, it is easy to also see them as useful for mediators. They are the foundation for how we work as mediators, in organizations. As you review these competencies, ask yourself: What exactly do leaders do? How do they think? How do they approach problems? Where you want to place your emphasis as a leader in mediation? What are some competencies you want to address and develop, both as a mediator and as a leader?

The following competencies are described my book with Warren Bennis, *Learning to Lead*. Warren was a university president who originally studied at Massachusetts Institute of Technology when Douglas McGregor and Abraham Maslow were teaching there. Warren was one of the youngest lieutenants in the European theater during World War II, and he said that he learned about leadership from the team of young soldiers he led as a lieutenant. He went on to become an internationally honored expert on leadership.

The first competency is that leaders *master the context*. They see the big picture and do research to understand it. They read the news. They perceive global threats and economic crises, and the need for immediate response to danger. The mediator as leader understands that conflict is a threat that impinges on every day relationships in the organizations or couples or families who are our clients.

For example, I was consulting with Xerox Corporation when it was facing possible bankruptcy, and there was tremendous stress in the organization that appeared in multiple conflicts. There was one team of people, one department where everybody wanted to work, and people didn't want to leave. It was headed by a woman, and most people wanted to work with her because she understood the big picture. She understood that all the jobs could disappear, and worked to retrain staff and help them support one another in case they lost their jobs. They felt part of a team, and were able to survive the temporary setback.

Knowing yourself is the second important competency for a leader, and certainly for any mediator. Mediators have to be aware of their life patterns and inherited family histories. When mediators are able to learn from new experiences they can understand their leadership skills, and places where they need to grow and improve.

When we are in mediation, we sometimes find we are facing a conflict where we feel intimidated or uncomfortable or unable to address the problem. We may ask someone to co-mediate with us so we have a partner who has more experience with that conflict, or feels more comfortable handling it. Leaders know themselves. And they know when they need help and are not afraid to ask for it.

Third, leaders *create visions and communicate meaningfully*. This means when we begin a mediation, we want to let the parties know how mediation might help them. We create visions for their future relationship that they can hold onto. We help them look into the future and commit to an inspiring plan to get there. or assist them in aligning with it and moving to implement it. In organizations, mediators can help staff create visions for the organization to address the conflict and allow people to listen to each other. In doing so, we start to make that vision real for them, by creating a clear path as a leader.

Another competency of leadership is *empowering others through empathy, integrity, and constancy*. Empathy means the mediator walks in the other person's shoes and knows where they are coming from, and listens to them with their separate mediator's agenda to one side. When parties trust their mediators, they listen to them, and hearing them, feel empowered. If the mediator demonstrates integrity and engages in actions that are consistent with their espoused beliefs, they are more likely to be followed.

The final competency is *translating intentions into action*, and producing results. This is behavior Ken describes calls "nailing it to the floor." I have seen Ken mediate for 24 hours straight. Meals were provided, coffee offered, parties stayed up all night, to resolve a complex organizational conflict. Ken was committed to translating his belief that the conflict could be resolved through action.

There is a distinction Warren Bennis makes between managers and leaders. This means that instead of managers merely administering and copying or trying to do things the way they were done in the past, they also need to be leaders who are innovative, original, and do the work in ways nobody has done it before. They focus on developing themselves and other people, and investigate reality rather than surrendering to it. The role of managers is partly to do things the ways it has always been done. The leader asks "why do it that way?" Leaders investigate, ask what's really going on and how can we change it?

The leader also focuses on people, rather than solely on structures and systems. We have seen many organizations where people take a beginning level job, and have grown and developed and given significant input into designing and changing the organization, creating organizations that are livable and successful by being leaders who focus on the human beings who are essential to success.

Leaders inspire trust and keep a long-range perspective. Their focus is less on what do you are doing today than on where are you heading. They ask if you are building for the long term. Often, managers ask, how are you going to do it? When are you going to produce a finished product? Leaders ask, where are you heading? Why does this need to happen? What really needs to happen for you to be satisfied?

The manager looks at the bottom line, the leader has his or her eye on the horizon. The manager imitates, the leader originates. The manager accepts the status quo, the leader challenges it and asks why. The manager is the classic good soldier, the leader is his or her own person. Here's the bottom line that Warren famously defined: **The manager does things right, the leader does the right thing.**

The mediator, coach, and conflict resolution consultant can be leaders who are risk takers, change agents, and role models. In relation to the past; they are conflict resolvers, learners, and evaluators. In relation to the present; they are supporters, champions, and spokespeople for mediation. In relation to the future; they are leaders, systems designers, synthesizers, and strategists, creating what is new.

Introducing Conflict and Organizational Change (Ken)

Clearly, every organization experiences change throughout its existence, and every organization has different attitudes and approaches to change. Some of these attitudes and approaches to change generate chronic conflicts, and leadership can have a direct impact on both personal and organizational change.

Organizations, on some level, can be seen as efforts to prevent change from happening. Yet at the same time, all organizations are systems that exist in a larger environment that is constantly changing. So the inability to change in a successful way is at least as dangerous as change that is too rapid and unhinged to a strategy or set of values, or grounded in basic principles.

In addition, we can describe conflict resolution as essentially a change process. We are trying to change people's attitudes and experiences of one another, and the way they talk to each other, so as to move them in the direction — not just of change in the abstract — but, of *improvement*, especially in the ways they engage and participate in conflicts.

So let's begin with a famous quotation from Niccolo Machiavelli:

> It must be considered that there is nothing more difficult to carry out, nor more doubtful of success, nor more dangerous to handle, than to initiate a new order of things. For the reformer has enemies in all those that profit by the old order, and only lukewarm defenders in all those who would profit by the new order, this lukewarmness arising rising partly from the incredulity of mankind, who do not truly believe in anything new until they have had actual experience of it.

What happens in most organizations during the change process? In a chart called "Stages in the Mismanagement of Change," we start with wild euphoria, then come growing concerns, near total disillusionment, unmitigated disaster, search for the guilty, punishment of the innocent, and promotion of the uninvolved. Does this sound familiar to you? This is something we have all seen quite a bit, and continue to see in organizational settings.

So the first question in response is, "What happens to our attitude toward change if this has been our experience?" And for the most part, what people say to themselves is, "this too shall pass," and drop out of the change effort, or see it as negative rather than positive. There is no guarantee, of course, that any change will result in improvement. What creates improvement is the answer to a deeper question we want to explore by looking at change in a deeper way.

Here are a few more often cited quotations on change. Leo Tolstoy wrote, "Everyone wants to change the world, but no one wants to start with themselves." Yet what leadership consists of in the change process is the willingness to begin with ourselves. Peter Senge wrote, "People don't resist change. They resist being changed." And Anton Chekhov observed,

> If you cry, 'Forward!' you must be sure to make clear the direction in which to go. Don't you see that if you fail to do that and simply call out the word to a monk and a revolutionary, they will go in precisely opposite directions."

In organizations, the word "change" hides many suppressed, strangled, and unfulfilled conversations, conversations that have not taken place around what we want and why we want it. We may have a vision for the future, or a theory of change, yet these are rarely openly discussed, yet are essential in order to avoid future difficulties.

Let's start with a basic, deceptively simple question: "If it ain't broke, why fix it?" Why reinvent the wheel? You hear this a lot in organizational change efforts. Here are six answers. First, it may actually be broke and you haven't noticed. Second, your competition is busy trying to fix it. Third, when you stop trying to fix it, you stop caring about it. Fourth, it's not really about being broke, it's about improving it. Fifth, unless you consistently try to fix it, you'll grow accustomed to dysfunction, and new ways of fixing or improving it will escape your attention. And sixth, who cares whether it's broke? It's challenging and fun to try to fix it anyway.

So for these reasons, we want to introduce the idea of change as a constant in organizational evolution, as well as in the evolution of our skills in conflict resolution. So once we decide to stop trying to improve our skills and capacities, we begin to lose the ability to intervene in conflicts in constructive ways. Here is a nice quote by George Ainsworth Land that we referred to earlier:

> In any system, once a relative orderliness has been achieved, the only means by which a broader and more complex interrelationship among the various elements can be achieved is by introducing or generating disorder.

The idea I would like to suggest we keep in mind, based on this statement from George Ainsworth Land, refers back to a point we made at the very beginning as an alternative definition of conflict, which is that it is "the sound made by the cracks in the system," or "the voice of a new paradigm waiting to be born."

What we discover, not only with organizations, but with families, couples, communities, and anywhere systems exist, is that this "creative disintegration and reintegration"— this creative disorder, is produced by the gradual erosion of the established order due to the energy required to protect the system from change. Here are some of the ways systems actively resist change:

- Marginalization of ideas, people, perspectives, or insights and making them look unimportant or irrational or impossible to achieve
- Negative framing, exaggeration, or stereotyping;
- Personalization of the change effort
- Reducing ideas to individual people, then discrediting or lionizing them — we see this particularly in connection with political change
- Sentimentalization; seduction; alignment, that is communicating that in order to exist or succeed or be happy, it's necessary to conform to the system regardless of all of its faults
- Legitimation
- Simplification
- False polarization
- Selective repression
- Double binds, or the creation of double standards that require people to live divided lives and make it difficult for them to act with integrity

These are based on several assumptions about change, most of which are at least marginally false. These include the idea that the future can be envisioned, that initial conditions can be known; that change can be designed and planned strategically; that timing can be controlled; that impact and outcomes predicted; that resistance can be anticipated; that change can be efficiently managed; that culture will change by itself; and that change can ever be complete and finished. If we look at organizational change efforts, we can see that these are not correct, yet they continue to pervade most organizational change efforts. What we require, then, is a fundamentally different attitude on the part of systems towards change.

Management consultant and professor Henry Mintzberg describes seven fallacies of change. These include:

1. The fallacy of models — that you can use a model, successfully, to identify what is happening inside a complex organization
2. The fallacy of prediction
3. The fallacy of reductionism — meaning you can breaking things down into tinier and tinier parts, without losing sight of the whole
4. The fallacy of the separation between planning and doing
5. The fallacy of good intentions
6. The fallacy of formalization
7. The fallacy of completion

Over several years, we have looked at a number of research studies on why organizational change efforts fail, and have come up with a number of interesting and useful answers. The first is that the change is either too timid or doesn't include strategic or systemic objectives. Or the change takes place on such a tiny level that it doesn't impact the larger system. Or critics with useful ideas are excluded. Or internal and external conflicts are allowed to continue unresolved. These conflicts can be seen not only as impacting the potential success of the change effort, but as efforts by the system to prevent the change from succeeding.

Change efforts also fail because skills in communication and conflict resolution are not improved, or people create a plan and fail to implement it. Often, people believe they won't benefit from the change, or that the change will actually be harmful to them. Or they don't know how to put the change into practice. Or changes are seen as a cure all. Or there is a failure to improve the change process itself,

The *Harvard Business Review* published an article several years ago by Richard Pascale, Mark Milleman, and Linda Gioja., in which they looked at several hundred organizational change efforts that had failed and asked the question: why did these organizational change efforts fail? The single answer they came up with was the failure to change organizational culture. And what they then did was very interesting. They broke organizational culture down into these four components:

> First, power and vision. Do people believe that they have the power to make things happen or to create change? Is there a clear and compelling vision for the future?

> Second, identity and relationships. With whom do people identify inside their organization? Their teams? Their functional units? Their professions? Or the organization, as a whole? Does the organization value relationships? And if so, how does that happen?

> Third, communication, negotiation, and conflict. What behaviors do people engage in when they have a conflict? How do others respond? Is it swept under the rug or discussed openly? How do conflicts finally get resolved? How do people communicate? How do they negotiate with each other?

> Fourth, learning and assessment. How does the organization learn? How does it grow? How does it evolve? How do people respond to new information that doesn't fit?

So in connection with leadership, we need to start with the idea that change is always going to be chaotic and unpredictable, which does not mean that it can't be led. In order to lead, it is more important to understand *why* a change is happening then to know when or where it will happen. It is more important to have an evolving strategy based on feedback, than an investigation of what took place that is designed to fix blame. It is more important to have a vision than a prediction of the future; and to be democratic, spontaneous, and responsive, rather than autocratic, centralized, and controlling; to invite active participation rather than discourage it. And it is more important to act with integrity than it is to succeed or fail.

This requires some explanation. Fundamentally, all of the attention and energy in organizational change efforts, as well as change efforts in families and in couples, is on success and failure, which are linked to specific outcomes. The difficulty is that the best definition of success for leaders and mediators is the willingness to fail. And the best definition of failure is being overly preoccupied or concerned with success. So the most important thing is to change our attitudes and the *way* we change, and not just the specific change we are seeking.

Advice for Change Agents (Joan)

Most of us, mediators and leaders, see ourselves as change agents and find it useful to have advice about how to behave, how to survive, and how to be successful with simple ideas about change, based on work by Ozzie Bermant that is especially important for mediators who are tasked to change individuals and organizations that are stuck in conflict.

The first step is to *walk your talk,* as you are being watched to see if you are consistent in what you say and do. You are observed to see if you are living your values; and if you suggest changes, first make the changes yourself, make them explicit in your behaviors, and in talking about them with commitment and enthusiasm.

Second, *don't drink the water,* and that means separating yourself from the organizational culture, and the ways most people operate or express, expectations or make decisions. If you mimic what you see and do the same things everybody else is doing, you will get lost in their conflict culture, and become ineffective.

Third, *fix systems, not people* ... It is up to each of us to choose whether to change and it's difficult to change others. You can be a role model and support others in changing themselves, and by changing yourself, you automatically start to change others.

The fourth piece of advice is to remember that *there is no such thing as neutral observation.* In social science and physical science research it has been noted that if something is observed, it starts to change. Just the fact of it being observed can stimulate a change, and allow people to observe themselves through the eyes of an observer.

Fifth, *look with peripheral vision.* If you're looking straight ahead or have blinders on, you're not going to see resistance to change coming from behind or the sides. Be thorough in looking all around you to find both support and resistance.

The sixth point comes from Muhammad Ali, who was a hero of mine since we both grew up in Louisville, Kentucky at the same time. He said, "*Float like a butterfly, sting like a bee;*" meaning, be light on your feet and able to move quickly; and look for opportunities to get in there with all your energy and commitment and make your mark

The seventh is to *search for preventative opportunities* and look for ways that you can prevent dangers, failures and losses.

Eight is *take a longer to make things right*. Don't be in a rush. Let people create a slower pace of change if that is what works for them.

Ninth is *think of conflicts as opportunities*. When conflicts emerge, rather than resisting them, look at them ways to use the conflict to leverage a change.

Tenth, *try to change me vs. them into us vs. it,* and try not to make others into opponents, but enlist their support.

Eleventh is *don't stand between an addict and their dope*. That is a shorthand to remind you that people can become addicted to conflict behaviors in organizations, or in families that are negative and destructive . If you try to take away these comfortable and needed behaviors,, they will dig in and resist. If you can get them to own their addiction and want to recover, change becomes possible.

Twelve is to *be optimistic and realistic* so you won't get bogged down in the negative, yet are realistic about what people are capable of doing.

Thirteen, *let go, and give up false expectations*. If you hold onto false expectations, the change is more likely to fail.

Fourteen is to remember that *not everything works for everyone,* so it is important to give each person a chance to figure out the changes they want, and the process of change, and the approach that are best suited to making innovation possible.

Fifteen is remember that *change always takes longer than planned*. so don't try to tightly control the timing. Leave room for others to participate at whatever pace works for them.

Sixteen, *there are no magic wands*. Change is not magical, but takes effort.

Finally, *don't be afraid of success*, so go for it!

And throughout, remember the advice of author George Bernard Shaw,

> A master in the art of living knows no sharp distinction between his or her work and play, his labor and his leisure, his mind and his body, his education and his recreation. He hardly knows which is which. He simply pursues his vision of excellence through whatever he's doing and he leaves others to determine whether he's working or he's playing. To himself he always seems to be doing both.

SESSION 3 LECTURE SLIDES

One's philosophy is not best expressed in words, it is expressed in the choices one makes. In the long run, we shape our lives and we shape ourselves. The process never ends until we die. And the choices we make are ultimately our responsibility.

ELEANOR ROOSEVELT

Douglas McGregor: Theory X and Theory Y

TRADITIONAL (THEORY X)	POTENTIAL (THEORY Y)
1. People are naturally lazy; they prefer to do nothing.	People are naturally active; they set goals and enjoy striving.
2. People work mostly for money and status rewards.	People seek many satisfactions in work: pride in achievement; enjoyment of process; sense of contribution; pleasure in association; stimulation of new challenges, etc.
3. The main force keeping people productive in their work is fear of being demoted or fired.	The main force keeping people productive in their work is desire to achieve their personal and social goals.
4. People remain children grown larger; they are naturally dependent on leaders.	People normally mature beyond childhood; they aspire to independence, self fulfillment, and responsibility.
5. People expect and depend on direction from above; they do not want to think for themselves.	People close to the situation see and feel what is needed and are capable of self-direction.
6. People need to be told, shown and trained in proper methods of work.	People who understand and care about what they are doing can devise and improve their own methods of doing work.
7. People need supervisors who will watch them closely enough to be able to praise good work and reprimand errors.	People need a sense that they are respected as capable of assuming responsibility and self-correction.
8. People have little concern beyond their immediate, material interests.	People seek to give meaning to their lives by identifying with nations, communities, churches, unions, companies, causes.
9. People need specific instruction on what to do and how to do it; larger policy issues are none of their business.	People need ever-increasing under-standing; they need to grasp the meaning of the activities in which they are engaged.
10. People appreciate being treated with courtesy.	People crave genuine respect from their fellow men.

© Kenneth Cloke and Joan Goldsmith

78

The 48 Laws of Power and Toxic Leaders

Among the recommendations in *The 48 Laws of Power* by Robert Greene are the following toxic, power-based ideas, each of which generates chronic conflicts:

- Conceal your intentions
- Court attention at all costs
- Get others to do the work for you, but always take the credit
- Learn to keep people dependent on you
- Use selective honesty and generosity to disarm your victim
- Pose as a friend, work as a spy
- Crush your enemy totally
- Keep others in suspended terror: cultivate an air of unpredictability
- Do not commit to anyone
- Play a sucker to catch a sucker – seem dumber than your mark
- Play the perfect courtier
- Play on people's need to believe to create a cult like following
- Control the options: get others to play with the cards you deal
- Discover each man's thumbscrew
- Be royal in your own fashion: act like a king to be treated like one
- Create compelling spectacles
- Think as you like but behave like others
- Despise the free lunch
- Strike the shepherd and the sheep will scatter
- Preach the need for change, but never reform too much at once

79

Maslow's Hierarchy of Needs

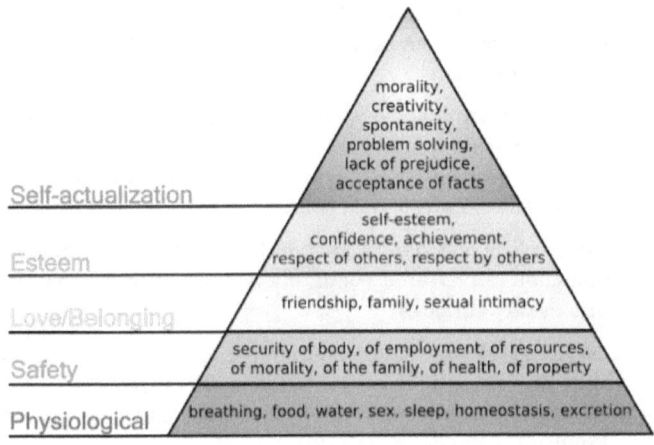

Source: http://en.wikipedia.org/wiki/Maslow%27s_hierarchy_of_needs
See also M. Rosenberg: http://www.cnvc.org/needs.htm

© Kenneth Cloke

Webs of Association

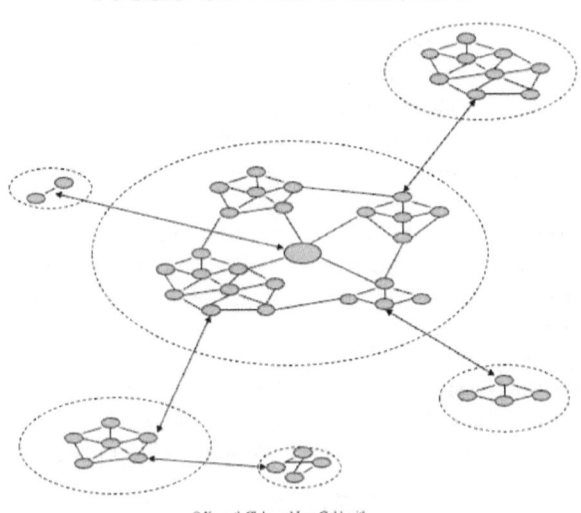

© Kenneth Cloke and Joan Goldsmith

Common Responses to Orders

- *Silent obedience* and surrender of organizational responsibility, resulting in loss of energy, initiative, awareness, creativity, and active collaboration

- *Passive-aggressive acquiescence* or "public compliance and private defiance," resulting in hypocrisy, silence, deceit, subtle forms of sabotage, suppressed rage, cynical obedience, and a seemingly endless cycle of unresolved conflicts

- *Active rebellion* and refusal to comply, resulting in discipline or termination, adversarial communications, and a hardening of positions on both sides

- *Strategic engagement* and commitment to participation, both within oneself and in collaboration with others, resulting in personal transformation, team involvement, and organizational learning

© Kenneth Cloke and Joan Goldsmith   82

Managers vs. Leaders

- The manager administrates; the leader innovates.
- The manager is a copy; the leader is an original.
- The manager maintains; the leader develops.
- The manager accepts reality; the leader investigates it.
- The manager focuses on systems and structure; the leader focuses on people.
- The manager relies on control; the leaders inspire trust.
- The manager has a short-range view; the leader has a long-range perspective.
- The manager asks how and when; the leaders ask what and why.
- The manager has his/her eye always on the bottom line; the leader has his/her eye on the horizon.
- The manager imitates; the leader originates.
- The manager accepts the status quo; the leader challenges it.
- The manager is the classic good soldier; the leader is his own person.
- *The manager does things right; the leader does the right thing.*

Warren Bennis and Joan Goldsmith, Learning to Lead: A Workbook on Becoming a Leader
© Kenneth Cloke and Joan Goldsmith   83

The Competencies of Leadership

Master The Context

Understand the big picture, be aware of the policy implications of your work, be current on research and reform efforts, take time to continue to be a learner.

Know Yourself

Be aware of your life patterns, your ability to learn from experience, your heroes who model leadership and your skills in working with conflicts, mistakes and failures.

Create Visions and Communicate Meaningfully

Look to the future, have a passionate commitment to an inspiring vision and be able to communicate this vision so that others are aligned with it and move to implement it.

Empower Others through Empathy, Integrity and Constancy

Build trust through empathy, empower others to be all they can be, take positions of integrity and be consistent in beliefs and actions.

Translate Intention into Action

Bring your vision into reality, demonstrate your commitments, act strategically and realize intention through action.

Prevent and Resolve Conflicts through Collaboration (The Mediator as Leader)

Warren Bennis and Joan Goldsmith, *Learning to Lead: A Workbook on Becoming a Leader*

EXEMPLARY LEADERSHIP

In Service of Constituent Needs	Leaders Provide	To Help Create
Direction/ Meaning	Purpose	Goals and Objectives
Trust	Integrity/ Authenticity	Reliability and Consistency
Hope	Optimism	Energy and Commitment
Results	Bias Toward Action/Curiosity	Confidence and Creativity

© 1998 Warren Bennis. All rights reserved.

5 Leadership Skills

1. Linking Integrity with Behavior: Skills in Leading by Values

2. Linking Change with Ideas: Skills in Revolutionary Thinking

3. Linking Feelings with Balance: Skills in Emotional Intelligence

4. Linking People with Each Other: Skills in Relationship Building

5. Linking Intention with Results: Skills in Committed Action

[Kenneth Cloke and Joan Goldsmith, *The End of Management and the Rise of Organizational Democracy*]

Roles for Organizational Leader/Mediator

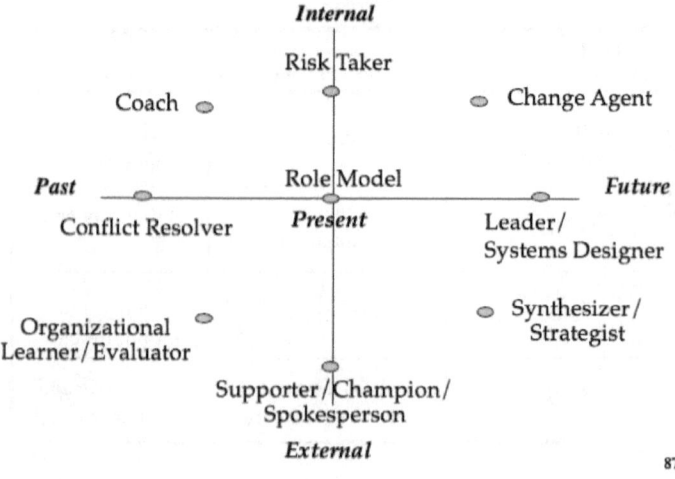

Leadership, Conflict, and Organizational Change

It must be considered that there is nothing more difficult to carry out, nor more doubtful of success, nor more dangerous to handle, than to initiate a new order of things. For the reformer has enemies in all those that profit by the old order, and only lukewarm defenders in all those who would profit by the new order, this lukewarmness arising...partly from the incredulity of mankind, who do not truly believe in anything new until they have had actual experience of it.

NICCOLO MACHIAVELLI

Everyone wants to change the world, but no one wants to start with themselves.

LEO TOLSTOY

People don't resist change. They resist being changed.

PETER SENGE

If you cry, 'Forward!' you must be sure to make clear the direction in which to go. Don't you see that if you fail to do that and simply call out the word to a monk and a revolutionary, they will go in precisely opposite directions?

ANTON CHEKHOV

Stages in the Mismanagement of Change

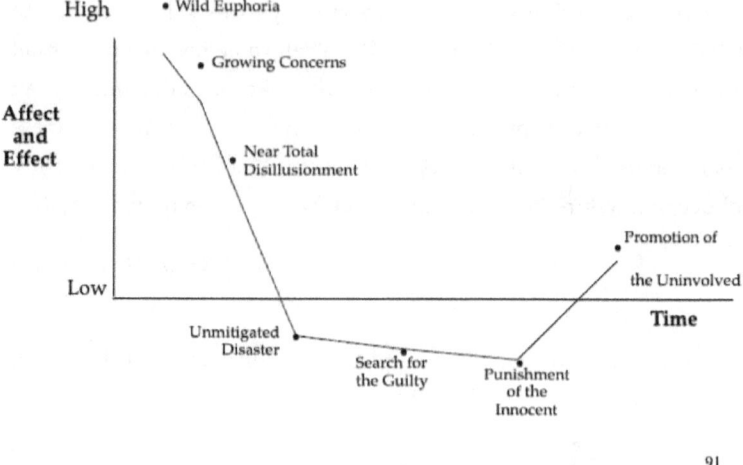

Why Fix It?

When faced with organizational or personal change, many people respond by saying: "If it ain't broke, why fix it." Here are some reasons for fixing it:

1. It may actually be broke and you haven't noticed.
2. Your competition is busy trying to fix it.
3. When you stop trying to fix it, you stop caring about it.
4. It's not about being broke, it's about improving it.
5. Unless you consistently try to fix it, you will grow accustomed to dysfunction, and new ways of fixing it will escape your attention.
6. Who cares whether its' broke, it's challenging and fun to try to fix it.

In any system, once a relative orderliness has been achieved, the only means by which a broader and more complex interrelationship among the various elements can be achieved is by introducing or generating disorder. The system can come apart to be put together in a much more integrated way. Any system that resists this creative disintegration and re-integration can only suffer the gradual erosion of its established order due to the energy required to protect the system from change.

GEORGE AINSWORTH LAND

12 Ways Systems Resist Change (1)

1. *Marginalization:* Making ideas, people, perspectives, or insights that could threaten the system appear unimportant, irrelevant, irrational, or impossible to achieve.

2. *Negative Framing:* Using language that frames new ideas and critics negatively so that nothing that threatens the system can be thought or communicated successfully.

3. *Exaggeration:* Stereotyping or exaggerating one part of an idea in order to discredit the other parts and the whole.

4. *Personalization:* Reducing ideas to individual people, then discrediting or lionizing them.

5. *Sentimentalization*: Using sentimental occasions, ideas, emotions, and language to enforce conformity and silence criticism.

6. *Seduction:* Describing the potential of the existing system in ways that unrealistically promise to fulfill people's deepest dreams and desires and blame the failure to achieve them on others.

94

© Kenneth Cloke

12 Ways Systems Resist Change (2)

7. *Alignment:* Communicating that in order to exist, succeed, be happy, or achieve influence, it is necessary to conform to the system regardless of its faults.

8. *Legitimation:* Considering only existing practices as legitimate and all others as illegitimate.

9. *Simplification:* Reducing disparate, complex, subtle, multi-faceted ideas to uniform, simplistic, superficial, emotionally charged beliefs.

10. *False Polarization:* Limiting people's ability to choose by falsely characterizing issues as good or evil, right or wrong, either/or.

11. *Selective Repression:* Selecting individual critics as examples, bullying them for disagreeing or failing to conform, and ostracizing them.

12. *Double Binds:* Creating double standards that require people to live divided lives, or make it difficult for them to act with integrity.

© Kenneth Cloke

Some Assumptions About Change

We often enter into the process of planning change based on a set of unexamined assumptions, including these:

- The future can be envisioned
- Initial conditions can be known
- Change can be designed and planned strategically
- Timing can be controlled
- Impact and outcomes can be predicted
- Resistance can be anticipated
- Change can be efficiently managed
- Culture will change by itself
- Change can be complete and finished

© Kenneth Cloke and Joan Goldsmith

Seven Fallacies of Change

1. The Fallacy of Models

2. The Fallacy of Prediction

3. The Fallacy of Reductionism

4. The Fallacy of Separation Between Planning & Doing

5. The Fallacy of Good Intentions

6. The Fallacy of Formalization

7. The Fallacy of Completion

[Based on Henry Mintzberg, *The Fall & Rise of Strategic Planning*]

© Kenneth Cloke and Joan Goldsmith

Why Change Efforts Fail

- The change is too timid and does not include strategic or systemic objectives
- Critics with useful ideas are excluded from the process
- Internal and external conflicts are allowed to continue unresolved
- Skills in communication and conflict resolution are not improved
- Change is viewed as an important event, as opposed to something that occurs daily
- Improvement in the design of systems, processes, relationships, communications, and technology are not prioritized
- Bureaucratic work takes time and energy from change efforts
- Not working strategically when facing emergencies or uncertainty
- Creating a plan and not implementing it
- Thinking only tactically or incrementally about change
- People's belief they will not benefit from the change
- Not using teamwork and collaboration to bring the change about
- Not assisting outsiders in understanding the need for change
- Not making the change an objective of the entire group, as opposed to the team that worked on it
- Not changing the culture of fear regarding change
- Not implementing the change at all levels
- Not being able to visualize what is planned or intended
- Unclear priorities or vague objectives
- Inadequate financial resources
- People don't know how to put the change into practice
- Changes are seen as a cure-all

© Kenneth Cloke and Joan Goldsmith

Organizational Culture and Change

1. *Power and Vision:*
   Do people believe they have the power to make things happen, to create change? Is there a clear, compelling vision for the future?
2. *Identity and Relationships:*
   With whom do people identify within the organization? Do they identify with their teams? Their functional work units? Their professions? Or the organization as a whole? Does the organization value relationships?
3. *Communication, Negotiation and Conflict:*
   What behaviors do people engage in when they have a conflict? How do others respond? Is it swept under the rug, or discussed openly? How do conflicts finally get resolved? How do people communicate? How do they negotiate with each other?
4. *Learning and Assessment:*
   How does the organization learn? How do people respond to new information that doesn't fit? How honest and real are they in assessing problems?

Based on work by Richard Pascale, Mark Millemann and Linda Gioja

Leading Organizational Change

Change is always chaotic and unpredictable, but this does not mean it cannot be lead.

1. It is more important to understand why a change is taking place than to know when or where it will happen.
2. It is more important to have an evolving strategy based on feedback than an investigation of what took place.
3. It is more important to have a vision than a prediction of the future.
4. It is more important to be democratic, spontaneous and responsive than autocratic, centralized and controlling.
5. It is more important to invite active participation than to get it done quickly or efficiently.
6. It is more important to act with integrity than it is to succeed or fail.

Mistakes and Lessons in Change (1)

Mistakes In Creating Change	Lessons for Leaders and Teams
1. Changing a Process Instead of Improving It	
2. Killing Ideas	
3. Neglecting People's Values and Beliefs	
4. Being Willing to Settle for Minor Results	

Mistakes and Lessons in Change (2)

Mistakes In Creating Change	Lessons for Leaders and Teams
5. Placing Prior Constraints on the Definition of the Problem and the Scope of the Change Effort	
6. Allowing the Existing Culture and Management Attitudes to Prevent the New Culture from Getting Started	
7. Trying to Make Change Happen Only from Top Down or Bottom Up	

Axioms of Change (1)

- Change is inevitable, improvement is optional.
- The pace or rate of change also changes.
- Without action, ideas about the future remain in the future.
- Real change is really difficult and takes real time.
- Change is painful, and pain is evidence that real change is taking place.
- If it's going smoothly, it isn't really changing.
- Change is a search rather than a solution.
- False starts, wrong turns and negative results are inevitable.
- Everyone is for change as long as nothing important changes.
- Change means doing things differently, not just harder or longer.
- Civility and conformity are obstacles to change.
- Letting go is more difficult than adding on.
- People suspect whatever they don't understand.
- Leaders are most successful at doing what most needs to change.
- We are all either agents of change or targets of change.
- Change means taking time to get things right.
- Tradition and inertia, and apathy and cynicism are enemies of change.
- Radical problems require radical solutions.
- The risks of not trying are greater than the risks of changing.

[Based partly on work by Adam Urbansky]
© Kenneth Cloke and Joan Goldsmith

Axioms of Change (2)

- Change generates opposition and unity. The deeper the change, the more powerful and committed the opposition.
- Opposition can be expressed negatively or positively.
- Negative opposition recreates what it opposes. Positive opposition leads to improvement, learning, and deeper unity.
- Small changes can trigger unpredictability and chaos.
- Higher levels of order can emerge out of chaos.
- Incremental changes can lead to transformational change.
- The more complex and transformational the change the less it can be forced.
- Changing part of a system can change the system as a whole.
- Changing people doesn't necessarily change the system.
- All change is two steps forward, one step back.
- Profound changes occur only when people are dissatisfied with the old ways and have a positive vision of the future.
- Real change takes place at the level of actual human behaviors.
- What people expect of change becomes a self-fulfilling prophecy.

© Kenneth Cloke and Joan Goldsmith

Axioms of Change (3)

- Change is more successful when people know where it is headed, and when goals and outcomes are collaboratively and clearly defined.
- Change can't be predicted. It is a journey, not a blueprint.
- During the transition nothing is clear and no one is satisfied.
- To complete the transition, it is necessary to change the culture.
- Changing culture means changing the hidden, unspoken context.
- Change induces loss, insecurity and fear, which fuel resistance.
- Anyone who is not involved in the change may actively resist it.
- Those who resist can be won over, or moved to neutrality or support by having their interests satisfied or acknowledged and their objections answered.
- Change is personal, and begins by changing ourselves.
- Change takes place more smoothly when feedback, evaluation and self-correction are built into the process.
- Change is reinforced through communication and celebration.
- The effects of change last long after the change is over, and need to be managed as much as the change itself.
- Change is outdated the moment it is born, initiating a new cycle of change.

How We Change

Individuals and organizations change by:
- Changing their language, culture, and physical environment
- Altering not just content, but context, process and relationships
- Changing roles and responsibilities
- Using imagination to explore alternatives, creating a vision of what life could be like, then integrating vision into the way people actually work
- Identifying what is dysfunctional or doesn't work, and linking it to paradigms and systems that need to be changed
- Including outsiders in examining the possibilities and implications of change
- Altering the way decisions are made
- Changing what is counted and how score is kept
- Opening new lines of communication and letting information flow more freely
- Altering expectations, challenging underlying assumptions, and rejecting what has been accepted, or is merely based on authority

Change, Conflict and Community

Attitude to Change	Conflict Style	Form of Community
Apathy and Cynicism	Avoidance	Isolation / Non Community
Obedience and Passivity	Accommodation	Civility / Pseudo Community
Resistance and Reaction	Aggression	Hostility / Negative Community
Acceptance and Compliance	Compromise	Tolerance / Legal Community
Ownership and Affirmation	Collaboration	Synergy / Diverse Community

© Kenneth Cloke and Joan Goldsmith

Some Things that Need to Change

1. Command and control style of management
2. Organizational visions, mission statements and goals written by executives, managers or HR for employees
3. Purely monetary incentives
4. Class distinctions and inferiorities
5. Uniformity in race, gender, and culture
6. Multi-page top-down performance appraisals
7. Detailed job descriptions
8. Adversarial negotiating, including collective bargaining
9. Promotion to management based on technical competency alone
10. Rule-driven values vs. value-driven rules
11. Gossip, dishonesty, public humiliation and bullying
12. Obscene salary discrepancies
13. Avoidance of responsibility for unethical conduct
14. Punishment of whistle-blowers
15. Conflict suppression, avoidance, settlement and reactiveness

© Kenneth Cloke and Joan Goldsmith

What Needs to Change?

Values Changes	Process/Systems Changes	Attitude/Behavior Changes	Relational Changes

© Kenneth Cloke and Joan Goldsmith

How to Change the *Way* We Change

- Bring in people who don't know how it should be done
- Increase awareness, especially of hidden rules and habits
- Create a context of ethics, values and integrity
- Speak the "unspeakable"
- Listen closely to critics and dissidents
- Ask "silly," "ridiculous" or "stupid" questions
- Give and accept genuine, honest feedback
- Change how evaluation and assessment take place
- Alter the ways people succeed or fail
- Shift work to teams, networks, and webs of association
- Include people or groups that have not been included before
- Engage in small acts of love and kindness
- Change ourselves
- Model what we want from others

© Kenneth Cloke

Advice for Change Agents

- Walk your talk.
- Don't drink the water.
- Fix systems, not people.
- Changing yourself automatically changes others.
- There is no such thing as neutral observation.
- Look with peripheral vision.
- Float like a butterfly, sting like a bee.
- Search for preventive opportunities
- Take a little longer to make it right
- Think of conflicts as opportunities
- Change me vs. them into us vs. it.
- Don't stand between an addict and their dope.
- Be optimistic and realistic.
- Let go. Give up your expectations.
- Not everything works for everybody.
- Change always takes longer than planned.
- Learn from each other.
- Don't control the process - leave room for others.
- There are no magic wands.
- Don't be afraid of success.

© Kenneth Cloke and Joan Goldsmith

A master in the art of living knows no sharp distinction between his work and his play, his labor and his leisure, his mind and his body, his education and his recreation. He hardly knows which is which. He simply pursues his vision of excellence through whatever he is doing and leaves others to determine whether he is working or playing. To himself he always seems to be doing both.

GEORGE BERNARD SHAW

CHAPTER 4

ORGANIZATIONAL CULTURE & CONFLICT

THE NARRATIVE STRUCTURE OF CONFLICT STORIES

Organizational Culture and Conflict Stories (Ken)

In previous sessions, we have spoken a lot about the importance of diversity, not only as a source of conflict, but also as a source of creativity and problem solving, and it's important for us to take a closer look at culture, and diversity in relationship to culture, in order to understand how conflicts arise, and how people get stuck in them.

To begin, here is a wonderful statement by Mary Parker Follett, one of the founders of mediation, writing in the 1910s and 1920s:

> Our 'opponents' are our co-creators, for they have something to give which we have not. The basis of all cooperative activity is integrated diversity. What people often mean by getting rid of conflict is getting rid of diversity, and it is of the utmost importance that these should not be considered the same. We may wish to abolish conflict, but we cannot get rid of diversity. We must face life as it is and understand that diversity is its most essential feature. Fear of difference is dread of life itself. It is possible to conceive conflict as not necessarily a wasteful outbreak of incompatibilities, but a normal process by

which socially valuable differences register themselves for the enrichment of all concerned.

It is a fundamental goal of conflict resolution to turn diversity — in views, in culture, in beliefs and ideas — into methods for achieving higher forms of cooperation. To do this, we have to understand the role of diversity in relation to culture, because it is precisely culture that provides the mechanism whereby diversity registers itself at the deepest possible level.

Let's begin with a simple question: what is culture? If we look at cultural anthropology as a field where a great deal of research and thinking has taken place on this topic, we can think about culture in a variety of ways.

First, culture is a way of approaching our environment. It is how we group together, and how we divide and separate from one another. It is how food is produced and consumed;; how gender is perceived and displayed; the ways space and boundaries are established between individuals and between groups; how time is defined and used; how learning takes place. It is how goods are made and possessed, used, exchanged and distributed. It is the ways people play and laugh, how they play, and what they laugh at. And, it is what people do when there are conflicts, how they are resolved, why they are not resolved, and how they behave when they are not resolved.

Here are some additional ideas about culture. Culture is a way of perceiving and processing reality. It is a set of shared behaviors, beliefs, attitudes, customs, ways of life, ways of differentiating ourselves from others, how we satisfy our needs in a given environment. And here, we begin to come up with a definition of culture that directly impacts organizations, and particularly, the conflicts that take place inside of organizations. Culture is a set of agreed upon *meanings* of symbols, events, sensations, behaviors, and communications in general, and ways of attributing meaning.

The most important element in any conflict is its' meaning for each person. Culture is the primary way meaning is attributed to what other people do, and to what we do. It is an accumulation of successful adaptations and a prescription for success. Finally, it's what everyone knows and no one talks about, allowing culture to remain largely beneath the surface and take place at a level that is far deeper than conscious attention.

Therefore, it requires a great deal of work for mediators to surface what culture is and how it results in the meanings people attribute to a given set of behaviors, or events, or sensations, or communications. How exactly does this happen? It happens in a variety of different ways, but fundamentally, these ways can be thought of as a set of cultural rules or norms.

The anthropologist, Edward T. Hall, has written a number of books, one of which is *The Silent Language*. He studied indigenous cultures, especially Hopi, Navaho, and other Native American cultures in the southwest of the United States, and looked at cultures in other areas as well.

Hall described culture as a set of rules, essentially, for how to interact with the environment, to associate with others, to subsist, and achieve some of the purposes I referred to. But the most important aspect of culture in determining meaning is what Hall called *context*. Culture is a way of categorizing context, and organizational cultures in particular provide a set of cultural norms and rules for understanding the context, and consequent meaning of any communication. These contexts are different, not only for different vertical levels within an organization, but horizontally across silos or departments as well.

It is easy to see how cultural differences and diverse norms can create conflict. For example, there is a difference between cultures in their orientation to precision versus ambiguity in communication. And we need to understand that these include family cultures, and subcultures within families, where individuals may approach communications differently.

Conflicts can also arise over open versus closed approaches to personal information. How open are we? How closed are we? What kinds of things do we communicate and what don't we? There is also verbal versus written as a basis for tradition, and there is high versus low context, which we will return to in a moment. There is consensus building versus individualism in decision-making, formal versus informal in processes, competitive versus collaborative in relationships, direct versus indirect in delivering feedback, authoritarian versus democratic in organization, deference versus rebelliousness in relationship to authority, exclusive versus inclusive in relation to outsiders.

If we ask which of these approaches is correct, we will soon realize that they are *both* correct, in different circumstances. And therefore, a diversity of approaches to these cultural differences will lead to a more complex and potentially successful set of solutions to a wider range of problems.

If we are only competitive and not at all collaborative, we will be able to solve a certain variety of problems, but not others. And if we are only collaborative and not competitive, we will solve another set of problems, but not all, and the same goes for each of these categories. Here are a few others: linear versus non-linear in thinking, gestalt (meaning holistic) versus detailed in overview, appropriate versus inappropriate in humor in play, demonstrative versus restrained in emotional expression. There is also permissive versus directive, fixed versus fluid, open versus closed, individual versus group in orientation, and within conflict resolution, what we describe as an interest-based approach to solving problems, versus a power- or rights-based orientation.

At a fundamental level, we can see that each of these cultural differences can give rise to conflicts, and that each of these conflicts can have two fundamental solutions: First, an exclusive solution in which one side wins and the other side loses. In which case, we have eliminated a great deal of the complexity that could be helpful in solving problems. Second, there is a synergistic, combined approach that brings these cultures into communication with each other, and searches for whichever approach is best in any particular circumstance, but tries to combine them in creative ways in order to solve problems. This is the fundamental approach of conflict resolution in organizations. The difficulty is, how do we bring conflicted parties into dialogue with each other? How do we decide which approach is most appropriate in any particular situation? And this is a place where conflict resolution offers several tools that are helpful.

If we look at time or space, as an illustration, cultures differ considerably in their perceptions of both. Edward T. Hall studied time and space in different cultures, and the role of context in communications. The question that he began with is, how much context is required in any culture to determine the meaning of a particular experience or statement?

For example, if we consider law as a culture, we will see that there are many definitions of behaviors in the law, and very little context is required to determine what the meaning of something is. Whereas emotional communication or romantic or sexual communication are very dependent on context and require a great deal of context in order to identify the meaning of any particular statement.

If we think about intimate communications in particular, we can see that the same statement can be interpreted in many different ways. Even the word 'hello' can be said in a romantic way, an angry way, a lewd way, a way that is frightened, a way that is sad. The question is, how do we know what the real meaning of that word 'hello' is? And some part of that is determined by context.

Similarly, conflict, as a culture, requires an enormous amount of context in order to understand the meaning of anything. That is why we require communication and dialogue between people in conflict and understanding their conflict cultures, in order to determine what something means to one person, and how that differs from what it means to someone else. Our focus is therefore on eliciting from each person and each culture the meaning of what has been said or done, and we do this in many ways.

Here, for example, are two questions you can ask: First, what role would you like me to play in this conversation? The answer will identify a set of cultural assumptions about conflict in general.

Second, what is the meaning of what she just said to you? Why do you believe that is what she means? Do you think she agrees with your understanding of what she meant? Why don't you ask her right now? In these ways, we can surface the underlying cultural assumptions, so that instead of culture becoming something that "everyone knows and no one talks about," it becomes something that everyone talks about in order to discover what it means to each person.

Levels of Organizational Culture and Cultural Approaches to Conflict (Joan)

It is important to analyze this concept of organizational culture and try to understand it if you're living in an organization, acting as a change agent, a mediator, an ombudsperson, or offering support for leadership.

First of all we need to realize that there are levels of organizational culture that offer ways of thinking explicitly about it, and understanding how it influences organizational life. Some of these elements have to do with feelings, thoughts, needs, wishes, interests, desires, hopes, fears, emotions, and feelings among people in the organization.

Here is a personal example. I became an in-house consultant in the headquarters in San Francisco of a very large international organization. It was a nonprofit that offered personal growth programs for individuals in centers all around the world. Soon after I had arrived I noticed a woman who seemed quite powerful and I wanted to get on her good side, early in my new role. She was very close to the founding president and eventually they married. In reading the culture, I realized that most staff looked up to her and had underlying, unspoken, implicit assumptions and expectations about her. So I reported to her the following; "Harriet has been not very welcoming to me and she'd not been very nice to me." The response I received surprised me when this perceived leader looked at me and said, "Joan, in our organization, we don't gossip about other people. If you have something that concerns you about Harriet, tell her."

What a surprise! I felt I had been slapped in the face. In previous organizations I had used gossip as a way of getting close to others, or at least size them up. But in that organization, there was a shared value, expressed in the culture that you talk directly work with others so you could resolve a conflict or deal with an issue.

Ken and I consulted and mediated for a science museum to assist the leadership in redesigning and rebuilding the organization.. It is a wonderful institution and a beautiful museum, and the staff committed to recreating it from scratch. There was a lot of tension in the staff as they saw themselves as two different groups: those paid by the county government to work there, and those paid by grants from private foundations. And between these divisions, gossip was rampant in their culture.

We worked with the leadership team to explicitly communicate their shared values and indicate that among their shared values were: not gossiping and resolving conflicts openly and directly. The leadership team agreed and wanted to articulate vision, mission, goals, and strategies for everybody to adopt, shift the culture to being more open, and reduce gossip.

We conducted a workshop with the entire staff and included people from every department — those who worked for the county, and those who worked for private foundations. As a result they came up with a plan to create large buttons that everybody would wear, which had the word "gossip" in the middle with a red line drawn through it. They wanted to end the gossip element of their culture and have underlying issues revealed and discussed so expectations could be clear and open.

In any organization, it is best to begin at the top of the pyramid in the hierarchy, and create rules, policies, and procedures that make the culture explicit, with clear expectations and communication styles.

We have also created processes in some organizations where team members meet on a regular basis and talk with each other about the behaviors they can use to support the team process and those that might block the team process. In this exercise, we offer a chart for each person to fill out for themselves, listing the behaviors they need to cease, because they're blocking team effectiveness, including:: stopping coming late to meetings, or interrupting, or avoiding gossip. Each person also identifies the behaviors they can use to support the team process including: bringing coffee or food to team meetings, thanking those who created the agenda, contributing to the agenda, making sure meetings begin and end on time, etc..

After each person shared the behaviors they were using that were blocking or supporting team behaviors, everybody gave each other feedback. We asked the team leader to be the first to articulate what she needed to do differently and how she could help build and improve the team culture.

There are two basic approaches to dealing with conflict in organizational cultures. The first is suppressing and avoiding it. The second is understanding it as normative, so that in the team example, it was expected and normal for someone to say that they need to do more to support the team process, and for others to give feedback by saying, they are not recognizing how much they take over the agenda and talk in meetings. The conflict between that person and those who give feedback then becomes normative, expected, positive, and leads to personal growth.

This approach views the self as *relational* and when in conflict, the focus is on the effects of the individual's behaviors on the group, and the security and self-worth of all are achieved through building cooperative relationships. The boundaries of conflict extend beyond the individual, the family, the community and reach the spiritual world, with repercussions beyond time. This is very important because, if the boundaries of conflict extend into larger spheres, the issues impact all of us and we need to understand and deal with conflict at every level where it occurs. There was a very important shift in thinking about the psychology of the individual and conflict that was developed after World War II in the U.S., when it became clear that to create a true democracy, we need to recognize how we're related to each other, the nature of that relationship, and how conflict occurs between us.

In this view of democracy, it is no longer just up to me, it's up to both of us to work out our disagreements and resolve our conflicts This very important shift doesn't take responsibility away from the individual, but rather invites the individual to look at how they're related to other people, including their opponents, and then conflict can be seen as binding people together in creating new understandings and conditions,. As a result, we understand that those to whom we are most closely bound are the people with whom we're most often in conflict.

We invite you to look at your family, the organization where you're working, at your mediation or consulting or coaching practice, and see who rubs you the wrong way or gives you trouble in feeling good about yourself. That reaction; "oh, damn, here comes a text from him again" can let you see that this person may be someone you can improve your skills and relationship with.

The first approach considers conflicts as destructive to harmonious relationships, and suggests that you should avoid facing them and sweep them under the rug. But when they do not go away, they become disruptive if they're not immediately addressed. The boundaries of conflict are narrow, defined by those who are directly involved, and naturally occur in the present.

We worked with a large cable television organization in New York, and the head of finance and the head of information systems were in a continual disruptive conflict with each other. They each saw their position as just and blamed the other for the stress. Their direct reports and the direct reports of their direct reports throughout each organization lined up behind the positions of their bosses. The conflict wasn't contained and everybody was in conflict with everybody else. The outcome was that finance people refused to give budget information to technology staff to indicate the funds for equipment to buy, so they could support other departments in the organization; and the technology people refused to build or buy applications for finance staff or fix their equipment or make technology useful for them in providing services for the rest of the organization.

Each person's approach to conflict was too narrow, and they both missed a huge opportunity for collaboration. When we were working with technology and finance staff and leaders to resolve their issues, the leader of finance said, "You know what? We solved the conflict with technology. And guess what? They agreed to everything we suggested." And when we talked to the head of tech, he said "You know what? Finance bought everything we suggested and ended the fights." Another aspect to remember about this approach is that the self is autonomous, individuated, and mostly speaks of self-interests in conflict. Security of self comes from individual achievement, as well as economic success. Thus, if an individual believes that they can steamroller over you any time to get ahead and climb the ladder over your back, then their approach creates more unresolved conflicts, pain, and does a disservice to the entire organization. With this dysfunctional approach people can rise to the top and earn huge salaries and benefits and feel they are doing well. However the organization pays a huge price for their behavior because they create dissatisfied and disgruntled people all around them.

We invite you, when working with organizations to understand and shape the culture, include staff on every level, and determine the culture they want to build and support. Ask them to defend the explicit and implicit cultures of conflict that they want. Find ways to reveal the visible and invisible structure for dealing with conflict. Determine the rules, policies, strategies, values and implicit assumptions and the feelings and thoughts that need to be resolved.

Differing Types of Cultures as They Relate to Conflict (Ken)

Culture plays a very subtle and often hidden role in conflict. Sometimes, it's quite explicit and directly at issue in conflict, particularly in organizational settings. The clearest case of a direct clash of cultures takes place when two organizations combine, when they merge, or when one is taken over by another.

There are, we find, six alternative approaches to the mixing of different cultures, looking at it from a large-scale point of view. We can then think about how to translate these back down to what happens in families, or couples. On a small scale, when people get married, many of these issues arise because they are simply alternative outcomes for what happens when we mix two different things together.

If we think about it in terms of differences, we can see that the first option is *subjugation*, or suppression of differences. That is, one culture becomes suppressed or subjugated to the other culture. Second, there is *plunder*, which is the appropriation of differences and their transfer from one to the other. Plunder implies a lack of reciprocity. So it's not sharing, but the more powerful culture taking from the less powerful one.

A third alternative is *amalgamation*, where there is a complete disappearance of differences. There is full and total amalgamation, so you can no longer identify what divides these cultures from one another. This is not necessarily the most optimal outcome, however.

Fourth, there can be *coexistence*, which is where differences are separated and interact with each other, but remain separate and coexist with each other side by side. Fifth, there can be *compromise*, which is a kind of negotiation of differences. And particularly, in organizational mergers, a great deal of what happens takes place at the level of compromise. One element is picked up from one culture, something else is picked up from the other culture. And marriage, as an institution, is a kind of collaborative negotiation of differences, including cultural differences, having to do with time, space, and all the different cultural categories we've described.

Sixth, and finally, there is *collaboration*, which is where different cultures combine and, in their combination, create something new, giving rise to a new culture that is not just the sum of its parts, but greater than both.

If we want to consider how we can get to collaboration, we first need to take a look at another place where culture forms an essential part of conflict. And that is in relation to whether the cultural message being sent is *congruent*. That is, whether the *explicit* message and the *implicit* message match, whether the *ideal* is the same as the *real*, whether the walk matches the talk.

In many organizations, there is a huge difference between these opposite messages, and they can be charted. For example, it is very common in organizations for there to be an ideal that "management has an open door policy." The implicit message is: "criticism is welcome. You are invited to come in and offer feedback." Yet it often happens that the door is ajar, but the mind inside the room is shut.

A second example is: "we promote risk takers," where the implicit message is that criticism is safe. But the real message, explicitly, may be that those who criticize are not listened to, and the implicit message is that criticism is, in fact, not valued at all in the organization.

Thus, a principal source of conflict in any organization is the separation between what is explicit and what is implicit in connection with a given cultural message, or a significant difference between what is ideal and what is real. The goal of conflict resolution then becomes, first, to surface these differences, bring them out into the open, by inviting people to identify the message and its meaning, and describe what is ideal and what is real for them. Second, it is to discuss openly how to return to congruence.

People can begin this process by small groups writing their responses on a flip chart, and you will be able to discover quickly what the reality is in most organizations because they will tell you, unless the fear is so great that nobody is willing to even put on a flip chart what their difficulties are. In that case, it's best to use a paper and pencil exercise where people can write down their answers so the facilitator or mediator can feed it back to the group without anyone's name attached to it.

Cultures where there is congruence between the explicit and the implicit, between the ideal and the real, are more likely to be collaborative, as opposed to being competitive. Collaborative cultures are more collegial, whereas competitive cultures have more norms of privacy, which also has an impact on the form of decision making, the form of problem solving, and the way work is shared, so we can tell by looking at a number of different characteristics how collaborative a culture is.

There is also a way of looking at competitive and collaborative cultures in terms of processes. Instead of looking at the culture itself, we can look at the processes within the organization. Hierarchical processes correspond to competitive cultures, whereas *heterarchical* (that is, not just up and down, but both and sideways), and what we described as matrixed organizations are much more collaborative and democratic as opposed to competitive and authoritarian. They are team-based as opposed to individualistic.

There are obvious differences in the orientation of each of these cultures to conflict. And collaborative processes, of course, typically offer much more support for a variety of conflict resolution methods and procedures, as opposed to competitive cultures that emphasize conflict avoidance or aggression.

What we can see, therefore, is that a small shift in culture, including in the direction of conflict resolution, can have a very large impact and influence on the culture, in moving it in a more collaborative direction. This can, in turn, lead to fundamental shifts in many of the other processes that are used in the organization. Most are mixtures of these two types of processes and two types of cultures.

Among the characteristics of collaborative cultures in organizations are shared vision and goals, high levels of interaction and teamwork, innovation, support for risk taking and criticism, tolerance of failure, which doesn't mean low levels of standards, but that everybody is pulling together and trying out new approaches that sometimes fail to create successful outcomes.

One of our definitions of collaborative cultures, and of team-based cultures, is *ownership* of the whole. So instead of promoting conformity and shaming and blaming people who don't comply or have failed at some task, there is orientation, support, and a commitment to learning from mistakes and celebrating the success of others.

Our way of saying this in conflict resolution is: *it doesn't matter whose end of the boat is sinking*. If the boat belongs to all of us, we all need to pitch in and figure out how to survive together. Therefore, fundamentally, we are looking at how we can convert organizations from belonging to a few people at the top, and not to others in the middle or at the bottom of the hierarchy; into organizations that belong to everyone, to all the people who work there, and everyone has the ability to participate in shaping its operations, influencing its processes, and creating its culture.

Another characteristic of collaborative cultures is that there is a great deal of dialogue, and *generative* conflict, with very little impasse, and *adversarial* conflict. This does not mean there are no disagreements, but that we need to differentiate between conflicts and disagreements based on the support given by collaborative cultures to positive emotional interactions between people with different status, leading to fewer experiences with intense negative emotions like anger and fear.

Finally, in collaborative cultures there is the presence of enjoyment and fun. And if these are able to take place in the work environment, there will be greater bonding between people. Enjoyment and fun are creative forces in any organization because they lead too much higher levels of motivation, tolerance of differences and difficulties, and greater motivation and creativity in problem solving.

The question then becomes: how do we create collaborative cultures? Here are a few ways of doing so. We can create a sense of inclusion by maximizing opportunities for collaboration, and locating work in teams and networks. We can help create a sense of vision and have everyone participate in defining that vision. We can celebrate diversity, and realize that it is not simply a source of conflict, but of innovation, growth, change, and deep understanding, and a gift to all of us. We can increase process awareness, encourage open and honest communication, support risk taking, and promote individual and team ownership of results. We can support what we call paradoxical problem solving, that is, solving a problem that is a paradox in ways that allow for multiple correct answers.

We can also encourage the idea that everyone is a leader in an organization, and everyone leads in slightly different ways with regard to different topics using different skills. Instead of thinking of leaders as a small group at the top of a hierarchy, we can strengthen democratic, collaborative, humanized organizations where everyone considers themselves responsible for helping move in a direction that is beneficial for everyone. Personal growth and satisfaction become essential in these organizations, along with seeing conflict as an opportunity, and embracing change.

One of the difficulties, in connection with change, is that the culture of an organization can create obstacles to change and improvement. These can include conditioned passivity and reactiveness; rewards for high levels of competition, narrow focus, and selfishness; fear of failure or punishment; cynicism and apathy; a control orientation, as opposed to a learning orientation; blind obedience to whatever information or direction is received from above; stories of victimization and demonization; reliance on external discipline and authority from above; isolation, lack of communication, and social fragmentation; conflict avoidance, accommodation, and aggression; acceptance of covert behavior and mediocrity, and a lack of ownership of "someone else's problem."

I did a mediation involving a law firm, and multiple conflicts between the lawyers, and also between the legal secretaries. One source of conflict was that if one legal secretary was overburdened, the others would not jump in to offer support. The core difficulty was that these legal secretaries had each been hired by individual lawyers and gave their loyalty to their lawyer, but not to each other. So they viewed all the burdens another legal secretary was facing simply as someone else's problem.

As a result, the entire law firm was losing clients because some legal secretaries were overwhelmed and unable to do their work. Instead, what was required was for everybody to pull together to solve the same problems. That is one of the fundamental goals, not only of organizational collaboration, but conflict resolution in general, because conflict is often responsible for identifying the issue as someone else's problem, when the truth is that every problems in every relationship, in a family, couple, or organization, belongs to everyone.

Exercises to Analyze Cultures and Address Conflicts (Joan)

As change agents, organizational consultants, and mediators dealing with organizational conflict, you may be wondering: how can I apply this analysis of organizational cultures? First, we recommend that you use these ideas and distinctions to enable people in the organization to better understand the hidden dynamics of the culture in which they are living, and the one they create through their responses to conflict.

Here are a set of questions that can help make culture more explicit, that staff can discuss and answer while working in small groups: First they can analyze "work rules." We can ask: What are the explicit and implicit rules in the organization. and what is the reality regarding work?" They may find that the explicit rules are; you should work as hard as you can, as fast as you can, as late as you can. The implicit rules, however, may be that you can get away with goofing off, and colleagues will cover for each other in trying to buy a little time for their personal lives. This implicit rule becomes obvious in a small way when people are waiting for a meeting to begin and everybody is on their cell phone with their kid, or husband, or wife, or best friend. The implicit rule is that it's OK to buy a little time for personal communication with your cell phone while waiting.

A second set of questions is: What are the values of the organization, and what are the ideals that people want to believe in? How real are these values? There may be values, for example, regarding having a diverse staff, in terms of age, race, gender, sexual orientation, or culture, and yet there is a homogeneous area where there is no diversity.

A third question relates to: Who are the "heroes" and "villains" in the organization? Who are the people who are looked up to or down on? What do they do? How do they behave? Who are the positive and negative role models? Who is liked and not liked? Who are the ones to copy and the ones to avoid?

We worked in an organization in Los Angeles that is a leader in the global entertainment industry, and the president of the organization had a very short temper, blowing up often with the people who reported to him, and they were shutting down and turning off their creative impulses.

He asked us to work with him on conflict resolution, and said, "I really don't know what it is that triggers my anger. But I just blow up, and become the villain. And I really need some help with that." So with everyone in the room, including not only his vice-presidents and direct reports, but secretaries and bottom-level staff, we asked, "Who here is willing to point out to him when he's gone over the edge, or is about to blow?" After a few moments of silence, his secretary raised her hand and said, "I'll do that." She said that she could sense when he was about to go from being a hero to being a villain. He was very relieved, thanked her publicly, promised to do better, agreed to have her play this role, and they made it work! And she became a hero among the entire company for having the courage to be honest with the boss.

Another question that is useful in clarifying organizational culture and hidden conflicts is: What are the rites and rituals in this organization? What are the ceremonies, and what do they communicate? We were working with an internationally known aerospace organization that had a contract to deliver airplanes on a very fast timeline. To meet this requirement they established a ritual. Every morning all the employees who were working on the project met in front of a flip chart for the first hour of the day to go over what would be accomplished that day, who was going to take on which responsibility, and how that plan would impact the rest of the organization. This meeting gave each person the information they needed for their team to understand their roles and responsibilities and avoided conflicts arising between the teams.

Another useful discussion regarding culture is to make explicit the communication and power dynamics in the organization. Staff can meet in small groups to discuss their formal and informal means of communication, and look at what is said at the water cooler, or in the cafeteria, or in informal emails that pass among staff. When these topics and results are made explicit, there are fewer conflicts among divisions and departments. Staff can also discuss how power is organized, become clear about how the people who have power in the organization communicate, and how they can use their power to empower others. They can discuss what happens when there is conflict, how collaboration is established, and how people can collaborate more effectively in dealing with conflict by sitting down and discussing what's going on.

I advised a team at AT&T that won the Baldridge Award for excellence in work. They won the award by dealing with a terrible situation that came about when the entire phone system and computers and electricity went down in a building, it took AT&T many hours, and sometimes days to get the systems up and running again.

The head of this division told his organization to try any approach, any idea, and work together in any way possible, to have conflicts and get over them, I don't care what happens, I'll take the blame and you'll get the credit when we find a solution. The team came up with a plan that solved this breakdown within minutes, and when they received the award, the team said they wanted to stay together and tackle all the unsolvable problems at At&T. In this way, the head of the division transformed their conflicts into opportunities for finding innovative and solutions that were unimaginable before the crisis.

The Narrative Structure of Conflict Stories (Ken)

Perhaps the most important place where culture has impacts conflict is in what we call "the narrative structure of conflict stories."

Every conflict takes the form of a story, or dual, adversarial stories, and in every organization people tell stories to each other. The story then becomes an *explicit* presentation of the conflict and, at the same time, an expression of the *implicit* cultural assumptions that led to the conflict in the first place. So it is useful to look at how conflict stories are structured, in order to identify methods for transforming the stories, and turning them in the direction of resolution.

Novelist Javier Marias writes,

> Storytelling is almost always done as a gift, even when the story contains and injects some poison, it is also a bond, a granting of trust, and rare is the trust or confidence that is not sooner or later betrayed, rare is the close bond that does not grow twisted or knotted and, in the end, become so tangled that a razor or knife is needed to cut it.

Conflict stories have this characteristic: they are complex and often twisted or knotted in ways that make it difficult to figure out what the story is actually about. The very first step is to recognize the relationship between the facts and the stories that people tell about them.

Consider what we can think of as the "field" of conflict stories. If, for example, you put 20 or 30 dots on a blank page and assume that very dot represents a fact, A's story will consist of a line connecting perhaps 10 of those dots, and B's story will consist of a different set of connected dots. Each of these stories is *factually* correct, in the sense that it connects a number of facts. And some of those facts may even be in common, connecting different stories.

Yet each of these stories is also false, because many facts have been left out. A's story often has little in common with B's. There may be some facts that are shared, but the interpretation is entirely different. Fundamentally, what we need to understand is that the point of the conflict story is *not* primarily to relate a set of facts, but to convey the emotional experience and *meaning* of those facts to the person who experienced them.

If you have a choice in telling a story about a conflict that happened to you, between *factual* accuracy and *emotional* accuracy, which will you choose? Nearly everyone chooses emotional accuracy over factual accuracy, because the point of the story is to help the listener understand what it *felt* like to be treated that way. The purpose of the story is to communicate to the listener what it felt like to be *you*, and to have experienced the conflict the way you did.

There are several ways of describing conflict stories that are useful. First, there are three sub-stories in every conflict story. First, there is the *external* story we tell others about what happened. Second, there is the *internal* story we tell ourselves about what happened. And third, there is the *core* story, which are the reasons we made up those other two stories.

There is a second set of three distinctions in conflict stories that can help us understand what the story means, and what it is actually about. First, every conflict story takes the form of an *accusation*. Second, beneath every accusation is a *confession*. And third, beneath every confession is a *request*.

It therefore, becomes possible, in listening to conflict stories, to hear not only what someone did, but how the person it was done to felt about it. That is the confession. The request is, what are you really asking the other person for? How would you have liked them to have treated you or behaved instead? We can, in this way, jump directly from the accusation to the request.

For example, a simple conflict story might be "Fred is lazy." That is an accusation. What is the confession? The confession is "I'm working hard here, and Fred isn't helping, and I feel bad because Fred doesn't care enough about me to be willing to help. Therefore, maybe Fred really doesn't like me. Maybe Fred is upset with me. I don't believe I did anything to deserve this, and I feel bad and would like Fred to do something to show me that he cares about the circumstances, and more importantly, about me." Or, "I wish I could take time off like Fred is doing, but don't give myself permission to do so, and am jealous."

What's the request? "Can you give me a hand?" There is no difference, except in form, between the accusation, the confession, and the request. In every conflict story, there is an "ask," a request, and if we can discover what that request is, we can help the conflict story transition from a place of being stuck, to a search for emotional completion, and from there to a place of problem solving.

The fundamental purpose of the conflict story is to lead us in the direction of emotional completion and problem solving, except that the *form* of the story keeps us from getting there. How does that happen? Well, there's been a lot of research into storytelling and the "emotional arcs" in storytelling, which take various forms. And there has been some research that has been done on 1,700 classical stories throughout history showing how these emotional arcs shift.

By paying attention to these emotional arcs, we can discover how to turn the story in the direction of emotional completion. And in order to get there, we have to understand the narrative structure of each conflict story, as an emotional experience.

It is helpful to begin by asking the question, "Who are the main parties in classical conflict stories?" If we look at conflict stories as a whole and take as an illustration fairy tales, we can define the characters more or less as follows. There is a princess. There is an evil perpetrator. There is a hero. These three form a very stable triangle, which can be relabeled as "victim, perpetrator, rescuer".

Over time, we can see that *everyone* who tells a conflict story is a princess describing something done by a villain to someone they hope will become their hero and rescue them from the conflict. But in order to tell the story this way, the princess has to reject responsibility for creating the problem, and at the same time reject responsibility for solving it. These rejections define the story of the princess.

The story then more or less takes this form. Once we see that there is a victim, a perpetrator, and a rescuer, we can also see that the victim has the least amount of power in the story and is responsible for describing the harm done by the conflict, the rescuer is responsible for solving the problem, and the perpetrator is responsible for creating the problem in the first place. Except that when the perpetrator tells the story, he or she becomes the princess, and the person who was the princess in the previous story now becomes the villain.

How do we resolve this conflict? It turns out there are three obvious ways. First, the mediator who has been positioned to be the rescuer can pass responsibility for solving the problem back to the victim and the perpetrator. The mediator is not the judge, but is instead responsible for assisting both parties in working together to solve their problems.

Second, we can ask the princess to take some responsibility for creating the problem, either by action or by inaction, and some responsibility for solving it as well. Third, we can extend empathy and compassion even to the villain or perpetrator, so that instead of slipping into patterns of demonization and victimization, which lead to loss of empathy and moral rationalization, we can search for ways these three can come together to create a common story.

So in interpreting conflict stories, we want to acknowledge that *all* of them are *relatively* true. That is, they are true as *emotional descriptions*, but not necessarily as precise factual statements. The more they are believed, the more they are *felt* to be true. The deeper meaning emerges only when we look carefully at the story and ask both parties what it is concealing, and what it is trying to tell us. And between any two opposing conflict stories, a fresh synthesis can be created that is also true.

We can also consider the elements of conflict stories. The most important is that every conflict story is told *about* someone else, the one we feel is responsible for creating the conflict. Whatever the storyteller did is described as logical and just, and whatever the perpetrator did as illogical and unjust.

Moreover, there are two fundamental resolutions to every conflict story. First, it can end in victory over external enemies, vanquishing our foes, and triumphing over evil. This leads to a *retributive* form of justice that punishes the evildoer. Second, the story can end in victory over *ourselves*, vanquishing our own weaknesses and temptations, triumphing over our own selfishness, anger, and willingness to be taken advantage of. This leads to a *restorative* form of justice that returns all the parties to a more equal, fair, and non-adversarial relationship. It is the second of these, obviously, that is the point of conflict resolution.

Every conflict story creates a stereotype of the other person. And if you want to know about stereotyping, you don't have to look very far. Every conflict generates hostility through stereotyping. Here are a set of methods or instructions on how to stereotype: pick a characteristic, blow it out of proportion, collapse the person into the characteristic, ignore individual differences, ignore subtleties and complexities, ignore our common humanity, make it match our own worst fears, and make it cruel. That is also how most conflict stories are told.

Notice, however, that each of these can be taken apart and reversed. We can make people more subtle and complex, we can look at individual differences and variations, we can separate the person from the characteristic, etc.. The purpose of stereotyping is to demonize the other person and thereby create a set of moral rationalizations, like: "He did at first." "All I did was …" "He's much worse than I am." "She made me do it," *et cetera*. The purpose of moral rationalization is to lead us to moral disengagement, that is, a state of mind in which we feel we are not responsible for the harmful impact we have on others.

The main mechanisms of moral disengagement are rationalizing, obscuring, denying, blaming, dehumanizing others, demonizing the perpetrator, magnifying the harm, distancing ourselves, and similar methods. The object of conflict stories is then to lead us to a place where we feel we are no longer responsible for what we do. And we can now see that one of the purposes of the conflict story is to give ourselves a backwards justification for doing harm to someone our own empathy and compassion would rise up and prevent us from doing. Finally, Rebecca Solnit writes,

> Stories save your life. And stories are your life. We are our stories, stories that can be both the prison and the crowbar to break open the door to that prison. We make stories to save ourselves or to trap ourselves or others, stories that lift us up or smash us against the

stone wall of our own limits and fears. Liberation is always in part a storytelling process. Breaking stories, breaking silences, making new stories.

This is the goal of conflict resolution.

What to Listen *for* in Conflict Stories (Joan)

When a client starts to tell you a story about a conflict, or several people or a team or an organization brings a conflict story to your attention, you may think, I'm going to listen and hear what's going on. But no matter who practiced we are in listening to conflict stories, there are aspects that we often miss.

Ken and I were working with an early childhood education project, and we asked the children in the Head Start classroom, "What happens when you come home from school, what do your parents say?" And one girl said, "Well, my mom asks, what happened today, and then turns her back and starts cooking. My dad asks, 'What happened in school today?' and when I try to tell him he starts reading on the internet or doing email or watching a TV program."

If you are going to support others in resolving their conflicts, or if you want to show your interest in a conflict story, you need to pay attention and listen with your whole being, even if the story is threatening, dangerous, or difficult for you to hear. This means listening not only to the *facts* but to the subjective *emotions*, as well as the intentions, interests, dreams, and visions. It means listening to the humiliations, the family patterns, defensiveness and denials. We need to listen for openings to dialogue, requests for acknowledgment, cries for help, mistakes in interpretation, and missed perceptions.

We can also listen for insults, metaphors, and stereotypes, which can be threatening if we recall our own experiences. Ken and I were doing a mediation regarding sexual harassment in a law firm and when the woman described her experience of being stereotyped and abused, I remembered being stereotyped when I was an organizational consultant by the president of a major insurance company, and whenever I spoke, he would turn his back to me, ignore my comments and turn to do email, but when my male colleague spoke, he would listen attentively.

Our meeting with him was followed by lunch in the president's dining room and I was outraged and embarrassed when he put his hands all over the woman who was waiting on our table, abusing her in front of us. I felt sad for the woman who was being humiliated in front of us and furious about his behavior.

At the next meeting with this client, my colleague insisted that I make the entire presentation. The client paid attention when he realized his organization was paying a hefty fee for our work, and he had better give up his stereotypes of women and pay attention to me. Years later, in a sexual harassment mediation Ken and I conducted with the partners of the law firm, my earlier emotional reaction got re-triggered and began to show on my face as I was listening. Ken noticed my response and suggested we take a coffee break in the mediation so that we could discuss my feelings. That strategy worked well and I was able to regain my balance, set my experiences aside, and join in working with the couple so they could apologize, reach forgiveness and rebuild their firm.

The conflict stories you hear, and the underlying issues that emerge as you listen will include the roles that people believe they are playing, their unspoken expectations, fears, ego defenses, and self doubts. They may be blaming themselves for the conflict, or exaggerating the other person's responsibility for the conflict. They may feel they won't ever be good enough to be respected, and reject the possibility of forgiveness, And sometimes, just having a mediator, leader, or conflict resolver listen to the story is enough to resolve a conflict.

Transforming Conflict Stories (Ken)

The last part of our work together on culture and conflict stories is to look at ways of transforming both the culture and the story, by turning them in the direction of problem solving. Instead of being adversarial, we want to support cultures and encourage stories that invite collaboration; that can end with the words "and they lived happily ever after."

When we listen to someone tell a story about a conflict they have experienced, there are several things that we can do as mediators. First, before they begin, in your own mind, insert the words "once upon a time," and you will be listening in exactly the right frame of mind to understand the narrative purpose of the story. And that the purpose is more deep and emotional than superficial and factual.

In order to transform a conflict story, we have to work at that deeper level. Fundamentally, there are several things we are looking for. First it is important capturing what is true in each person's story; that is, to summarize what is true and useful in each person's story, leaving out the parts that demonize or victimize the other party.

So, for example, if someone tells a story in which they say, "Joe is a bully," that is an adversarial story, it is an accusation. And Joe, if he is present and hears this story, will predictably respond defensively, or with a counterattack. But another way of telling the same story is, "I felt intimidated when Joe yelled at me." That is a confession. And we can discover the intent of Joe's story by asking the question, "Did you feel intimidated when he yelled at you?"

It is also possible to take the story to the next level and convert it into a request, as in: "How would you like Joe to communicate differently, so you don't feel intimidated when he yells at you?" Here we begin to discover what the story was designed to do, — that is, somehow, without knowing exactly how, to lead us in the direction of a solution to the underlying problem.

Every conflict story is a *request for help*, and the help we want to provide comes in part out of the nature of the story. One way of looking at conflict stories, one exercise we use, is to ask each person to write down the story of what happened. We ask them now to write the *other* person's story, as best they can imagine it. After they're done, we may ask them to read their stories to each other and ask if they got it right. Finally, we ask them to write a third story that combines their earlier stories together, leaving out all the demonization and victimization.

We may also ask them to tell a story that is positive and acknowledging about the other person. Even the story that "Joe is a bully" can be told as, "Joe cares a lot about this issue and is trying very hard to get what he needs." It is also possible to tell the story as part of a dialogue, in which each person contributes something towards a common understanding and solution to the problem.

We may also suggest they change the pronouns in their story. The usual pronouns in most conflict stories are the words "you," or "they," or "he or she." But if the word is "you," the *form* of the pronoun is an accusation, and the likely response will be a denial or counterattack. If the story uses the pronoun "they," as in "They are lazy," the form of the story is a stereotype, and the likely outcome will be prejudgment or prejudice, etc..

But if the story is told as an "it"— for example, if we say, "There is a lot of work to be done. How should it be divided?" that question is identical in *content* to the "you/they are lazy" stories, but there is no reason any longer for anyone to be defensive or to respond with a counterattack, or feel stereotyped.

We can also reframe the story using "I" statements, that is, as a confession: "I feel disrespected and uncared for when you see me working and don't offer to help;" or as a request: "I need a hand, can you give me some help." And we can reframe it using "we" statements — that is, "We have a lot of work to do; how shall we divide it?", in which case it becomes an invitation to collaborate.

We can also ask each person to clarify the *context* in which the story occurred. What were the circumstances? What influenced the outcome? We can then offer a contrary, empowering interpretation. So if someone says, "I was frightened," we can say, "It must have taken a lot of courage for you to have shown up in the face of your fear. So it sounds to me like you were pretty brave. Or, if they say, "I'm so angry," we can respond by saying, "You must care a lot about this issue." Because all anger is about caring, or another way of saying the same thing is: *nobody* gets angry over things they don't care about.

We can also clarify people's expectations. "What did you want him to say, as opposed to what he just said?" Or: "What would you most like him to say to you right now?" Sometimes, this may take the form of a request for acknowledgment, or for respectful communication. We can also identify the hidden judgments in the story. And we can *map* the evolution of the conflict, and ask people to correct what happened in their conflict step-by-step.

We call this *microsurgery*, where we try to completely fix one small piece of what went wrong, in the hope that doing so will have an impact on the conflict as a whole. We can ask people to compare the cultural influences on their perceptions. "How did you interpret what he said to you in light of your culture, the culture in your family of origin or the group culture that you come from?" Or: "How did that sound to you? What led you to hear it that way?"

We can then identify ways for people to be clear about their cultural influences, and to contrast their stories with what they want to achieve, or with their goals. For example, I did a mediation involving a mother and her teenage daughter. The mother was criticizing everything her daughter was doing, and the daughter sat silently, sinking lower and lower in her chair. I asked the mother a question, "What kind of life do you want for your daughter?" She began talking about all the beautiful things in life she wanted for her — for her to be happy, to feel good about herself and self-confident. I then asked her, "Is there anything in common between the stories you have been telling about her and the kind of life you want for her?" And she had to say there wasn't, and began to cry. I then asked, "Can you tell a story about your daughter that could convince her that she can have the kind of life you want for her?" She immediately saw the point and began to tell stories about how smart and capable her daughter is, and the daughter began picking herself up, responding, and smiling, and the conversation ended in a really beautiful way.

As mediators, we may also ask people to jointly or separately investigate the factual assumptions behind their stories. We may ask,

"How do you know whether that is actually true?" "Can you investigate and try to find out if it's true?" "Are you willing to do that together?" Or, we may ask: "What are the gaps in your stories?" "What was left out?" Or, we may ask each person to identify the gaps in the other person's story.

We can also ask questions that reveal their unspoken assumptions about causation, or the other person's intentions, and suggest a joint need to improve skills and responsibility for communicating more effectively. Even identifying the specific skills that are needed in a particular situation, or asking each person "What skills do you think the other person might develop that would lead you to respond differently?" can be helpful.

We may also find it useful to look at the larger systems, especially the family and organizational systems that impacted their story – for example, the culture of competition, or absence of peer mediation in an organization; or the presence of racial or gender inequalities, etc. The form this question most commonly takes is simply this: "What is one thing people in this organization *could* have done that might have prevented this conflict, or made it easier to handle?"

We may also try to clarify what we call the "ghost roles" in the story, those played by people who are not directly included in the story, yet have impacted it. In every organization, there are countless influences on every conflict, and often these are lost sight of. For example, in conflicts between mothers-in-law and daughters-in-law, often it is the son/husband who plays a "ghost role" in the story.

We may ask questions about the *meaning* of the story to each person, and separate facts from interpretations. We can use a flip chart, for example, and draw a line down the center, with facts on the left, and interpretations on the right. So what is the fact? Perhaps it is that Barbara didn't say hello to me at work when I came in this morning. What is the interpretation? First, Barbara hates me. Second, Barbara isn't feeling well today. Third, Barbara is distracted because she's got something on her mind and just forgot about it,. Soon, they will discover that there are countless possible interpretations for every fact, and each interpretation is something they have chosen.

Finally, and most importantly, we can help them create a *third* story that doesn't rely on demonization or victimization, and ends in learning, collaboration, and problem solving. I sometimes ask people to create this third story themselves, and find away to end it with the words "and they lived happily ever after," then read their stories out loud to each other and talk about how they can make the ending real.

In every subgroup in every organization, every, there are stories and narratives about the other subgroups. Sales and marketing tells stories and creates narratives about legal, or HR, who do the same about other groups in the organization. It is possible to take these subgroups, put them in separate rooms and ask them to identify the narratives and stories they are telling about the other group, what they believe the stories are that others are telling about them, and then ask them to present these stories to each other, identify the interests and requests behind each story or narrative, and talk about how it feels and who they actually are.

Here are some questions they can answer, and present their answers to the other group: "What is one thing you would like to acknowledge or thank people in the other group for in relation to the stories they tell?" "What is one thing you think they contribute to the organization as a whole?" "What are the deeper underlying subjective or emotional truths that are contained in each story or narrative?" "What are the interests, expectations, and desires that are expressed in those stories?"

If the story is, "they're not pulling their weight," the underlying interest is in having a more equal and collaborative workload and a more egalitarian relationship. The expectation is that they will jump in if they see that we are overburdened and decide to help us out. You can then ask: "How might you reframe the narratives, stereotypes, or misunderstandings of your group as *requests* for improvement?" " What commitments or promises are you willing to make in response to the other group's requests?" "What expectations still need to be negotiated between your groups?" "What do you most want people in the other group to understand about your group, its culture, and the context of your work?"

We can then add to this more difficult and "dangerous" questions, like: "What is one thing that you never ever want to hear again, as a story or stereotype about your group?" "What is one question you have for the other group that you always wanted to ask but we're afraid to?" " What is one thing your group could do to make sure no one ever tells this story again?" And, "What is one thing you learned from this exercise, and plan to do differently in the future? "

SESSION 4 LECTURE SLIDES

Our 'opponents' are our co-creators, for they have something to give which we have not. The basis of all cooperative activity is integrated diversity.... What people often mean by getting rid of conflict is getting rid of diversity, and it is of the utmost importance that these should not be considered the same. We may wish to abolish conflict, but we cannot get rid of diversity. We must face life as it is and understand that diversity is its most essential feature... Fear of difference is dread of life itself. It is possible to conceive conflict as not necessarily a wasteful outbreak of incompatibilities, but a normal process by which socially valuable differences register themselves for the enrichment of all concerned.

MARY PARKER FOLLETT

What is Culture?

- How we approach our environment
- How we group and divide
- How food is produced and consumed
- How gender is perceived and displayed
- The ways space and boundaries are established
- How time is defined and used
- How learning takes place
- How and when people play and laugh
- What people do when conflicts are not resolved
- How goods are made, possessed, used, exchanged and distributed
- Ways of perceiving and processing reality
- Shared behaviors, beliefs, attitudes, customs or ways of life
- Ways of differentiating ourselves from others
- How we satisfy our needs in a given environment
- Agreed upon meanings of symbols, events, sensations and behavior
- An accumulation of successful adaptations
- What everyone knows and no one talks about

Cultural Rules and Norms

Cultural anthropologist, Edward T. Hall outlined the elements of culture in his classic book, *The Silent Language*. Cultures, including organizational cultures, contain rules for:

- Interacting with the environment
- Associating with others
- Subsisting
- Understanding gender and other biases
- Navigating territoriality
- Monitoring temporality
- Learning
- Playing
- Using property
- Fighting

Examples of Cultural Differences

- Precision vs. ambiguity in communication
- Open vs. closed in personal information
- Verbal vs. written as a basis for traditions
- High vs. low context in establishing meaning
- Consensus vs. individualistic in decision making
- Formal vs. informal in processes
- Competitive vs. collaborative in relationships
- Direct vs. indirect in giving feedback
- Authoritarian vs. democratic in organization
- Deference vs. rebelliousness in relation to authority
- Exclusive vs. inclusive in relation to outsiders
- Linear vs. non-linear emphasis in thinking
- Gestalt vs. detail in orientation
- Appropriateness vs. inappropriateness in humor and play
- Demonstrative vs. restrained in emotional expression
- Permissive vs. directive in child rearing
- Fixed vs. fluid attitudes toward time
- Open vs. closed attitudes toward space
- Individual vs. group orientation in norms and values
- Interests vs. power or rights orientation in dispute resolution

© Kenneth Cloke and Joan Goldsmith

Cultural Perceptions of Time

Differences in Perception of Time

Monochronic vs. Polychronic

Linear vs. Circular

Logical vs. Emotional

Being on Time vs. Being in Time

Time as Money vs. Time as Sacred

Limited vs. Unlimited

Controlled by Schedules vs. Flexible Schedules

Unitary vs. Flowing

© Kenneth Cloke and Joan Goldsmith

Cultural Perceptions of Space

Differences in Perception of Space
Closed vs. Open

Functional vs. Aesthetic

Space as Separation vs. Space as Connection

Empty vs. Filled

Space as a Thing vs. Space as a Relationship

Personal Space vs. Social Space

Face to Face vs. Side by Side

High Context/Low Context Cultures

High Context: Implicit/Indirect	Low Context: Explicit/Direct
Knowledge is acquired through a built in expectation of what is customary within a culture	Information and rules are abundant and clearly stated. Focus on rules and literal meanings of words
Non-Verbal Messages/Gestures are Important	Statements taken at face value, little about the process is assumed
Saving face and tact are important	Expectations are discussed
Rules are implicit	Direct questions are not meant to offend
Little use for formalized agreements, the parties "know" from experience	Indirect cues may be ineffectual

Levels of Organizational Culture

Two Cultural Approaches to Conflict

First Approach

Second Approach

Conflict is normative; potentially positive; can lead to personal growth.

Conflict is disruptive to harmonious relationships.

Boundaries of conflict extensive; extend beyond family to spiritual, natural world ; repercussions extend in time.

Boundaries of conflict narrow; defined by those directly involved, occurs in the present.

View of self as relational; in conflict, focus is on the effects of individual behavior on the group; security and self worth achieved through relationship.

Self as autonomous, individuated; can speak of "self interests" in conflict; security of self comes with individual achievement (as with economic success)

Conflict binds people tightly together.

Conflict is divisive and separates people.

When Cultures Meet

When divergent cultures meet, including organizational cultures, there are many possible outcomes, which may take place rapidly or slowly, including:

1. *Subjugation* (suppression of differences)
2. *Plunder* (appropriation of differences)
3. *Amalgamation* (disappearance of differences)
4. *Coexistence* (interaction of differences)
5. *Compromise* (negotiation of differences)
6. *Collaboration* (synergy of differences)

Organizational Culture and Congruence

In organizations, culture can be *congruent*, in which case the explicit and implicit messages match and the ideal is not fundamentally different from the real, or it can lack congruence, in which case they do not match. For example:

	EXPLICIT MESSAGE	IMPLICIT MESSAGE
IDEAL	"Open door policy"	Criticism is welcome.
REAL	We promote risk-takers.	Criticism is safe.
	Those who criticize are not listened to.	Criticism is not valued.
	People who play it safe do not get ahead.	Criticism is not rewarded.

Competitive vs. Collaborative Cultures

Collaborative Cultures	Competitive Cultures
Norms of Collegiality	Norms of privacy,
Work is Innovative	Work is Routine
Support for Learning	Bureaucratic, Rule Bound
Commitment to Success of Others	Low Expectations of Others
Dynamic Content	Static Content
Community of Inquiry	Acceptance of Existing Practices
Constantly Changing	Static
Challenging	Boring
Active	Inert
Distributed Expertise	Isolated Expertise
Democratic Decision Making	Authoritarian Decision Making
Informal Problem Solving	Whining and Complaining
Work is Shared	Work is Proprietary
Focus on Process	Focus on Blame, Fault Finding
Supporting Others	Classifying Others.
Interconnected	Isolated, Conflict Ridden
Expectation of Maturity	Infantilization
Responsible for Professionalism	Professionalism is Imposed

(Based partly on work by Milbrae McLaughlin on professional community)
© Kenneth Cloke and Joan Goldsmith

Competitive vs. Collaborative Processes

Collaborative Processes	Competitive Processes
Heterarchical	Hierarchical
Democratic	Authoritarian
Innovative, Creative	Rule Driven, Routine
Interactive and Social	Isolated and Private
Support for Diversity	Support for Conformity
Team-Based	Individualistic
High Expectations of Others	Low Expectations of Others
Critique of Existing Practices	Acceptance of Existing Practices
Constantly Changing	Static
Focus on Risk Taking	Focus on Safety and Security
Situational Leadership	Fixed Management
Informal Problem Solving	Whining and Complaining
Successes/Failures are Shared	Successes/Failures are Personal
Focus on Problem Solving	Focus on Blaming, Fault Finding
Acknowledgement of Others	Criticism of Others.
Interconnected/Relational	Isolated/Cliques
Expectation of Maturity	Infantilization
Conflict Resolution	Conflict Avoidance or Aggression

© Kenneth Cloke and Joan Goldsmith

Characteristics of Collaborative Cultures

1. Shared vision and goals
2. Higher levels of interaction and teamwork
3. Innovation
4. Support for risk taking and criticism
5. Tolerance of failure
6. Commitment to the success of others
7. Democratic decision making
8. Honesty and openness
9. Acceptance of challenge
10. Distributed expertise
11. Widespread leadership
12. Creative problem solving
13. Shared effort
14. Individual responsibility for the whole
15. High standards for all
16. Lots of dialogue with little conflict
17. Constant reflection, evaluation and feedback
18. Awareness of unity and similarity
19. Valuing and respect for differences
20. Enjoyment and fun

127

© Kenneth Cloke and Joan Goldsmith

14 Values to Humanize the Way We Work

1. Inclusion
2. Collaboration
3. Teams and networks
4. Vision
5. Celebration of diversity
6. Process awareness
7. Open and honest communication
8. Risk taking
9. Individual and team ownership of results
10. Paradoxical problem solving
11. Everyone is a leader
12. Personal growth and satisfaction
13. Seeing conflict as an opportunity
14. Embracing change

128

[Excerpt from Kenneth Cloke and Joan Goldsmith, *Thank God It's Monday!*, Irwin Publ., 1996]

Cultural Obstacles to Change

- Conditioned passivity and reactiveness
- Rewards for competition, narrow focus and selfishness
- Fear of failure or punishment
- Cynicism, apathy, control-orientation and obedience
- Stories of victimization and demonization
- Reliance on external discipline and authority from above
- Isolation, lack of communication and social fragmentation
- Conflict avoidance, accommodation and aggression
- Acceptance of covert behavior and mediocrity
- Lack of ownership of "someone else's problem"

Some Questions on Organizational Culture

1. *Work Rules*
   - What are the explicit rules in the organization?
   - What are the implicit rules? What is the reality?
2. *Values*
   - What are the ideal values, concepts and beliefs? Which of these are real?
   - How is success defined? How is failure defined?
3. *Heroes and Villains*
   - Who are the positive role models? What did they do?
   - Who are the negative role models? What did they do?

Some Questions on Organizational Culture

4. *Rites and Rituals*
   - What are the day to day routines or rituals?
   - What does the organization stand for in its ceremonies?

5. *Communication and Power*
   - What are the primary formal and informal means of communication?
   - How is the hidden power organized?

6. *Relationships and Conflict*
   - What happens when there is conflict?
   - How does collaboration happen?

(Based partly on work by Deal & Kennedy, Corporate Cultures)

Organizational Culture and Change

	Old Culture	New Culture
Work Rules		
Values		
Heroes and Villains		

Organizational Culture and Leadership

	Old Culture	New Culture
Rites and Rituals		
Communication and Power		
Relationships and Conflict		

© Kenneth Cloke and Joan Goldsmith

The Narrative Structures of Conflict Stories

[Story]telling is almost always done as a gift, even when the story contains and injects some poison, it is also a bond, a granting of trust, and rare is the trust or confidence that is not sooner or later betrayed, rare is the close bond that does not grow twisted or knotted and, in the end, become so tangled that a razor or knife is needed to cut it.

JAVIER MARAIS

The Field of Conflict Stories

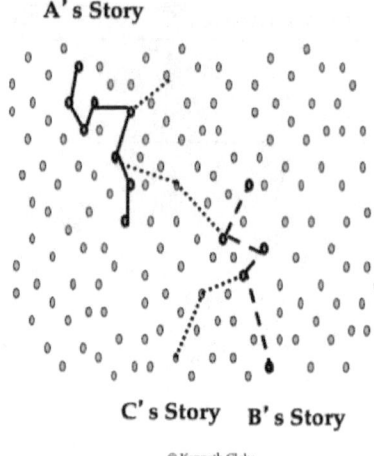

Emotional Arcs in Conflict Stories

Andrew Reagan at the Computational Story Lab at the University of Vermont in Burlington used sentiment analysis to map the emotional arcs of over 1,700 stories, and data-mining techniques to reveal their most common arcs. They found that the six basic emotional arcs of stories are:

1. A steady, ongoing rise in emotional valence, as in a rags-to-riches story such as *Alice's Adventures Underground* by Lewis Carroll.
2. A steady, ongoing fall in emotional valence, as in a tragic story such as *Romeo and Juliet* by William Shakespeare.
3. A fall then a rise, as in a "man falling in a hole and getting out story," as discussed for example by Kurt Vonnegut. [See YouTube video at https://www.youtube.com/watch?v=oP3c1h8v2ZQ.]
4. A rise then a fall, as in the Greek myth of *Icarus*.
5. A rise-fall-rise, as in the romantic story of *Cinderella*.
6. A fall-rise-fall, as in the tragedy of *Oedipus*.

3 Emotional Arcs

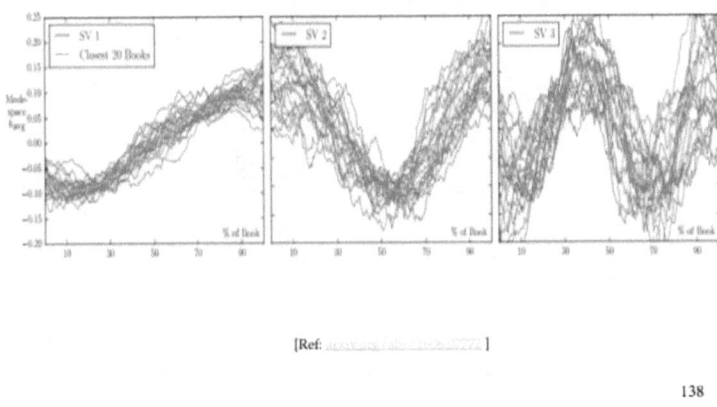

[Ref:]

The Narrative Structure of Conflict Stories

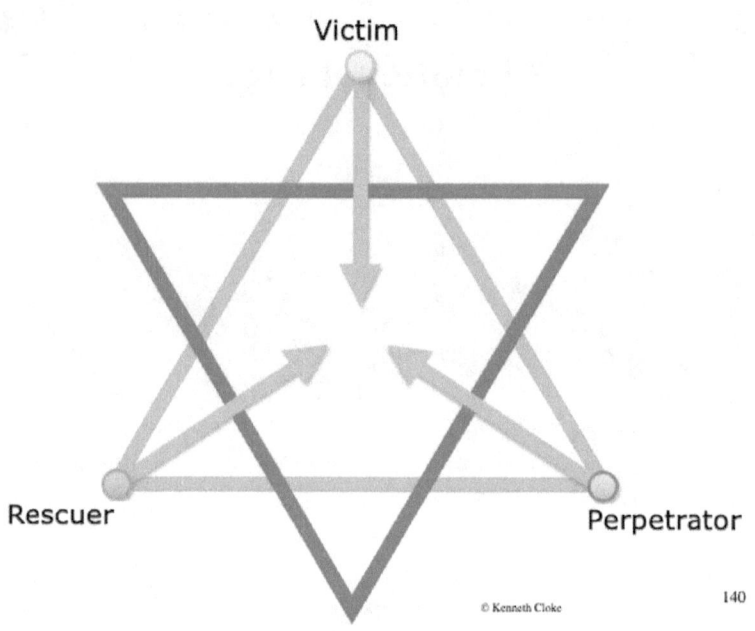

How should we be able to forget those ancient myths that are at the beginning of all peoples, the myths about dragons that at the last moment turn into princesses; perhaps all the dragons of our lives are princesses who are only waiting to see us once beautiful and brave. Perhaps everything terrible is in its deepest being something helpless that wants help from us.

RAINER MARIA RILKE

Interpreting Conflict Stories

1. All stories and interpretations are potentially and relatively true, though none is exclusively or absolutely true. In other words, there are degrees and varieties of truth and all metaphoric truths are relative to the observer.
2. If the meaning is believed, that makes it true, to the extent that it is believed. Or rather, believing and truth are the same for the listener.
3. A deeper level of meaning is one that arises when we ask why the story is told. What are we trying to convince ourselves of by telling this story? Our own innate goodness? Our lack of self-control? Our suffering? Our innocence? Our guilt or "original sin"?
4. Another layer of meaning is derived by looking at who the story is told to. For example, if the Adam and Eve story is told by a parent to a child, or a religious leader to a congregation, the message is clear: "Obey the rules or you will be punished and lose my affection and protection."
5. Between any two stories, a synthesis can be created that is also true.

Elements of Conflict Stories (1)

1. The storyteller is a victim who is more acted upon than acting.
2. The other party is the creator, initiator or cause of the conflict.
3. Whatever the storyteller did is related as rational and just.
4. Whatever the other party did appears irrational and unjust.
5. The symbolic and metaphoric content of the story points to its real meaning to the teller.
6. The story that is told collapses all other perceptions, possibilities and versions into one. It appears to exclude all other stories.
7. All stories about conflict are metaphorically true.
8. The stories people tell create their lives. As they tell the story, it happens.
9. Stories are rituals designed to comfort the teller with their familiarity.
10. The more the story is repeated, the more it is believed to be true. As Lewis Carroll had it: "I've said it once, I've said it twice, I've said it thrice--it must be true!"
11. The central purpose of conflict stories is to maintain the self-image and self-esteem of the storyteller.
12. Conflict stories merge emotionally charged symbols with action and events so that it is nearly impossible to separate them.

Elements of Conflict Stories (2)

13. Stories help fulfill wishes or dreams, or explain why they failed to occur.
14. Conflict stories are organized around a central unstated myth about the other which is subconsciously perceived to be only partially true.
15. Conflict stories link together perceived facts to favor the teller. Inconsistent facts are denied, dismissed or disconnected from the story.
16. Most conflict stories reveal in their imagery and language a set of emotional assumptions that have more to do with the conflict than the story itself.
17. Most of the stories we tell ourselves about ourselves are compensatory, revealing in their satisfaction the existence of an underlying need.
18. Most of the stories we tell ourselves about others are relational, creating others as a way of creating ourselves through our relationship with them.
19. Thus, even the stories we tell about others often end up being about ourselves, about what we admire in others because we lack it in ourselves, or what we dislike in others because we reject it, yet are simultaneously drawn it to in ourselves.
20. Stories create listening and a powerful bond with the listener, even when the listener is an opponent or adversary.

2 Meta-Resolutions of Conflict Stories

The two most common resolutions that are implied or suggested by the adversarial structure of conflict stories are:

1. Victory over one's external enemies, vanquishing one's foes, triumphing over evil, plus a *retributive* form of justice that punishes the evil-doer;

2. Victory over oneself, vanquishing one's weaknesses and temptations, triumphing over our own selfishness, anger, and willingness to be taken advantage of, plus a *restorative* form of justice that returns the parties to a more equal, fair and non-adversarial relationship.

How to Stereotype

1. Pick a characteristic
2. Blow it completely out of proportion
3. Collapse the whole person into the characteristic
4. Ignore individual differences and variations
5. Ignore subtleties and complexities
6. Ignore our common humanity
7. Make it match your own worst fears
8. Make it cruel

© Kenneth Cloke

Elements of Demonization

- *Assumption of Injurious Intentions* - they intended to cause the harm we experienced
- *Distrust* - every idea or statement made by them is wrong or proposed for dishonest reasons
- *Externalization of Guilt* - everything bad or wrong is their fault
- *Attribution of Evil* - they want to destroy us and what we value most, and must therefore be destroyed themselves
- *Zero-Sum Interests* - everything that benefits them harms us, and *vice versa*
- *Paranoia and Preoccupation with Disloyalty* - any criticism of us or praise of them is disloyal and treasonous
- *Prejudgment* - everyone in the enemy group is an enemy
- *Collapse of Neutrality and Independence into Opposition* - anyone who is not with us is against us
- *Suppression of Empathy* - we have nothing in common and considering them human is dangerous
- *Isolation and Impasse* - we cannot dialogue, negotiate, cooperate, or resolve conflicts with them
- *Self-Fulfilling Prophecy* - their evil makes it permissible for us to act in a hostile way toward them, and *vice versa*

[Based partly on work by Kurt R. and Kati Spillman]
© Kenneth Cloke

Mechanisms of Moral Disengagement

1. *Rationalizing* the possible beneficial consequences of otherwise wrong behaviors that are imagined to outweigh their negative consequences. ("If I make enough money by doing this I can help people later.")
2. *Obscuring* or lessening personal responsibility for participating in the wrongful activity. ("I just did what I was told." "I just played a small part." "Other people do the same thing, so why can't I?")
3. *Denying* the seriousness of harmful effects on others. ("He won't mind." "He's going to be fine." "It was only a small thing." "He can claim it on his insurance.")
4. *Blaming*, dehumanizing, or derogating the victim. ("He was stupid." "She was a bitch." "It served him right." "She shouldn't have ...")
5. *Demonizing* the perpetrator. ("He is vicious." "He's not human." "He should be shot.")
6. *Magnifying* or exaggerating the harm that occurred. ("What he did [if a minor infraction] is intolerable.")
7. *Distancing* or separating from both sides. ("A plague on both their houses." "It has nothing to do with me.")

(Based on work by Albert Bandura)
© Kenneth Cloke

Commonly Cited Moral Rationalizations

- *Moral Justification*: "He did it first."
- *Euphemistic Labeling*: "All I did was ..."
- *Disadvantageous Comparison*: "He's much worse than I am."
- *Displacement of Responsibility*: "She made me do it."
- *Diffusion of Responsibility*: "Everyone is doing it."
- *Disregard/Distortion of Consequences:* "What I did wasn't that bad."
- *Dehumanization*: "He deserved it."
- *Blaming the Victim*: "She was asking for it."

(Based on work by Albert Bandura)
© Kenneth Cloke

Stories save your life. And stories are your life. We are our stories, stories that can be both prison and the crowbar to break open the door to that prison; we make stories to save ourselves or to trap ourselves or others, stories that lift us up or smash us against the stone wall of our own limits and fears. Liberation is always in part a storytelling process: breaking stories, breaking silences, making new stories ...

REBECCA SOLNIT

What to Listen *For* in Conflict Stories

- Facts
- Subjective Experiences
- Emotions
- Intentions
- Interests and Positions
- Dreams and Visions
- Humiliations
- Family Patterns
- Defensiveness
- Denials
- Insults
- Metaphors
- Stereotypes
- Openings to Dialogue
- Requests for Acknowledgement
- Universality
- Cries for Help
- Interpretations
- Modes of Perception
- Roles
- Expectations
- Wishes and Desires
- Fears
- Ego Defenses
- Self-Esteem
- Resistance
- Confessions
- Self-Doubts
- Subconscious Meanings
- Prejudices
- Offers to Negotiate
- Need for Support
- Uniqueness
- Desire for Forgiveness

© Kenneth Cloke   151

Transforming Conflict Stories (1)

- Summarize what is true and useful in each party's story, leaving out the portions that demonize or victimize the other party;
- Ask each party to write their own story, then the other person's story, and then combine them;
- Ask them to tell a story that is positive and acknowledging;
- Ask them to change the pronoun in their story to it or I or we;
- Ask each party to clarify the context in which their story occurred;
- Offer a contrary, empowering interpretation, i.e., if the person says "I was frightened," you say "You were brave." Or if they say "I am so angry," you say "You must care a lot";
- Clarify expectations. Ask: "What did you want him to say?"
- Identify the hidden judgments in the story;
- Map the evolution of the conflict, identifying steps 1, 2, 3, etc.;
- Ask the parties to correct the conflict step by step;

152

© Kenneth Cloke

Transforming Conflict Stories (2)

- Ask the parties to compare the cultural influences on their perceptions and responses to each others stories;
- Contrast their stories with what they want to achieve, with their goals;
- Ask them to jointly or separately investigate their factual assumptions;
- Identify the gaps in their stories. Ask them what was left out?
- Reveal their assumptions about causation and suggest a joint need to improve skills and responsibility for outcomes;
- Identify the larger systems, processes and conditions that impact their story, i.e., the absence of peer mediation, gender inequalities, etc., and extend the mediation to include the field" in which the conflict took place;
- Clarify the" ghost roles" including organizational policies and procedures, parents, people who are apathetic;
- Clarify the *meaning* of the story to each party;
- Separate facts from interpretations;
- Create a third story without demonization or victimization.

153

© Kenneth Cloke

CHAPTER 5

MEDIATING ORGANIZATIONAL CONFLICTS

Mediating Organizational Conflicts (Ken)

We now want to look at organizational conflicts in ways that describe, in the first place, why we get stuck; and second, how we get unstuck, and in the process identify a number of specific techniques for mediating organizational conflicts. To do this, we have to begin with a fundamental idea that goes back to the philosophical bases for conflict resolution that we described earlier.

The basic idea is this — no matter how experienced you are in conflict resolution, *every* conflict is going to be different from the one before. And within each conflict, things will shift from moment to moment, and you will discover complex places where it is difficult to find your way to a solution. This means *there is no technique* that will work always or everywhere or with everyone, and therefore, there is a *continuous* need in mediation to innovate, to be creative, to discover where people are stuck and why.

The primary reasons why we get stuck are emotional, as captured by poet Killarney Clary, who wrote this powerful prose poem to capture the feeling of being stuck in alienating work:

Because the ones I work for do not love me, because I have said too much, and I haven't been sure of what is right and I've hated the people I've trusted, because I work in an office and we are lost, and when I come home, I say their lives are theirs, and they don't know what they apologize for and none of it mended, because I let them beat me and I remember something of mine which not everyone has, and because I lie to keep myself and my hands, my voice, on the phone, because I swallow what hurts me, because I hurt them. I give them the hours I spend away from them, and carry them even in my sleep, at least as the nag of a misplaced shoe. For years after I have quit and gone on to another job, where I hesitate in telling, and I remember, and I resent having had to spend more time with them than with the ones I love.

So what is it that gets us stuck in conflict in the first place, and what keeps us there? Here are several reasons we get stuck that pop up in many organizational settings: First, conflicts define us and give our lives meaning. Having an enemy is a quick, easy source of identity, and if you are new at work, there are two ways of quickly creating relationships with coworkers. One is based on who you both hate, and the other is based on who you are, and what like about each other. The first is clearly easier. It takes less effort. It's far less risky. But it ends up creating cliques and prioritizing adversarial and conflicted relationships.

Second, conflicts give us energy, even if it's only the energy of anger or fear or other negative emotions, and we can become addicted to these emotions and to the intimacy of combat.

Third, conflict ennobles our misery and makes it appear that we are suffering for a worthwhile cause. Otherwise, we might be suffering in vain, and one of the clear characteristics of suffering is that no one wants to suffer for nothing. If you are going to suffer, at least let it be for something.

Fourth, conflict safeguards our personal space. It is a way of keeping people from violating our boundaries. It encourages other people to recognize our needs and respect our privacy. It creates intimacy, and as we've indicated, even negative intimacy.

Fifth, conflict camouflages our weaknesses. It powerfully communicates what we honestly feel. Sixth, it gets results, especially from faceless bureaucrats, clerks, service representatives who only seem to respond when we yell at them, no matter how humiliating that may feel for us. Seventh, it makes us feel righteous. Eighth, it prompts change. Many people believe that change emerges only from conflict, and often this is the case. It doesn't have to be the case, but it often is.

In addition to these, there are many other reasons people prefer to be stuck in conflict rather than resolve it. The deepest, and I think the most profound of these, is simply the inability, from inside a conflict, to understand what it looks like from the outside. That is, to be so immersed in it that we lose perspective.

In addition, we often also lose our sense of self, which has been defined now by someone else, and their actions towards us. This is the advantage we gain in adversarial conflicts – that we can deprive our opponents of an accurate sense of themselves, and make them lose energy through negativity. These are just a few of the very many reasons we get stuck in conflict.

Mediation in Organizations (Ken)

If these are the reasons we get stuck in conflict, let's take a closer look at what gets us unstuck. If conflict, for example, represents a loss of perspective on what has happened, how do we regain that perspective? How do we get to look at our conflicts as though from the outside, and discover ways out of them?

Sometimes this happens through the conflict itself, but ordinarily, we simply get re-triggered, our emotional responses take over, and we lose whatever capacity for insight we may have otherwise accumulated over the course of our lives. So it helps to have a third person enter the conflict, someone who is outside it and can bring perspective as though from the outside, and this is the essential definition of a mediator.

We often think of mediation as a three-party process, but it can involve many more than three parties, and sometimes it is simply a one-on-one process where we are mediating between the internal aspects of conflict inside of us. Workplace and organizational mediations are just a few of the many forms of mediation, and it's important to recognize that while conflict resolution takes a different form in each variety of conflict, all of them can learn from the others. We can improve our techniques by looking at sexual harassment mediations or divorce mediations or family mediations and, with a little adaptation, use them successfully in the workplace.

There are also many different conflict resolution processes, and each is a field in itself. Appreciative inquiry is a field, nonviolent communication is a field, emotional intelligence is a field. And each of these has been developing relatively rapidly over the last several decades, primarily because of the need for innovative approaches to impasse and the places where people get stuck.

Consensus building is a conflict resolution technique, as are team building, conflict coaching, conflict resolution consulting, conflict resolution systems design, participatory feedback and evaluation, etc. These are explicit solutions to organizational conflicts that will be very important as we proceed.

There are also a large number of meditative-style interventions in conflict that help to explain why conflict resolution can be so powerful. For example, transparency. A mediator can ask, "What just happened in the conversation we were having right now? What took place? Who said what, what was your response?" We can be transparent about conversations, the organizational settings in which they took place, and how each person felt about what happened.

We can also intervene in conflicts by asking: "What do you think should be done?" "Why do you think so?" We can be supporting, by appreciating the other person's willingness to be present and contribute to the conversation. We can use acknowledging, refereeing, summarizing, *et cetera*, and each of these will be useful in some settings and not in others. So what we require is an understanding of what makes process interventions useful in one moment and not in another, and to understand that, we have to gain an understanding of what happens in the moment of conflict itself.

If we assume, for example, that B tells a story in which A is said to have attacked B, what is B likely to do or say in response? The answer is to counter-attack, defend, leave, surrender, gossip to C, or try to undermine A. This is essentially the fight, flight, or freeze response, triggered by the emotional processing centers of the brain, especially by the amygdala and the limbic system, which is responsible for many of our emotional responses.

But in addition to these responses, there are also collaborative ones. First, A and B can bring in a mediator who triangulates the antagonism between them and draws it in a new direction so that it isn't perceived as an attack. Second, they can focus on the problem as in "it," rather than as a "you." Third, they can focus on the future rather than on the past. Fourth, they can focus on interests rather than positions. Fifth, they can welcome their differences, invite the conflict in, and try to learn from it. Sixth, they can create introspection around their responses to the conflict. Seventh, they can acknowledge their emotions. Eighth, they can reframe the issues. Ninth, they can forgive each other and themselves. Tenth, they can let it pass through them without reacting. These are a few of the collaborative options that are possible.

So what can they do to get from the first set of responses to the second? Doing so requires a higher order of skill in being able to deal with conflicts. We believe there are six orders of skill in conflict resolution. First are skills in exercising *power*. Power is a highly successful method for resolving disputes at one level. But it uses intimidation and gives orders, is grounded in aggression, is fear-based, is directive and oriented to action and outcomes, it results in win-lose outcomes, and creates hierarchies of domination and subordination.

A second order of skill is in expanding and defending *rights*. That is, using the legal system, or policies and procedures, or rules and regulations, or a grievance process, to resolve the conflict. This requires the use of rhetoric and advocacy, is grounded in competition, is anger-based, focused on rules, oriented to facts and issues, results in compromise and settlement, and is usually either win-lose or lose-lose. Even if you go to court, or if you vote, those are rights-based processes, in which one side wins, and the other side loses.

The third order of skill is in working with *emotions*, which requires the use of emotional intelligence. It is feelings-based, focused on experience, oriented to self, results in closure, and is not any longer about winning or losing, because when we are talking about subjective emotions, victory and loss are no longer the most relevant descriptions or categories.

A fourth order of skill is in satisfying *interests*. Here, we use the art of asking questions, which may be grounded in emotions, as well as in interests. Interests are collaborative, empathy-based, focused on listening, transformative, oriented to relationships, and usually win-win, and described in more detail in other sections.

A fifth order of skill is in building *relationships*, and we can see how each of these skills incorporates, builds on and transforms the ones before. Relationship building skills use caring, integrity, and insight, are grounded in wisdom and spirituality, and are ethical and heart-based, and seek to move people beyond ideas of winning and losing.

A sixth order of skill is in *designing* conflict resolution *systems*, which uses systems thinking to identify the chronic sources of conflict and design techniques to create preventative system-wide enhancements. These result in restructuring, process improvement, and mutual gain.

Thus, each conflict presents us with problems that are resolvable using different orders or sets of skills, and there is an *evolution* in the nature of our conflicts, with a parallel evolution in the order of skills required in order to resolve them, which continues beyond the primitive level that takes place when power-based ideas and cultures dominate the conflict.

These skills can be taught even at early ages. We have helped teach mediation to children in schools and designed conflict resolution systems for children, parents, teachers, and administrators in schools. Here, for example, are 10 simple, easy to remember questions that can be asked by anyone in any conflict, even young children, that can help them move in the direction of resolution:

1. What happened?
2. How did it feel?
3. What do you want?
4. Why do you want it?
5. What are you doing in order to get it?
6. Is that working?
7. What do you think you might do instead?
8. What is one thing the other person could do that could help resolve this problem?
9. What have you learned from this experience that you want to do differently next times?
10. Is there anything else you want to say to each other before we end?

There are other questions that can be asked as well in response to whatever the person answers. The complex issues facing workplace organizations are sometimes also amenable to these simple questions, but we also need to look at how we mediate more complex organizational issues. What is most important in organizations is to begin by evaluating the conflict at its source, and the primary way of doing that is to interview people in advance, then collaboratively design an approach based on their answers, try the most likely approach out, see what works and what doesn't, and continuously improve. It is important to recognize, as we said before, that no technique or approach is going to work always or everywhere or with everyone. Even listening may not be the right thing to do in every situation, so we constantly have to revise and revisit the methods we use to resolve organizational conflicts.

Organizational Interventions (Joan)

I'd like to introduce to you some simple organizational interventions and techniques for resolving conflicts that can be useful in conflicts either between individuals or with teams in organizations.

A very simple technique is round-robin brainstorming, for example, on words or phrases that define the conflict, which is a way for each person to define the conflict for themselves and present it to the group, and you can continue going around the room until all the ideas are out and everyone says, I pass, I don't have anything new to add. Then, they can brainstorm solutions, and come to consensus on how they will resolve the conflict.

Another is group interviews, in which each person in the group interviews someone else, even in the opposing group. When they interview each other, they may ask, what started it, how do you feel about it, all the questions we described earlier. Then the person who was interviewed can be debriefed in front of the group, offer feedback, and have a chance to correct what was reported.

A different technique is called "single document/multiple draft." This technique is used where the mediator tries to accumulate points of consensus, either from scratch, or conversation, or a proposal by one side or the other. Then it gets modified, going back and forth between all the people in the conflict until it results in a single document that everybody agrees to. In fact, our colleagues, Roger Fisher and William Ury, used this technique during the Camp David meetings between Begin and Sadat from Israel and Egypt many years ago, who were about to go to war with each other but reached agreement instead, so it can be a powerful technique.

Another technique is what we call "line-ups" and "stations," which are different versions of the same method. You create different areas of the room and name them for alternative solutions. So those who think the solution to the conflict should be X go to one corner. In another corner, there are people who feel that the solution should be Y, etc.. Everyone goes to different corners, talks with their neighbors, and comes up with bridging solutions or new options, and those are presented to the group, and the room can be reorganized to redefine those options and work on next steps in implementing a solution.

Another method is the Samoan circle, which is a wonderful technique, and the way this works is this: you set a table in the middle of the room, with chairs around the table, usually four, one on each side of the table representing different positions on the issue. Then ask volunteers to go and sit in each of the chairs and talk about their perspective on the conflict. Anyone who also wants to speak about the conflict comes and stands behind the person sitting in that chair, and the person seated completes their comments, gets up, gives the chair to the one who is waiting, and they keep rotating who's sitting in the chairs so everyone can speak.

One person facilitates this process, pulls together what's being proposed, and may, if the group is ready, start looking for ways of negotiating agreements or points of consensus. The moderator can also freeze-frame the discussion or ask for comments from everybody who is outside the circle so everyone feels heard.

Another method is named for Professors Blake and Mouton, who came up with a method for "solving costly organizational conflicts." This is especially useful in organizations where people are deeply divided. First, there is a brief orientation to how they are going to work together, then the conflicting groups separate and identify their goals for their relationship with the other group. Then they return and present, and discover that many of their goals are shared or mutually agreeable. Then, they separate again to identify the barriers to achieving their goals, or the problems in their relationship, and again they present to each other and agree on the problems.

Then they meet in joint problem solving teams to brainstorm how they can overcome their barriers and achieve their goals and propose concrete action plans. Finally, they critique their group process, acknowledge everyone's contributions, review their progress and plan future sessions. What's important here is that both sides feel they have had a voice in describing and determining the goals they have for their relationship, the conflicts or problems in their relationship, and what they will do together to overcome their problems.

Another method is simply strategic planning. Whenever there is a conflict, we can bring people together to create a common vision of where they want to go, how they want to get there, examine the barriers to achieving their vision (and the barriers are usually the conflicts), and work together to create strategies for overcoming the barriers, and action plans to implement the strategies.

Often it is possible to reach agreement on a vision for the future, even if there are conflicts. People can unite on where they want to go, what their dreams are for their organization for the future. Then they identify the barriers, what are they? What's really standing in the way? Then we often divide people up into small groups, let each group choose a barrier they want to work on, and come up with strategies for overcoming that barrier. There is often a lot of commonality, and a lot of consensus on the strategies, which makes action planning much easier. And in action planning, it's not just the organization that needs to act or make changes and end the conflict, but each person is asked to say one action they will take to contribute to achieving the vision, overcoming the barriers, implementing the strategies, and ending the conflict.

Another method is called "sidebar consensus." I used this once when I was working with a task force on homelessness. There was a woman in the group who ran a shelter for homeless people and a developer who wanted to create high-end apartment buildings. I sent them down the hall to come up with something they could agree on, to reach a mini-sidebar consensus. And when they walked back into the room, smiling and announced their agreement, the whole conflict shifted. The entire group then came to agreement, we reached consensus on a plan for dealing with homelessness, and the city council adopted it, and years later, are still using it.

It is also possible to use "group sculptures." This technique originated with Peggy Papp, who was a family therapist, and Margaret Whittaker, another family therapist, who asked families to create living "sculptures" showing how they saw people in their families. Parties who are in conflict can also be asked to create fixed sculptures that depict their view of their relationship and what it feels like. One person picks people from the group and places them in the sculpture — fixed, standing, seated, frozen, or moving robotically — and each person describes how they feel, how they are perceived, and what they need to change. It's a very powerful technique, and I recommend you try it.

Another method we call "passion posters," where we take a flip chart and ask people to write or draw things they feel passionately about. People read these and sign up to discuss them. Then, in small groups, individuals make lists of ways they can bring what they feel passionately about into the organization or use it to resolve their conflicts. Then they post those lists and describe the commonalities in their lists.

Breaking Impasses, Bullying and the Limits of Mediation (Ken)

We know that conflict resolution is not an easy process, and that it requires a great deal of dedication and work to overcome impasse. In this section, we will look at some of the techniques for breaking impasse, some issues that reveal potential openings and interventions, like the issue of bullying, and some of the limits of mediation as a process.

We begin with the idea that the natural state of conflict is impasse. Therefore, it's important not to get upset just because whatever you have done up until now hasn't worked — that means you now have permission to try something new. It's helpful to recognize that there are many reasons for impasse, and people rarely directly communicate *why* they are at an impasse, or what it would take to get them unstuck. Instead, their impasse takes the general form of being unwilling to budge.

Consequently, it is necessary for mediators to explore areas of impasse, which are by definition difficult explore, in part because people may be holding on to the conflict for a variety of reasons that they are unwilling to discuss. Another part of what makes it difficult to resolve conflicts is the lack of permission — not only for the mediator, but extending globally to virtually everyone — to inquire into the sources of impasse for the individual involved.

We therefore need to *mediate our way* into the mediation. We have to take some risks, and some of those risks are described in my book *Mediating Dangerously*, because there is a danger in asking questions about any conflict, particularly sensitive questions about where they are stuck and why.

Here are a few very simple techniques for breaking impasse. First, break the issue down into smaller pieces, subdivide them, isolate the most difficult issues, and come back to them later. We may decide to work on the easier issues in order to create a sense of momentum in the direction of resolution. We can also ask people why an alternative is unacceptable, then look for narrow solutions that are tailored to the reasons they offer. Or, we can simply move on to other issues. We can take a break. We can ask people to think about the various alternatives that have been presented. We can assign as homework for people during breaks or between sessions to think about why they are stuck and what they might do that could get unstuck, and to come up with three to five suggestions for how they might resolve the dispute that they think would be acceptable to the other side.

We can review the other side's priorities and search for common interests. We can bring in experts who may be able to advise on factual differences. Caucusing also often helps. There are some mediators who never caucus, and others who always caucus. Instead, we should think about the reasons for caucusing, and whether it is possible to achieve those reasons together, as there are great advantages to people speaking directly to one another if they can.

We can use a very simple mediator trick and just add two sums together and divide by 2, or split the difference. We can try to figure out what people originally thought their agreement would be. We can look for trade-offs, exchanges of services, or support for one another. We can encourage people to recognize and acknowledge each other's points of view. We can even tell people that we are stuck and ask for their advice on how to get unstuck. And we can ask people what they think would happen or change if they were able to reach a solution.

Sometimes, there is a deeper underlying problem in reaching a solution, or perhaps they feel they will be trapped in a relationship they don't want, or be forced to change in some significant way they aren't ready for. We can then give them permission to say they're not ready for resolution.

We can also compliment people on reaching earlier points of agreement, and encourage them to reach a complete agreement. We can remind them what will happen if they don't settle. We can ask for a minute of silence that invites people to just stop for a moment and think about what they want. I've discovered that when I give people a moment of silence, they return to understanding what the conflict means to them, independent of the actions of the other person, or what is uncomfortable about the conflict, or the reasons for not resolving it.

We can ask more questions. We can serve food or drinks to help people relax. We can end the session and give them homework, or do research ad come up with new information. We can ask people to brainstorm and ask, for example: "What are all the solutions you can think of?" Sometimes, just in the process of listing them, people come up with solutions that are mutually agreeable.

If these simple methods fail, you can tell the parties what alternative you think is fair and why, but this is going to take you out of your role as mediator, and you should ask for permission from the parties before doing this, and only use it as a last resort in exceptional cases. You can suggest arbitration before a mutually agreeable arbitrator, or perhaps bring in another mediator, or even paradoxically suggest that they *increase* the level of their conflict, as a way of pointing out its pointlessness. This has to be done very carefully, and by someone who is skilled in being able to handle whatever responses may get triggered.

If we look for a moment at what happens in impasse in a specific situation, for example, in cases where there is an accusation of bullying, we can see that the source of the impasse is actually the parties' lack of skill at being able to ask deeper questions that are able to reveal the *meaning* of bullying, or a perceived inequality in the relationship that expresses itself as bullying.

For example, one of the questions we might ask is, "What specifically did B do that you consider to be bullying?" This is an effort to identify bullying as an *activity* rather than as a global "personal judgment. Instead of stereotyping B as "a bully," we can ask, what B did that A regards as bullying. And, "What made that feel like bullying to you?" Here you invite an answer that identifies what is taking place inside the person who feels bullied, and you are likely to discover that bullying is a *relationship* between someone who cares deeply about an issue and is willing to be aggressive in order to get what they want; and someone who feels intimidated when they are yelled at, or treated in an aggressive fashion, and is unwilling to be "steamrollered" so the other person can get what they want.

We can now see that it is possible to solve the problem in two directions. Once we define it as a relationship, both people are doing things that contribute to it turning in the wrong direction. On the one hand, one person is engaging in aggressive behavior, and on the other hand, another person is feeling intimidated or treated badly, and neither is reacting skillfully to the other one's behavior.

We can then ask a series of questions, some of which are very risky: "What would you have *liked* B to have said or done instead?" That's not particularly risky, but the next one is—"Why did you allow yourself to be bullied by B?" The danger with this question is that it may feel as though you have taken sides, or that you are now focusing on one of them as the problem, or blaming the victim rather than the one who was aggressive.

One way of addressing this would be to ask, "What do you think you might have done in response, now that you have had some time to think?" Or, "Would you like some ideas about some what you might be able to do or say if this happens again?" And, "Would you be willing to try some of those now and see whether any of them work?" Or, "How could B have made the same point in a way that would not have been experienced by you as bullying?" This is a very useful question because B is listening while you are doing this.

Or, you can ask, "What do you think are some of the reasons people in general bully others?" And, "What are some of the rationalizations people offer for allowing themselves to be intimidated?" Again, this is a dangerous question, and you have to approach it carefully with a great deal of empathy and trust that you have built up beforehand. These questions are designed to help people identify the source of bullying inside them in ways that are non-adversarial and non-judgmental, but offer insight into the problem and suggests methods for resolving it.

Finally, you can ask, "Can you agree, as a ground rule for your communications in the future, that neither of you will act in ways that lead the other person to feel intimidated?" "Can you agree that it is OK to refuse to accept behavior that feels like bullying to either of you?" These questions will probably be answered affirmatively by both parties. Or, "Can you agree that you will both listen to what each other is saying and not engage in or encourage aggressive or bullying behavior?" The object of these questions is to create insight wherever possible.

Of course, we need to address the fact that there is commonly a power differential between the one who is engaging in bullying and the one who feels bullied, and one purpose of the accusation of bullying is to request or initiate a process of "power balancing" — that is, an effort to place the person who is most power-down in a more powerful position in the conversation so they do not feel intimidated, so that what happened that created the conflict will not happen again.

Power balancing is an important element in mediation, but there are a number of pitfalls or difficulties in using it that need to be considered when trying to address power imbalances, especially in rigidly hierarchical organizations. First, there may be an assumption of symmetry, a belief that oppressor and oppressed, powerful and weak, are exactly the same and ought to be treated equally, yet the organization is instead set up to maintain a power imbalance by those above over those below.

There can also be a tendency to ignore deeper underlying conflicts by mediators, an acceptance of the status quo, or pressure to compromise principles, and seeing dialogue as a substitute for action. In highly polarized cases, there can be pressure to renounce more radical allies and practices, or to join in judging third parties who are not present.

There can also be a danger of co-optation by those who have great status, wealth, or power; or efforts to use the mediation process for narrow, selfish, undisclosed personal or organizational purposes. This can happen in marriages and families as well, and what these dangers and difficulties lead to is an understanding of some of the *limits* of mediation as a process.

It is important to have an understanding of the likely *limits* of mediation as a process. Yet mediation is still in its infancy, and because we are still babies in this work, we don't actually know what its limits are. However, we can identify some likely or *potential* limits, which I have framed in the style of Mahatma Gandhi. Each of the eight limits that follow expresses an arena of concern, without finally deciding whether the issue is mediate-able or not. Instead, we need to keep an open mind and continue making *innovative* efforts to resolve it, and learn in the process what is mediate-able and what is not within each unique circumstance based on experience.

A first limit is what I call "power without purpose." Power is always an obstacle in mediation because it is nearly always distributed unequally and is a "zero-sum game," or "win/lose" process. If resort to power has a purpose, we can satisfy the purpose using interests and reduce the need to resort to power. But where power is used without any goal or purpose, as when it is addictive, or used simply for pleasure, satisfying interests is less likely to prevent people from using it.

A second limit is "insanity without comprehension." Everyone in conflict is a little bit crazy, so saying the other person is insane doesn't mean we are automatically off the hook in trying to mediate it, because there's a bit of insanity that is present in every conflict, and we can reduce that insanity through comprehension. But where the form of the insanity precludes comprehension, or the ability to understand what is happening at all, we are less likely to be able to mediate successfully, as consensus becomes impossible.

A third limit is "dishonesty without motive," as with someone who lies about what time it is, or about the weather, for no discernible reason. Dishonesty that has a motive can possibly be resolved by addressing the underlying motive, in which case the person will not feel the need to be dishonest anymore. Yet people lie to each other often, especially in organizations where a great deal of dishonesty is motivated by a desire to survive within the organization, retain a job, be promoted, be looked at favorably by colleagues, etc. But if there is dishonesty without a motive, it will be more difficult to reduce resort to dishonesty.

A fourth limit is "addiction without awareness." People can be addicted to many things, including conflict, but if we can create an awareness of the addiction, we may be able to create a 12-step type of process, or something similar, using methods that might help the person or organization break the addiction. But if they are addicted and unaware of how addicted they are, that can reduce our ability to resolve the conflict.

A fifth limit is "greed without gain." If people are getting something from their conflict, a mediator may be able to find a way of getting it for them without having to be greedy. In this case, greed is *conditional* and instrumental, rather than absolute or fundamental. But if they are greedy without any desire for gain, that creates an obstacle to empathy, learning, and collaboration that limits the effectiveness of mediation.

A sixth likely limit is "suffering without compassion." Initially, many people's experience of suffering drives out compassion for the suffering of others, but it is also possible for suffering to increase their capacity for compassion, and reduce their suffering. But to suffer without being able to experience empathy or compassion for the suffering of others can block understanding and create a limit on the likely success of mediation.

A seventh limit is "revenge without self-interest." My definition of revenge is "the willingness to harm yourself in order to harm someone else." The introduction of any form of self-interest therefore automatically begins to undermine the desire for revenge. But to be so committed to revenge that you are willing to harm yourself in order to hurt someone else makes it difficult to mediate.

An eighth limit is "trauma without meaning." Trauma is so senseless it becomes difficult for anyone who has experienced it even to be aware of the trauma of others, and unable to escape it. Yet if their suffering can find a larger meaning or higher purpose, it may still be possible to mediate. But to suffer trauma without any meaning at all can keep people trapped, and create a limit in mediation.

A ninth limit is "bias without empathy." We all have biases of many kinds, and the worst occur in those who are not empathetic. Yet empathy and awareness of bias, which are commonly techniques in mediation, reduce it by making others more complex, unique, and human than the bias allows. But being biased, un-empathetic, and unaware creates obstacles to mediated understandings and authentic agreements.

A tenth likely limit is "domination without dialogue." The desire to dominate and control others without allowing for dialogue or dissent, ends up partially excluding, silencing, or annihilating the other, effectively reducing two parties to one and eliminating diversity, whether in couples, families, organizations, or societies, making it difficult to mediate, solve problems, or find common ground. But to seek domination without making room at all for those who are being dominated contradicts the core values and principles of the mediation process.

There are many other potential limits on mediation, including limits created by rigidity and dogmatism, excessive vulnerability and emotional fragility, a need to control and manipulate, extreme narcissism and paranoia, a desire to dominate and humiliate others, or even the incompatibility of languages and cultures. Yet for every limit, there are possible approaches, methods and techniques that can help dismantle and reduce them at their chronic, hidden, and conflicted source. What is most important for mediators is that we not give in to these limits, but continue trying, and consecrate our failures to those who will come after.

Learning From Difficult Behaviors (Ken)

It is useful for mediators to consider how we respond to and are able to *learn* from difficult behaviors. To begin, we have three options regarding the way we think about difficult behaviors, especially the kinds that arise in organizations when there are conflicts.

First, we can think about the difficulties we face in conflict as attributable to "difficult people." But once we have defined the *person* as the problem, the only option left is to get rid of the person. And if we define a *group* of people as difficult, we may decide to get rid of the entire group, leading to genocide and lesser types of adversarial behavior directed against groups, like discrimination.

Second, we can think about these difficulties as attributable to "difficult personalities." But here, again, we have painted ourselves into a corner, because if the problem is a difficult personality, the only solution is to put them through years of psychotherapy, and that may not change their behavior. So what we have essentially done in both cases is say there is nothing we can do about the problem.

One of the ways of letting ourselves off the hook in any conflict is to define the problem as unsolvable. But what we want to do in mediation, and conflict resolution generally, is approach the problem differently. So instead of thinking of conflicts as created by "difficult people" or "difficult personalities," we can think of them in a third way, as attributable to "difficult behaviors."

Now, it is possible to recognize that everyone has changed their behaviors countless times over the course of their lives, and can continue to change their behaviors in response to feedback from others. How do we change difficult behaviors? The primary method mediators use is asking questions that reveal to the person the sources of difficulty within themselves and others, the consequences of that difficulty for themselves and others, as well as for the organization in which they are working, and assist them in developing their skills and identifying alternative behaviors that are less difficult to handle, and therefore more successful.

Here are some questions we can ask ourselves about difficult behaviors in conflict to help identify fresh approaches: "What have I contributed to making this conflict happen?" "With hindsight, how could I have handled it better?" "How would I evaluate my own responses so far?" "What have I done that's been effective?" "What hasn't been effective?" "What have I suffered as a result of my own actions?" "How have others suffered?" "What is this conflict asking me to let go of or learn to accept?" "What's the most important lesson I can learn from it?" "How would it be possible for both of our versions of what happened to be correct?" "What could I learn from this conflict that could improve my life?" "What would it take for me to let go of it completely?" "What would happen if I did?" "Has my communication been effective in creating understanding in the other person?" "What could I do to improve it?" "What skills could I develop in handling conflict or responding to negative behaviors?"

These are internally directed mediative questions. But here some more difficult, risky, and dangerous questions we have to be very careful before asking. Some are quite powerful, and, in the right circumstance, can immediately trigger the level of insight we are describing. Questions like: "What have you done to create the very thing you are most troubled by?" That's a very dangerous question to ask in conflict, and you have to have a high level of empathy and trust that has been built up during the mediation in order to be able to ask it.

Here are a few others: "What have you been clinging to or holding onto that it is now time for you to give up?" "What are you responsible for in this conflict that you have not yet acknowledged to the other person?" "What do you most want the other person to say to you that you haven't mentioned?" "What do you long for in your relationship with the other person?" "What is the refusal, or 'no,' that you have not yet communicated?" "What is the permission, or 'yes,' you gave in the past that you now want to retract?" "What is the resentment that you are still holding on to that the other person doesn't even know about?"

Here are some tough ones: "What is the promise you gave in the past that you were now betraying?" "What is it that they or you did that you are still unwilling to forgive?" The next questions feel like they encourage the person to see themselves as a victim, but they are followed by questions that counter that feeling. "What price have you paid for this conflict?" Or, "What price are you willing to pay for your refusal to forgive?" And, "How much longer are you prepared to continue paying that price?" "What promise are you willing to make with no expectation of return?" "What gift could you give the other person that you continue to withhold?" "Why?" "What are you prepared to do, unconditionally, without any expectation of reciprocity or recognition?"

Some of these questions originate with Peter Block, author and management consultant. These are dangerous questions, and we have to be careful in asking them. There are many others as well, and the question becomes more dangerous the closer it gets to the heart of the problem inside us, and that is where it begins to dismantle.

There are also safer questions that can be specifically designed and directed at difficult behaviors. We can ask, for example: "Why is that disturbing to you?" Or, "What do you think led the other person to act that way toward you?" These questions are partly designed to reveal that what makes any behaviors difficult is our lack of skills in being able to handle it. And it is possible for us to develop those skills.

One of the outcomes of difficult behaviors in organizations is that people are disciplined or fired from work, yet it is often the case that no one has ever communicated honestly and directly to that person what it was they did *specifically* that was difficult for others to handle, or helped them understand what they might have done differently before it reached the point of termination.

So one set of questions we can ask in mediation is: "Have you given the person honest, direct feedback about their behavior?" "Has the work group, as a whole, given them feedback?" "What feedback have you given them about their behavior?" "What feedback have you *not* given them, and why not?" "What would it take for you to give them fully direct, empathetic, and honest feedback?"" What could you do to help motivate them to change their behavior?" "How could you reward them for behaviors you find more acceptable?"

When people are terminated for poor performance, we often discover that there are dozens of questions that were never asked. Yet, by not asking these questions, we cheat the person out of an opportunity to improve, and ourselves out of the opportunity to learn new skills. Here are some questions we can ask people who are about to be disciplined or terminated for poor performance, as a way of revealing to them what the issues are and how they might be able to improve: "If you were the manager of this organization, what level of performance or behavior would you expect from an employee in your position?" "Do you think the organization has a right to expect employees to meet minimal standards? What do you believe those standards are?" "What do you think will happen in an organization where people do not meet those standards?" "Do you believe that you've met those standards?" "How could we test to make sure that you've met them?" "What kind of support do you feel you need in order to meet them?" "What should happen to an employee who fails to meet those standards?" *Et cetera..*

The purpose of these questions is to ensure that there is a sense throughout the organization of fundamental fairness in how employees are treated. One of the ways of testing for fundamental fairness is by looking at twelve elements of just cause for discipline. There is a book that has been written about seven elements of just cause, but we have expanded this list to encompass a number of areas we feel also deserve recognition in identifying what is just and fair about discipline or termination.

1. The rule or expectation is clear and reasonable.
2. The investigation is fair and objective.
3. The employee knows or should have known of the rule or expectation.
4. The rule or expectation is job-related.
5. There is substantial evidence of non-compliance.

6. The rule or expectation has been applied to all employees equally, and without discrimination.
7. The employee has actually been notified of the problem with their performance.
8. The employee has had a reasonable opportunity to correct the performance.
9. The employee has been supported in correcting their performance.
10. The discipline has been progressive and incremental.
11. The discipline takes into account the employee's entire record.
12. The discipline is proportionate to the severity of the problem.

These, of course, can each be mediated.

There is a last point we would like to make about mediating organizational conflicts, which is this: we think of conflict resolution techniques as things mediators *do* in conflict, but the mediator is *also* a technique — *you* are the technique, and what you bring to the conversation matters to those who are in conflict. Consequently, we are brought back to ourselves as instruments of openness, empathy, and honesty in conflict conversations.

There are ways of *being* that, by themselves, encourage people to resolve their disputes. This means, first, just showing up and being present and as authentic as we can possibly be; listening empathetically to what is hidden beneath words; telling the truth without blaming or judgment; engaging in poignant, vulnerable, heartfelt communications; being open minded, open hearted, and unattached to outcomes; acting collaboratively throughout the mediation and in all our relationships; displaying unconditional integrity and respect; drawing on our deepest intuition; working for completion and closure; being ready for anything at every moment; and being able to let go, but giving up on no one.

Conflict Mapping (Ken)

Conflict mapping is an effort to diagram in detail how a specific conflict took place by adapting a technique from management and organizational design called process mapping. What we basically do is look at any process — for example, how someone is checked into a hotel — and break it down into parts. Then we look at each of the parts and figure out how it can be improved.

In conflict mapping, we are doing the same thing. This can be done by individuals writing in their notebooks or diaries, or together using flip charts, or butcher paper along a wall, or a series of flip chart pages placed together along a wall that give people an opportunity to come up and insert information regarding any particular point. The process is quite powerful, but it is not used widely, so it is an innovative technique we would like to recommend you try.

Conflict mapping can be done with an opponent in mediation, in a group setting, by yourself, or with a conflict coach. It starts simply by writing down what we know happened in chronological order, and then supplementing and expanding the map by adding additional information.

Remember that "the map is not the territory." The recipe is not the food. It is a guide. It is not the journey. It is designed to help identify places where something may have been missed. So if we go back to the example we cited before, in which someone says, "You are a bully." We can ask, what happened immediately before that? Well, the answer creates a prior point on the map. And, between the yelling that gave rise to the comment and the reaction to it, something happened internally inside each person. Can we map that?

Perhaps the person who yelled felt a sense of guilt about what they did, or insensitivity to the responses of others. Certainly, a cascade of responses was taking place, and the ability to identify the elements in that cascade may be important. Then we can go back and ask, "Why did you feel you had to yell at her? What did she do that led you to yell at her?" This creates another point on the map. And, "Is there an intervention that could have taken place between what she did and your yelling that might have reduced the likelihood that you would have yelled at her? We can design similar questions for each mapping point.

There are several basic steps in conflict mapping. First, simply describe what happened. Then try to determine how much it cost each person and the organization, how long it took, what it meant to each person, the levels of personal dissatisfaction around what happened, and similar measures. Try to map all the events that took place in sequential order.

We next want to analyze the places where the conflict could have been shifted or impacted, consider what might have been done to improve the communications, the processes, and the relationships, and begin improving them in those ways. Finally, we want to monitor these changes to make sure that resolution is taking place and improvements are continuing.

An example of an initial conflict map might be: A insulted B. B felt bad. B insulted A back. A walked away. A told C that B walked out. B felt rejected. C told D what B did to A. B heard from D what A told D. A accused B of bad mouthing A. But why did A insult B? What happened that led A to do that? What could B have said or done just before the insult? Why did B feel bad instead of asking A why this happened? Notice that A could have apologized at some point, which might have led to a completely different outcome. So if we take any process and break it down into its subcomponents, we can identify opportunities for intervention that can prevent it, or make it easier to handle, or offer opportunities for resolution. We can then ask A, "Would you be willing to apologize to B right now?"

The purpose of process mapping is to stimulate a dialogue between people in conflict, with a point of focus that draws their attention to what happened in the process, rather than to what they did to each other, and invent alternatives rather than blaming each other. In other words, it moves the *vector*, or direction of attention, from our opponent to the process, and how we got trapped or stuck in ways that are avoidable.

SESSION 5 LECTURE SLIDES

Because the ones I work for do not love me, because I have said too much and I haven't been sure of what is right and I've hated the people I've trusted, because I work in an office and we are lost and when I come home I say their lives are theirs and they don't know what they apologize for and none of it mended, because I let them beat me and I remember something of mine which not everyone has, and because I lie to keep my self and my hands my voice on the phone because I swallow what hurts me, because I hurt them — I give them the hours I spend away from them and carry them, even in my sleep, at least as the nag of a misplaced shoe, for years after I have quit and gone on to another job where I hesitate in telling and I remember and I resent having had to spend more time with them than with the ones I love.

KILLARNEY CLARY

Ten Reasons We Get Stuck in Conflict (1)

1. *Conflict defines us and gives our lives meaning.* Having an enemy is a quick, easy source of identity, because we *are* whatever they are *not*. By defining our opponents as evil, we implicitly define ourselves as good.

2. *Conflict gives us energy*, even if it is only the energy of anger, fear, jealousy, guilt, shame, and grief. We can become addicted to the adrenaline rush, the flash-point intensity, and the *intimacy* of combat..

3. *Conflict ennobles our misery* and makes it appear that we are suffering for a worthwhile cause. Without conflict, we may feel we suffered in vain, and forced to critique our choices and regret the wasted lives we've led.

4. *Conflict safeguards our personal space* and encourages others to recognize our needs and respect our privacy. For many of us, conflict seems the only way of effectively declaring our rights, securing the respect of others, restoring our inner balance, and protecting ourselves from boundary violations.

5. *Conflict creates intimacy*, even if it is only the transient, *negative* intimacy of fear, rage, attachment, and loss. Every two-year old instinctively knows that it is better to be noticed for doing something wrong than not to be noticed at all.

© Kenneth Cloke

Ten Reasons We Get Stuck in Conflict (2)

6. *Conflict camouflages our weaknesses* and diverts attention from sensitive subjects we would rather avoid discussing. It is a smokescreen, a way of passing the buck, blaming others, and distracting attention from our mistakes.

7. *Conflict powerfully communicates what we honestly feel*, allowing us to vent and assuage our pain by unloading our emotions onto others.

8. *Conflict gets results* and forces others to heed us, especially faceless bureaucrats, clerks, and "service representatives," who only seem to respond to our requests or do what we want when we yell at them.

9. *Conflict makes us feel righteous* by encouraging us to believe we are opposing evil behaviors and rewarding those that are good. Our opponents' pernicious actions justify us in giving them what they "rightly deserve."

10. *Conflict prompts change*, which feels better than impasse and stagnation. Many changes only take place as a result of conflict—not because it is actually necessary to achieve a given result, but because people's fear and resistance make it so.

© Kenneth Cloke

25 Varieties of Mediation

1. Neighborhood and Community Mediation
2. Peer Mediation
3. Cross-Cultural Mediation
4. Prejudice and Discrimination Mediation
5. Sexual Harassment Mediation
6. Divorce Mediation
7. Family Mediation
8. Family Business Mediation
9. Marital and Relational Mediation
10. Prenuptial Mediation
11. Workplace Mediation
12. Organizational Mediation
13. Ombudsmanship
14. School Mediation
15. Victim-Offender Mediation
16. Restorative Justice Mediation
17. Public Policy Mediation
18. Social Justice and Advocacy Mediation
19. Environmental Mediation
20. Healthcare and Hospital Mediation
21. Commercial Mediation
22. Litigated Case Mediation
23. Insurance Mediation
24. Multi-Door Courthouses
25. Conflict Resolution Systems Design

© Kenneth Cloke

25 Conflict Resolution Processes

1. Active, empathetic and responsive listening
2. Appreciative inquiry
3. Non-violent communication
4. Emotional intelligence
5. Collaborative, mutual gain and interest-based negotiation
6. Consensus building
7. Prejudice reduction and bias awareness
8. Support for diversity and cross-cultural communication
9. Team building
10. Community organizing
11. Mediation
12. Dialogue facilitation
13. Circles
14. Opening heart-to-heart conversations
15. Restorative justice
16. Victim-offender mediation
17. Awareness, mindfulness and meditation
18. Informal problem solving
19. Conflict coaching
20. Conflict resolution consulting
21. Participatory feedback and evaluation
22. Conflict resolution systems design
23. Apology and acknowledgment
24. Forgiveness and reconciliation
25. Training and capacity building

© Kenneth Cloke

Some Mediative Process Interventions

- *Transparency* — "What just happened in the conversation we were having?"
- *Inquiring* — "What do you think should be done? Why do you think so?"
- *Supporting* — "I appreciate your willingness to speak up and express your opinions. Here is an example that supports your point."
- *Acknowledging* — "You took a risk in making that apology/concession."
- *Refereeing* — "What ground rules do we need so everyone can feel we are behaving fairly?"
- *Concretizing* — "Can you give a specific example?"
- *Exploring* — "Can you say more about why you feel so strongly about this issue?"
- *Summarizing* — "Is this what you are trying to say ... ?"
- *Challenging* — "Is that consistent with the ground rules/what the group has already decided?"
- *Coaching* — "Is there a way you could respond less defensively?"
- *Connecting* — "That point connects directly with what was said earlier ... ."
- *Re-orienting* — "I think we're lost. Can we get back on track? Are we talking about the real issue?"
- *Problem Solving* — "What do you see as possible solutions?"
- *Uniting* — "What can we agree on here?"
- *Contextualizing:* "Why did you decide to come together to discuss this issue?"

© Kenneth Cloke

Aggressive Options

If A attacks B (A⟶B), B can respond in several ways:

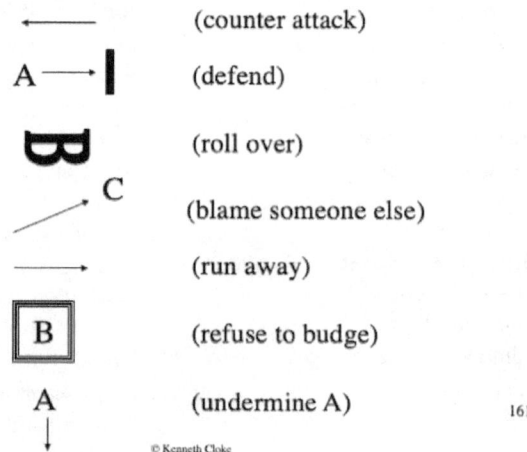

© Kenneth Cloke

Collaborative Options

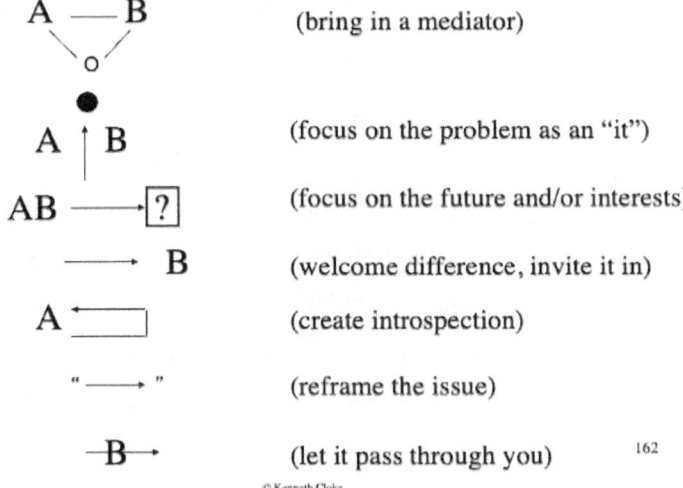

6 Orders of Skill in Conflict Resolution

1. Skills in Exercising *Power*: Uses intimidation and decisiveness – grounded in aggression, fear-based, directive, oriented to action and outcomes, resulting in win/lose, hierarchies of domination and subordination
2. Skills in Expanding and Defending *Rights*: Uses rhetoric and advocacy – grounded in competition, anger-based, focused on rules, oriented to facts and issues, resulting in compromise and settlement, usually lose/lose
3. Skills in Working with *Emotions*: Uses emotional intelligence – grounded in eliciting and acknowledging, feeling-based, focused on experience, oriented to self, resulting in closure, not about winning or losing
4. Skills in Satisfying *Interests*: Uses the art of asking questions – grounded in emotions and interests, collaborative, empathy-based, focused on listening, transformative, oriented to relationships, resulting in resolution and satisfaction, usually win/win
5. Skills in Building *Relationships*: Uses caring, integrity and insight – grounded in wisdom and spirituality, ethical, heart-based, focused on awareness, oriented to being, intimacy and living one's values, resulting in connection, learning and transcendence, beyond winning and losing
6. Skills in Designing *Systems*: Uses systems thinking to identify chronic sources of conflict and design preventative systems – grounded in science and art, systems-based, focused on prevention, oriented to amelioration, resulting in restructuring, process improvement and mutual gain

© Kenneth Cloke

10 Strategies to Resolve Conflicts at Work

Strategy One: Understand the Culture and Dynamics of Conflict

Strategy Two: Listen Actively, Empathetically, and Responsively

Strategy Three: Search Beneath the Surface for Hidden Meanings

Strategy Four: Acknowledge and Reframe Emotions

Strategy Five: Separate What Matters from What Gets in the Way

Strategy Six: Solve Problems Creatively and Paradoxically

Strategy Seven: Learn from Difficult Behaviors

Strategy Eight: Lead and Coach for Transformation

Strategy Nine: Explore Resistance and Negotiate Collaboratively

Strategy Ten: Mediate, and Design Systems for Prevention

© Kenneth Cloke and Joan Goldsmith

20 Ways to Reduce Conflict (1)

1. Stop arguing, accusing and insulting each other, and sit down together to talk.
2. Take turns speaking and listening without interrupting.
3. Summarize, clarify and acknowledge what the other person has said and feels.
4. Repeat what you think the other person is saying. Ask if you are correct. If not, listen again.
5. Avoid accusations. Say: "I feel ... when you ... because ..."
6. Focus on the future rather than the past. Offer unilateral concessions.
7. Focus on problems and behaviors rather than personalities.
8. Focus on interests rather than positions. Ask "Why do you want that?" "Why is that important to you?"
9. Break the problem down into smaller parts. Focus on the easiest.
10. Search for creative solutions. Brainstorm ideas.

© Kenneth Cloke and Joan Goldsmith

20 Ways to Reduce Conflict (2)

11. List, categorize and prioritize all possible solutions, then try to reach consensus on the best option.
12. Agree on criteria that will make the outcome fair and workable.
13. If you can't agree, take a break and come back to it later.
14. Write down what you want and what you are willing to do to end the dispute.
15. Move on to other issues and circle back after reaching smaller agreements.
16. Split the difference 50/50. Consider what you want in exchange for agreeing to something that is important to them.
17. Consider trade-offs and ways to "expand the pie."
18. Say what will happen and what you will do next if the dispute is not resolved, then ask if that is what you want and return to options.
19. Write down and confirm your agreements. Jointly evaluate your progress in implementing them.
20. Ask someone you both trust to mediate or arbitrate the issues. [166]

© Kenneth Cloke and Joan Goldsmith

12 Questions for Anyone in Conflict

1. What happened?
2. How did it feel?
3. What do you want?
4. Why do you want it?
5. What does the other person want?
6. Why do they want it?
7. What are each of you doing in order to get it?
8. Is that working?
9. What do you think you might do instead?
10. What could you each do to help solve the problem? Are you willing to try that?
11. What have you learned that you want to do differently next time?
12. Is there anything else you want to say to each other before we end? [167]

© Kenneth Cloke

Mediating Organizational Issues (1)

1. Use two or three mediators. Consider including small group (or "team") facilitators -- one for each group of 4-5 participants.
2. Begin by asking each participant to introduce themselves, state their position in the organization, and what they would like to accomplish in the session.
3. Establish clear ground rules. Obtain consensus on confidentiality. Agree to talk about what will be said to others who are not present about the mediation session and any agreements that may be reached.
4. Use a round robin process to allow each person to describe how he or she see the conflict.
5. If the true conflict does not surface, use a secret ballot. Ask everyone to write down the three most important problems in the organization.
6. Write these down on flipchart paper and post on the wall for all to see.
7. Discuss the problems, causes or metaphors, placing them in categories by analysis in large group discussion.
8. Break up into small groups by interest, divergent views, responsibility or random selection with a mediator or facilitator in each group. Let each group analyze and distill the problems to a concise statement by analysis.
9. Have each small group select someone to record ideas and another to present to the group as a whole. Applaud each presentation.

Mediating Organizational Issues (2)

10. Discuss the small group reports in the large group and look for ways of reaching consensus.
11. Ask each small group to brainstorm and prioritize a list of possible solutions.
12. Assign each small group follow-up "homework", to gather additional facts, narrow the list of options, consult with others who are not present, develop proposals for key options, etc.
13. Use force-field analysis and other techniques to identify what hindering and helping forces need to be identified.
14. Create an action plan, with specific responsibility for tasks and deadlines.
15. Reflect on the transformation from anger, resentment, cynicism and resistance to energy, enthusiasm, teamwork and commitment.
16. Evaluate the process and get feedback on the satisfaction of participants with the outcome and process.
17. Encourage participant to give constructive feedback to others.
18. Reduce agreements to writing, identify next steps to be taken, and who will be responsible for taking them.
19. Congratulate participants on their work, and celebrate their successes.
20. Schedule a follow-up meeting to track progress and maintain momentum.

The Deep Structure of Conflict Stories

1. Every conflict story takes the form of an accusation.

2. Beneath every accusation is a confession.

3. Beneath every confession is a request.

An Example:

1. "You are lazy."

2. "I am working hard and would like to take time off but don't give myself permission, so when I see you taking time off I feel jealous and disrespected."

3. "Can you give me a hand?"

Creative Group Techniques (1)

1. **Round Robin Brainstorming:** Each person in turn defines the problem, going around the room until everyone passes. The same process is used to brainstorm solutions and arrive at consensus.
2. **Group Interview:** Each person in the group interviews another person about their view of the conflict, then presents the results of the interview to the group as a whole. The person interviewed is then "debriefed" and asked for feedback.
3. **Single Document/Multiple Draft:** The mediator accumulates points of consensus, either from scratch or starting with a proposal from one side that is modified by the other back and forth until there is agreement.
4. **Lineups:** Make one spot in the room stand for one solution to the conflict and another spot stand for the opposite solution. Ask people to arrange themselves in relation to the strength of their feelings about the issue, then discuss it with those nearest.
5. **Stations:** Do the same exercise, but create four alternatives, one for each corner in the room and allow people to group themselves in front of the option they like best. Then ask everyone how they feel being divided, and ask them to talk to their neighbors and get them to recombine into fewer options to narrow the number of people supporting each choice.

Creative Group Techniques (2)

6. **Samoan Circle:** Place chairs in a circle or square with a table and 4 chairs in the center. Ask four volunteers to represent four perspectives on the conflict. Only those seated at the table may talk, and if others wish to speak they stand next to someone at the table and wait for a turn. A neutral person acts as facilitator to begin the process, or as moderator if needed. After discussion, the parties talk about how to negotiate an agreement. The moderator may switch roles or positions or freeze-frame and ask for comments on the process. Afterward everyone discusses the experience.

7. **Blake and Mouton Method:** (from <u>Solving Costly Organizational Conflicts</u>) After orientation, conflicting groups separately identify optimal goals for their relationship, then jointly consolidate and agree on goals; then separately identify problems in their relationship and jointly consolidate and agree on problems. They then meet together to develop concrete plans for changing their relationship to achieve their goals. They then critique their group process, acknowledge individual contributions, review their progress and plan further improvements.

8. **Strategic Planning:** The group jointly creates a vision of how they would like their organization or their relationship to be, then identifies barriers to realizing that vision, develops strategies for overcoming the barriers, and action plans to put the strategies into effect.

Creative Group Techniques (3)

9. **Side-Bar Consensus:** Ask two to four individuals with differing views of the problem to meet separately and develop a consensus recommendation for the group as a whole.

10. **Group Sculpture:** Ask each sub-group to use its members to create a sculpture that depicts what the relationship with the other group feels to them, asking people to freeze in position or use only robotic movements. Interview the sculpture to understand what each element feels like in position. Then look for ways of making the relationship less stressful through reworking the sculpture.

11. **Passion Posters:** Individuals write on flip chart paper one thing they feel passionately about. Everyone reads these and small groups are formed to talk in round robin fashion about why they feel passionately about that subject and what they might do to more effectively act on their passion. Each group reports on their results.

12. *Reductio ad Absurdum*: In dyads, individual members of conflicting groups list as many things that are wrong with the other group or reasons for not resolving their conflict as they possibly can, being urged repeatedly to keep on going. Afterwards they list as many reasons for resolving their differences as they can, and then compare their lists.

25 Techniques to Break Impasse (1)

1. Break the issue down into smaller parts, isolating the most difficult issues and reserving these for later.
2. Ask the parties why an alternative is unacceptable, then look for narrow solutions tailored to the reasons given.
3. Go on to other issues, or take a break and ask the parties to think about the various alternatives presented.
4. Review the parties' priorities and common interests.
5. Suggest consulting an expert to supply needed facts or advice.
6. Caucus with each party separately to explore hidden agendas and willingness to compromise.
7. Split the difference.
8. Try to obtain agreement on what the parties originally expected the solution would be.
9. Look for possible trade-offs or exchange of services.
10. Encourage the parties to recognize and acknowledge each other's points of view.
11. Tell the parties you are stuck and ask for their ideas.
12. Ask the parties to indicate what would change or happen if they reached a solution.
13. Make certain the parties prefer conflict resolution, as opposed to using HR or letting the conflict continue. If they don't, find out why.

© Kenneth Cloke and Joan Goldsmith

25 Techniques to Break Impasse (2)

14. Look at the impact of various solutions on allied third parties.
15. Test for emotional investment by asking what it would take to surrender it.
16. Compliment the parties on reaching earlier points of agreement and being willing to compromise, encouraging them to reach a complete agreement and put this dispute behind them.
17. Remind them what will happen if they don't settle--what each might lose.
18. Create a minute of silence for the parties to think about it.
19. Ask more questions about the problem, about feelings, priorities, alternative solutions, flexibility, hidden agendas, reluctance to compromise, anger at one another, etc., or return to agenda setting.
20. Serve food or drinks to get them to relax.
21. End the session and assign homework for the parties to return to the next session with written alternatives or reasons or financial data, etc.
22. Generate options by asking the parties to brainstorm without considering the practicality of a suggestion.
23. Tell the parties which alternative you believe is fair and why. This should only be done if all other options fail.
24. Suggest arbitration as a last-ditch alternative.
25. Suggest (paradoxically) that the parties increase their fighting, as a way of revealing the pointlessness of the conflict.

© Kenneth Cloke and Joan Goldsmith

Some Questions on Bullying (1)

- "What specifically did B *do* that you consider to be bullying?"
- "What made that *feel* like bullying to you?"
- "What would you have *liked* B to have done instead?"
- "Why do you *allow* yourself to be bullied by B?"
- "How could B have made the same point, but in a way that would not have been *experienced* by you as bullying?"
- "What do each of you think are the reasons people in general bully others?"
- "What are some of the rationalizations people generally offer for allowing themselves to be intimidated?"
- "What do you think B wants to *get* through what you call bullying?"
- "If we talk about those issues do you think B will still feel the need to push so hard for what s/he wants?"
- "Can you think of anything A did that encouraged you to engage in what s/he has called "bullying"?
- "What could s/he do in the future that would allow you to act differently?"
- "Would you be willing to try that approach right now and see if it works."
- "Why do you (B) think A felt afraid of, or intimidated by you?"
- "Was there anything you (A) did that encouraged B to think his behavior was acceptable?"

© Kenneth Cloke

176

Some Questions on Bullying (2)

- "Was there anything you (A) did that encouraged B to think his behavior was acceptable?" "Why did you do that?"
- "Did A do anything that made you (B) feel s/he accepted your behavior?"
- "Can you both agree that you could have a better relationship if the two of you did not engage in or accept bullying behavior?"
- "What are some of the ways your relationship could improve if you moved away from these behaviors?"
- "Was there anyone who was a bully or was bullied in the neighborhood or school where you grew up or in your family of origin?"
- "How did you respond to it then?"
- "Would you respond the same way to it now?" "Why?"
- "Can you agree as a ground rule for your communication in the future that neither of you will act in ways that make the other person feel intimidated?" "Can you also agree that it is OK to refuse to accept bullying behavior?"
- "Can you agree that you will both listen to what each other is saying and not engage in or encourage bullying behavior?"
- "B, is it acceptable to you if A lets you know in the future if s/he feels intimidated by you?" "If s/he does, can A raise it with you as a topic for discussion and negotiation?" "How would you like her/him to do that?"

© Kenneth Cloke

177

Potential Pitfalls of Mediation

1. *False Assumption of Symmetry:* It is mistaken to assume that oppressor and oppressed, occupier and occupied, powerful and weak are the same or that they can be treated as equally aggrieved.
2. *Tendency to Ignore Underlying Conflicts:* People in mediation often behave reasonably and want to reach agreements, and may ignore or avoid issues that could be disruptive.
3. *Acceptance of the Status Quo:* There is a tendency in mediation to accept and take for granted what is or have been the case for years, even when this is perceived by some to be wrong.
4. *Pressure to Compromise Principles:* People in mediation often feel pressured to surrender or compromise on points of principle in order to reach agreement, even when there are moral reasons not to.
5. *Dialogue as a Substitute for Action:* There is a tendency to substitute talk for action, especially for those who seek to change the status quo. Many see mediation as an end in itself, rather than as an effort to secure justice.
6. *Pressure to Renounce Allies and Practices:* Members of out-group and oppressed groups are often pressured to renounce violence, yet in-groups and oppressors are permitted to continue.
7. *Danger of Co-Optation:* Government authorities can misuse and co-opt mediation for their own purposes.

[Based on work by Palestinian Attorney Jonathan Kuttab.]

10 Likely Limits in Mediation

1. Power without purpose
2. Insanity without comprehension
3. Dishonesty without motive
4. Addiction without awareness
5. Greed without gain
6. Suffering without compassion
7. Revenge without self-interest
8. Trauma without meaning
9. Bias without empathy
10. Domination without dialogue

© Kenneth Cloke and Joan Goldsmith

Questions on Conflict

- What did I contribute to making this conflict happen?
- With hindsight, how could I have handled it better?
- How would I evaluate my responses so far? What have I done that has been effective? What hasn't been effective?
- How have I suffered as a result of my own actions or inactions?
- How have other suffered?
- What does this conflict ask me to let go of or learn to accept?
- What is the most important lesson I can learn from this conflict?
- How would it be possible for both of our versions of what happened to be correct?
- In what way could this conflict improve my life?
- What's funny or ridiculous about my role in this conflict?
- What would it take for me to let go of this conflict completely?
- What would happen if I did?
- Has my communication been effective in creating understanding in the other person? What could I do to improve it?
- What skills could I develop in handling conflict? In responding to negative behavior?

© Kenneth Cloke and Joan Goldsmith

Some Dangerous Questions

- What have you done to create the very thing you are most troubled by?
- What have you been clinging to or holding onto that it is now time for you to release?
- What are you responsible for in your conflict that you have not yet acknowledged to the other person?
- What do you most want to hear the other person say to you that you still haven't mentioned?
- What do you long for in your relationship with the other person?
- What is the refusal, or "no" that you have not yet communicated?
- What is the permission, or "yes" you gave in the past that you now want to retract?
- What is the resentment you are still holding on to that the other person doesn't know about?
- What is the promise you gave that you are now betraying?
- What is it they or you did that you are still unwilling to forgive?
- What price are you willing to pay for your refusal to forgive? How long are you prepared to continue paying that price?
- What promise are you willing to make to the other person with no acknowledgement or expectation of return?
- What gift could you give the other person that you continue to withhold? Why?
- What are you prepared to do *unconditionally*, without any expectation of recognition or reciprocity by the other person?

[Based partly on work by Peter Block]
© Kenneth Cloke and Joan Goldsmith

Questions for Improvement

1. What do I want to stop/start/continue?
2. What do I want to more of/do less of?
3. What am I going to do specifically? (List each action.)
4. When am I going to begin each action?
5. When am I going to finish each action?
6. What coaching or support do I need from others?
7. How can I get the coaching and support I need from others?
8. How will others know whether I have improved?
9. How could I undermine myself and not do it?
10. How could others undermine my ability to improve?
11. How can I support myself in improving?
12. What changes need to be made in the workplace for me to succeed?
13. What is in it for me to actually complete these actions and improve?
14. What will it mean and what will happen if I don't?

© Kenneth Cloke and Joan Goldsmith

Questions for Difficult Behaviors

- What is the specific behavior they are engaged in that you find most disturbing?
- Why is that disturbing to you?
- Why do you think they are engaging in it?
- Did anyone in your family of origin engage in similar behavior? How did you respond?
- How are you responding to the difficult behavior?
- Is the other person benefiting in any way from your responses to their behavior?
- Have your responses been successful so far in stopping their behavior?
- How could you change your responses to stop rewarding them for behaviors you find unacceptable?
- How are others in the organization responding to their behavior?
- Is there anyone who handles their behavior skillfully? What are they doing differently?
- What organizational benefits are they deriving from their behavior?
- Have you given them honest feedback about their behavior? If so, how did they receive it?
- Has the work group as a whole given them feedback?
- What feedback have you *not* given them about their behavior? Why not?
- What would it take for you to give them fully empathetic and honest feedback?
- What could motivate them to change their behavior? What would motivate you?
- How could you reward them for behaviors you find more acceptable? How could you support them in changing?

© Kenneth Cloke and Joan Goldsmith

Questions for Poor Performance

- If you were the manager of this organization, what level of performance or behavior would you expect from an employee in your position?
- Do you think the organization has a right to expect employees to meet minimal standards?
- What do you believe those standards are? Do you think they should be any different from what they are?
- Would you like to know in more detail what they are or why they were set?
- What impact do you think the failure to meet these standards will have on the team? On the organization?
- Do you believe you have met those standards?
- How could we test to make sure you have met them?
- What kind of support do you feel you need in order to meet these standards?
- What do you think should happen to any employee who fails to meet these standards?
- If you were a manager, how many warnings would you give an employee who failed to meet these standards prior to termination?
- What do you think is going to happen to you if you continue along this path?
- What would need to be done for any discipline or discharge to feel fair to you?
- What do you want to happen? What are you prepared to do to make sure it does?
- Are you sure you really want this job? Do you think you might be in the wrong position?
- If you really want this job, what are you prepared to do to keep it?
- How long should it take you to meet these standards? What should happen if you don't?
- Would you like some feedback from me on what you said in response to these questions?

© Kenneth Cloke and Joan Goldsmith

12 Elements of Just Cause for Discipline

1. The rule or expectation is clear and reasonable.
2. The investigation is fair and objective.
3. The employee knows or should have known of the rule or expectation.
4. The rule or expectation is job-related.
5. There is substantial evidence of non-compliance.
6. The rule or expectation has been applied to all employees equally, and without discrimination.
7. The employee has actually been notified of the problem with their performance.
8. The employee has had a reasonable opportunity to correct the performance.
9. The employee has been supported in correcting their performance.
10. The discipline has been progressive and incremental.
11. The discipline takes into account the employee's entire record.
12. The discipline is proportionate to the severity of the problem.

© Kenneth Cloke and Joan Goldsmith

What is Conflict Mapping?

- Conflict Mapping is a process for understanding *exactly* how and where we get stuck in conflict.
- Conflict mapping can be done in four basic ways:
    1. With your opponent -- especially in marital and relational conflicts
    2. With a group -- especially in workplace, organizational and social, political or public policy conflicts
    3. By yourself -- especially to see what you could do to shift the conversational dynamic in a more constructive direction
    4. With a conflict coach -- especially where you want to gain fresh insight into the places where you get stuck or learn new skills
- The mapping process begins by writing down what you know about what happened, moment by moment, then expanding and supplementing the map with increasing detail.
- Remember: the map is not the territory, the recipe is not the cake. It is a guide, but not the journey.

© Kenneth Cloke and Joan Goldsmith

Some Conflict Mapping Points

- Every point where something was said or an action was taken that impacted the conflict, either positively or negatively
- Every point where something was not said, or an action was not taken, but could or should have, that might have stopped the conflict or made it easier to handle
- What was the response, what was added or changed in the conflict or relationship as a result
- What it would have cost each person to say or not say it, to do or not do it, how long it would have taken, and how important it would have been to say or do it
- What it would have meant to each person in their relationships, and in personal satisfaction and morale
- What became possible or impossible for them to do or say as a result
- What might have been said or done instead that could have resolved the dispute or improved their relationship

© Kenneth Cloke and Joan Goldsmith

5 Steps in Conflict Mapping

1. *Evaluate*: Describe what happened, determine how much it cost, how long it took, what it meant, personal satisfaction, and similar measures
2. *Map*: List steps in sequential order
3. *Analyze*: Identify critical places where the conflict could be impacted
4. *Act*: Improve the communication, process and relationship
5. *Monitor*: Monitor the changes to make sure resolution is achieved, and that improvements continue.

© Kenneth Cloke and Joan Goldsmith

Initial Conflict Map Example

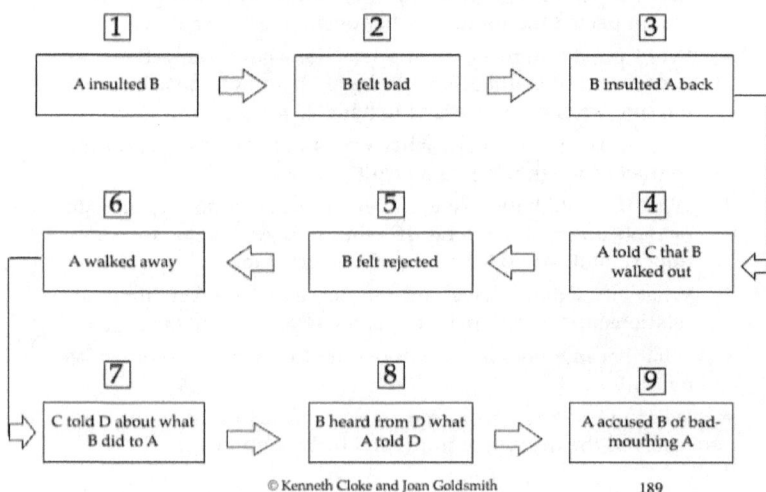

© Kenneth Cloke and Joan Goldsmith

Modified Conflict Map Example

Blank Conflict Map (to be filled in)

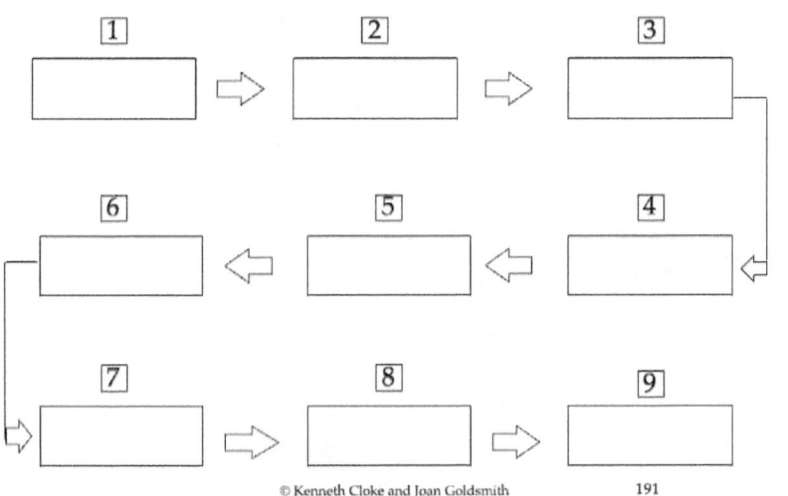

Some Limits in Mediation

- Power without purpose
- Insanity without comprehension
- Addiction without awareness
- Dishonesty without reason
- Suffering without compassion
- Greed without gain
- Revenge without self-interest
- Trauma without meaning

© Kenneth Cloke
(Based partly on ideas by Mahatma Gandhi)

192

How to *Be* in Conflict

1. Show up and be as present and authentic as you can be.
2. Listen empathetically for what is hidden beneath words.
3. Tell the truth without blaming or judgment.
4. Engage in poignant, vulnerable, heart-felt communications.
5. Be open-minded, open-hearted, and unattached to outcomes.
6. Act collaboratively in all relationships.
7. Display unconditional integrity and respect.
8. Draw on your deepest intuition.
9. Work for completion and closure.
10. Be ready for anything at every moment.
11. Be able to let go, but give up on no one.

© Kenneth Cloke

193

CHAPTER 6

CONFLICT RESOLUTION SYSTEMS DESIGN

Overview of Systems Design, Costs of Conflicts, and Reasons for Systems Design (Ken)

Perhaps the most powerful tool available for organizations in dealing with chronic conflicts is *conflict resolution systems design*, which was first described by William Ury, Steve Goldberg, and Jeanne Brett in *Getting Disputes Resolved*. The authors were invited into the coal mines to look at conflicts taking place among miners, between the union and the miners, labor and management, and in the group as a whole.

What they discovered was that there were a number of cracks and holes in the system they had set up to process conflicts. They developed an analysis, which led to the idea of systems design, and realized that it would be possible to act in a preventative way and develop systems to address and resolve chronic organizational conflicts.

In our view, there are three *orders* or generations of systems design. The first order or generation, as described by Ury, Goldberg, and Brett, focuses on the development of conflict resolution systems within an organization or group, and how to design conflict resolution systems for handling grievances, complaints, arguments, difficulties, problems, and internal conflicts within an organizational system.

The second order or generation of systems design looks at the problem differently, and sees that e very organization, as we described earlier, is itself a *conflict resolution* mechanism. This means, for example, that there will be more conflicts when there is poor leadership and fewer conflicts when there is good leadership. Therefore, leadership performs a conflict resolution function. We then want to think about how leaders can learn to be better mediators, and how mediators can learn to be better leaders, and lead people through the change process we call mediation.

We can then look at *all* organizational systems, including feedback and evaluation systems, reward and compensation systems, human resource systems, and a variety of other systems inside organizations that impact the level of conflict inside that organization. As mediators, we can ask the question, "How well is this entire system functioning from the perspective of conflict resolution, and how successful is it in preventing conflicts?"

We can also apply these ideas to large-scale social, economic, and political conflicts, not just within organizations, but within governments, economies, and societies, and the larger environmental systems that are national and international, and impact all of us. And this will be the subject of our last series of lectures.

There is a third order or generation of systems design, which is to redesign systems design itself so as to modify, customize, and reimagine it in fresh ways. For example, organizational aspects of systems design will be less effective in preventing conflicts in family systems, which require an appreciation of the system of caring or love, which will assume a different form in organizational conflicts.

Henri Frederic Amiel wrote, "Our systems, perhaps, are nothing more than an unconscious apology for our faults, a gigantic scaffolding whose object is to hide from us our favorite sin." And if our favorite sin is conflict, our systems may in fact be highly effective in doing this. What is it that we have hidden from ourselves? One item is the human, financial, and other *costs* of our conflicts, and if we take a look at the costs of organizational conflict, we can see that there are massive amounts of loss they experience every day.

In one study that looked at 1,600 employees, 22 percent of those interviewed said they decreased their work efforts as a result of conflict. 50 percent reported they had lost work time because they worried about whether the instigator of the conflict would do it again, and 12 percent reported they had changed jobs to get away from the instigator of the conflict.

If you add up these costs, they are simply overwhelming. They are a massive part of the hidden budget of every organization. What we want to do with systems design is identify the costs of conflict as accurately as we can, so the organization can then set aside resources to save those costs through conflict prevention and return most of them to the organization.

Here are some examples of savings that have taken place in conflict resolution. Brown and Root reported an 80 percent reduction in outside litigation expenses. Motorola reported savings in a similar percentage in litigation expenses, up to 75 percent per year over six years. NCR reported a reduction of litigation expenses of 50 percent. These are reported in Karl Slaikeu and Ralph Hasson's, *Controlling the Costs of Conflict*. The Air Force reported that taking a collaborative approach to conflict management involving the Army Corps of Engineers allowed it to complete a project 144 days ahead of schedule and $12 million under budget, etc.

Massive costs are incurred as a result of conflict, and massive savings can occur as a result of conflict resolution. So what are the options in terms of conflict resolution? There is a range that extends all the way from surrender to genocide and total war. What we want to do is expand the middle ground, reduce the resort to violence, revenge, and confrontation, even to arbitration and courts, by emphasizing interest-based approaches.

What are some of the reasons organizations might want to use conflict resolution systems design? First, in order to prevent conflicts before they occur. If we can do this, it would be very cost-effective. We also want to reduce the risks and costs of conflict; encourage settlement before those costs and attorney's fees accumulate; provide a forum for final resolution outside the courts; create inexpensive internal mechanisms to prevent, manage, and resolve conflicts; improve morale; and pinpoint and resolve the underlying reasons for the conflict.

Here are some additional ones, some identified by Ury, Goldberg, and Brett. Once conflict is seen as a system, it can be addressed in more than one way. The emphasis in the past has been on discrete, individual, tailored dispute resolution procedures, rather than on an *integrated* systems design approach. Systems design allows organizations to respond not only to single disputes, but the stream of disputes that arise in all organizations, the chronic disputes that are generated by its systems. In addition, some procedures work better in certain disputes than in others, and we can decide which procedures to use and create a rich mix of backup procedures we can use in case they don't.

Systems are also needed to encourage negotiation and de-escalation procedures throughout the life of a conflict. This allows a variety of diverse professionals to work on the same conflict from different perspectives, so HR can contribute something, line management can contribute something, etc..

Also, different parts of the organization may be able to impact the conflict in diverse and constructive ways. Finally, a systems approach can promote synergy, in which the whole is seen as greater than the sum of its parts. It can, in other words, draw an organization together and increase its internal unity, cohesion, morale, determination, and potential for success.

Conflict Audit (Joan)

The word "audit" can raise hackles and fears in organizations because financial audits often have the purpose of finding misuse of money, or mistakes, or financial misdemeanors, or corruption, etc. It is therefore difficult to talk about conflict audits because we can raise fears when we examine problems or difficulties, or what's not working and costing the company money, goodwill, good feelings about themselves, and perhaps even personal health. However without a careful and through examination of the source of chronic conflicts, they can remain hidden, denied, or papered over, and never be confronted or resolved. A conflict audit is therefore necessary for *systemic* resolution and organizational transformation.

The first step in creating a conflict audit is to recruit a team to work with you, as a coach or consultant, to jointly design the audit, frame the questions, brief everyone in the organization about the process, and include them in reviewing and analyzing the results, and recommending changes. We usually ask for a volunteer team composed of a wide range of diverse staff, across departments and the hierarchy.

We did a conflict audit with an entire a county government, and the team involved staff from every department who ranged in roles from cleaners in the parks and recreation department to the managing director of the entire county.

To begin the process we meet with the team, helping design the audit, and work with them to identify questions to ask in the audit. As advisors, consultants, and mediators, we propose questions, looking to the team to review, modify, give us feedback, and approve a final draft.. We often submit the final questions to everyone in the organization, top to bottom, across units, and do so in writing so people can respond in writing and we can model transparency.

If the organization is small and informal and we are working with a strong team, we will do the audit verbally through interviews, and if the organization is as at a distance, or very large, we may do them by telephone or email. It is interesting to note that often the people we want to reach will speak more honestly and openly when they're on the phone than they do when they are face-to-face, even with a mediator.

Some of our questions include: "How much money and time is being spent on lawyers, litigation, and human resources related to conflicts?" "What is the impact on morale and motivation?" And, "How might the organization succeed if it hadn't experienced these conflicts?" Or, "What are the main messages sent by the culture regarding conflict?" "How are negative conflict behaviors rewarded?" "How satisfied are employees with existing processes for resolution?" "What systems changes might prevent, reduce, or help resolve conflict?" These questions and others that emerge give us an idea of what people want or need to resolve their conflicts.

Once we get their answers, we feed them back to everybody who participated, taking out any information that might identify who told us what. The team then takes the results and feedback, and brainstorms some initial suggestions, recommendations, and changes in the systems, so that they can begin implement easy changes immediately. Everyone then feels, as a result of the audit, that they had a part in making their organization better and resolving conflicts. They feel more a part of the organization, and the organization's improvement.

Paradoxical Problem-Solving and Collaborative Bargaining (Ken)

Conflict resolution consists essentially of two parts. The first is listening, and the second is problem solving. If we don't listen deeply and empathetically, actively and responsively, to the other person, we may end up solving the wrong problem. And while problem solving seems relatively easy, just like listening, there are a number of subtleties and deep methodologies that can help us engage in that process much more effectively than we otherwise might. Some of these emerge out of the field of conflict resolution itself.

An initial question we want to ask is, "How do we solve a problem that is a paradox?" A paradox by definition has at least two correct answers. Thus, the square root of 16 is both four and minus four. And in any conflict that is not simple or trivial, or one of a kind disputes that don't occur again, the chances are quite good that there is more than one answer, and in some cases, multiple correct answers to the same underlying problem.

Here is a simple illustration. There are three *categories*, or kinds of questions I can ask any group. For example, "Who is the oldest or youngest person in the group?" There will be a single correct answer to that question for everyone. A second category of question is, "How old are you?" Now there is a single correct answer for each person in, no longer one for everyone. A third category of question is, "What does your age mean to you?" "What issues are you facing at whatever age you are at?" Now there are multiple correct answers for each person.

This, quite simply, is the methodology of conflict resolution, and of interest-based approaches to paradoxical problem solving that do not seek a single correct answer for everyone, but multiple correct answers for each person that may prove useful in a variety of different settings, so we will have a much richer array of potential solutions and sets of tactics that can enrich whatever strategies we may have selected for solving our problems.

There are four basic approaches to problem solving. We can think of these as belonging more or less in the following categories. First, we can take a *reductionist* approach to problems and try to reduce them to the smallest possible units. Secondly, we can approach problems *analytically* and try to analyze what their sources are, what kind of problems they are. Third, we can look at problems *holistically* and try to get a sense of the whole. And fourth, we can look at them *relationally* and try to understand their relationship to other problems. Similarly, we can think of problems as discrete, linear, continuous, or chaotic. We can approach them as particles (in a sense) or adopting a control orientation; or as waves, or in a kind of free-form quantum field approach each of which looks at the problem in a very different way.

What we want to do is to be able to use a number of different approaches that allow us to enter the stages of problem solving with an open mind and an attitude of curiosity and excitement around the *discovery* of problems, and then explore their nature.

If we begin with the attitude that there are multiple correct ways of solving problems, of looking at problems, of understanding them, and that we can approach them with curiosity and excitement, that's really step one. Step two is to listen to the problem, and that means listening to the people who have the problem — and not just to the words they use, but to what is said without words.

It is often helpful to form diverse teams that can investigate the problem within an organization, teams that are diverse horizontally and vertically, and to acknowledge and enlist emotions in helping prioritize problems and solutions. This may sound counterintuitive, but science has demonstrated that one of the side effects of having a stroke in the emotional processing centers of our brains is that we are no longer able to make decisions or solve certain simple problems because we make decisions, even on trivial matters, based on what we *like*.

Emotions can be quite helpful in solving problems because they allow us to consider quickly a wide range of options and get a *feeling* for what is going to work best for us. This isn't always accurate, but it is one element in what can *become* accurate. This is described in detail in Daniel Kahneman's *Thinking Fast and Slow,* where he describes both positive and negative elements of system one and system two thinking, or problem solving that is slow and logical, and that which is quick and intuitive or emotional.

We next want to identify the interests and paradoxical elements in the problem, and to initiate even "dangerous" conversations about the problem — that is, we want to encourage people to tell the truth, to discuss the issues and problems honestly and openly. We then want to collaboratively negotiate *complex* solutions to the problem, not just simple ones, but with enough complexity in the solution to match the complexity of the problem.

Predictably, if you face a complex problem and try to address it with a simplistic solution, the problem is going to remain and become chronic. Indeed, one of the sources of chronic conflict is simply the use of overly simplistic conflict resolution or problem solving procedures. We then want to mediate the remaining differences, elicit feedback, evaluate the problem solving process, and design self-correcting, preventative approaches to problem solving in the future.

One of the places where problem solving is most useful is in connection with collective bargaining, or collaborative bargaining, and negotiation in general. One definition of an organization is that it is a place where negotiations take place between people in different parts of the organization. A large part of organizational life consists of negotiation, and though it is not always thought of this way, people negotiate virtually everything all the time.

If we consider how we might improve the negotiation or bargaining process, whether it's collective bargaining or the simple kinds of negotiations that take place in every work unit, every team, every marriage, every family every day, we went to look at a range of possible solutions and techniques.

We can, for example, meet informally to discuss our past negotiation experiences and reflect on how we might improve the process. We can start by recognizing that we've negotiated in the past, and maybe that hasn't always worked well for everyone. We can then figure out how to build more trusting relationships through socializing, storytelling, and idea sharing.

We can also create a common vision of where we want to go, or get trained jointly in communication and collaborative negotiation techniques, or bring in a facilitator or mediator. We have played this role in a number of collective bargaining situations where we have been brought in to assist with the negotiation process.

There are many things we can do *before* bargaining begins, including jointly talking about what our needs, wishes, and interests are, or our goals for our relationship. We have seen many collective bargaining situations in many negotiations where neither side understood what was actually important to the other side, and the other side didn't tell them. There was no opportunity for them to get together and have an open and honest conversation about what is most important to each, or about what is at stake in this negotiation, or how we *want* to negotiate with each other.

Then there are a series of things we can do *during* the bargaining process. If you are in collective bargaining, instead of sitting at a table with everyone from labor on one side and management on the other, try sitting together in small groups and mixing it up a bit, and see what happens. We can also brainstorm options, form bilateral teams to jointly investigate, prioritize options, or agree on criteria for optimal solutions.

We can ask questions like, "Why is that important to you?" "How would that work?" "What would it take for you to give that up?" One of the techniques we have used successfully in collective bargaining, particularly over wage issues, is to ask, "If you were to agree to what the other side is asking, what would you want in exchange?" And when we ask each side that question, often privately, we discover there are a series of issues that lie in the middle, or to one side, or have been neglected, that actually influence the willingness to accept what the other side is asking.

We can also, at the *end* of the negotiation, ask each person to briefly identify what worked for them personally in the negotiation process and what did not, and then make sure those are included in whatever minutes they take and changes are made in future meetings. We can also do this *during* the negotiation simply by stopping the process in its tracks and asking, "Is this process working for you, because it's not working for me?" Or, "I would like to recommend that we stop for a minute and brainstorm some options to see what we could do better." Or, "Let's just go around the table and ask each person to say one thing that could be done to improve the effectiveness of this conversation." You will get some startling and useful answers.

After the negotiation process, you can ask people to summarize their experiences. You can publicize the work of the collaborative effort that took place, and acknowledge the work of the other side. You can create joint evaluation teams to report on what worked and what didn't. And, you can continue to meet after formal negotiations are over, not only to assess what is continuing to work and what isn't, but to identify in advance issues that are likely to require negotiation in the future. And, at the very end of the negotiation, you can bring new people into the process and jointly educate them about how it worked. Lastly, you can stop and celebrate what we have accomplished, as an important element in the continuing success of the process.

One part of every conflict resolution conversation is a negotiation, and every negotiation involves some kind of conflict or difference between the sides, and these inform one another. Using the systems design process, we can identify additional, very specific, concrete things that can be done to improve the process.

Consequences of Systems Design (Ken)

The use of conflict resolution systems design is not without organizational consequences. It is a deeply transformational methodology that impacts the entire system. So what are some of the consequences of the systems design approach? First, implicit within this process is a shift from hierarchy, bureaucracy, and autocracy to hierarchy, direct participation, and democracy — simply because, for systems design to be deeply effective, it has to place people on an equal level and give them a voice in how the process works.

A second consequence is that it can reduce inequalities in status, inequities in wealth, and autocracies in power, especially when used on a large scale. These may be small to begin with, but once the idea arises that chronic conflicts are created by social inequality, economic inequity, and political autocracy, the outcome of implementing these principles is likely to be a reduction in these arenas of conflict.

Another consequence is that the systems design process encourages people to forswear the use of military options and litigation, to invite direct public participation in significant decision-making, and to substitute dialogue for debate. In debate, there are serial monologues, in which the object is to win. In dialogue, there is genuine engagement with people we disagree with, in which the object is to learn.

It becomes possible, then, to reach consensus in a variety of adversarial situations, vote only as a last resort, shift from power- and rights- to interest-based solutions, and commit to open, honest, authentic communication, and the reduction of secrecy and restricted access to information. The object is to create a safe environment within which it is possible to be open, with an emphasis on collaboration and partnership, rather than antagonism and hyper-competition.

Another consequence is that it becomes possible to celebrate diversity in race, gender, and other categories, because people feel less threatened or challenged by those who are different. It also becomes possible to flatten hierarchical divisions within organizations by turning managers into leaders, reducing the ranks of middle management, whose role, in part, is sometimes to suppress or dampen the *expression* of organizational conflict.

How exactly do these consequences occur? I think it is through an *algorithm*, or set of operations that are performed more or less routinely. A simple algorithm is to take any number and add one; or take any number and divide by three. Here, the algorithm is a set of operations we can perform on conflict that are designed to increase inclusion and participation, strengthen consensus-based decision making and diversity, normalize the expression of differences, encourage dialogue, *et cetera*.

The basic idea at is that everyone is regarded as responsible for participating; improving content, processes, relationships, and culture; and creating synergies and transformations — and we do mean *everyone* in the organization. We worked, for example, with a school district in which there was an effort to reach kids who were "at risk," and been identified as a result of criminal arrests, or drug use, or behaviors in the classroom. Teams were formed to work with these kids, and on each team there was a classroom teacher, a counselor, an administrator, and a janitor or cafeteria worker. Guess which of these had the best contacts with the kids and the best ability to communicate with them? The answer was the janitors and cafeteria workers. No kid wanted to talk about their problems to a homeroom teacher, or classroom teacher, or administrator, or counselor. But they were willing to talk to the janitors and cafeteria workers. This is a counter-intuitive example of how people with the least amount of power within an organization can end up having the most influence.

Every chronic conflict can be traced to its' systemic sources, where they can be prevented and redesigned to discourage repetition, so that victory is obtainable by everyone and redirected toward collaborating and solving common problems, leaving no one feeling defeated. This is the fundamental goal of conflict resolution in our view.

We can think of organizational systems design as the answer to a set of questions. Here are 10 important questions for organizations and workplaces. There are many others, but these are key for expanding the systems design process into important organizational systems that can trigger chronic conflicts.

1. Who makes the decision to hire?
2. Who allocates work and assigns tasks?
3. How is work evaluated and improved?
4. Who selects leaders?
5. Who gets promoted, how, and by what criteria?
6. Who gets trained in what?
7. Who determines and enforces rules?
8. Who resolves conflicts and how?
9. How is compensation determined?
10. How are profits and losses divided?

Let's take the first question: Who makes the decision to hire? If we return to the example we gave earlier of legal secretaries who were fighting with each other, who hired the legal secretaries? The lawyers did. And as a result, the legal secretaries owed their allegiance to the individual lawyers who hired them, and not to each other.

But if we ask a very simple question, we will come up with a very different solution. Who knows more about whether a legal secretary is qualified, or experienced, or will be good at the job — a lawyer, or another legal secretary? The answer is clearly another legal secretary.

This doesn't mean the lawyers should have no say in the hiring of legal secretaries. It means that the legal secretaries should have at least an equal say, if not more. And if legal secretaries hire other legal secretaries, they will owe their loyalty to the secretaries as a team, and will jump in and help them when they are overburdened with work. This is a small example of how we can rethink organizational design by asking questions that flow from conflict resolution, and see that alternative solutions are possible. In each of these areas, that is the case.

For example, when organizational leaders are selected from above, as by boards of directors or upper management, without input from below, they are more likely to serve the interests of their boards of directors, and won't pay as much attention to issues or conflicts that emerge from below. Whereas if people on all levels in the organization participate in selecting the people who are going to lead them, those leaders will pay greater attention to their issues and act more effectively in solving them.

The first casualty in every conflict is trust, and if we look at how trust is broken in organizations, a variety of reasons can be found. One of these, of course, is the presence of a conflict in which people feel they have not been heard or listened to, or where their interests have not been satisfied. So, in addition to listening and eliciting interests, how can organizations rebuild trust? Here are a few ways we have found useful.

We can rebuild trust in any conflict by, for example, being honest about ourselves, being open about problems, having unconditional respect for people, being clear about boundaries, being consistent over time, acting based on our vision and our values, collaborating and engaging in joint action, empowering others through teamwork and joint participation, listening and empathizing, and being dependable in periods of crisis or hard times.

We can rebuild trust also by being congruent in our words and actions; having ordinary social interactions with people we don't trust or who don't trust us; by curiosity and asking open ended questions about what people want and what they mean; through personal sharing, especially about our own mistakes; by willingness to sacrifice something that is important to us, and by sincere apologies. Thus, using systems design, we can help rebuild trust in organizations where it has been broken. We can then transition to a form of restorative justice that seeks to rebuild relationships that have been broken as a result of conflict.

SESSION 6 LECTURE SLIDES

Our systems, perhaps, are nothing more than an unconscious apology for our faults — a gigantic scaffolding whose object is to hide from us our favorite sin.

HENRI FREDERIC AMIEL

3 Generations in Systems Design

- The first order or generation, described by William L. Ury, Jeanne M. Brett, and Stephen B. Goldberg, in *Getting Disputes Resolved*, focuses on strengthening conflict resolution systems in organizations or groups, and designing integrated conflict resolution systems for handling grievances, complaints, arguments, difficulties, problems, and internal conflicts inside an organizational system.
- The second order or generation of systems design regards organizations as *conflict resolution mechanisms*, and considers all systems from a conflict resolution perspective, including feedback and evaluation, reward and compensation, leadership, and similar systems that impact conflict, and evaluate how well the system is doing at conflict prevention and resolution.
- The third order or generation of systems design, undertakes to redesign systems design itself, and apply it not only to large scale social, economic, and political institutions and practices, but to relationship and family systems, and all the larger human systems that impact all of us.

© Kenneth Cloke

The Hidden Costs of Conflict

Conflict costs organizations in time, energy, creativity, and money. For example, in one study of 1600 employees:

- 22% said they actually decreased their work efforts because of conflict
- Over 50% reported that they lost work time because they worried about whether the instigator of the conflict would do it again
- 12% reported they changed jobs to get away from the instigator of the conflict

[Source: Karl A. Slaikeu and Ralph H. Hasson, *Controlling the Costs of Conflict*, Jossey Bass, 1998]

© Kenneth Cloke and Joan Goldsmith

Savings from Conflict Resolution

- In the first year of side-by-side comparison, Brown and Root reported an 80 percent reduction in outside litigation expenses by introducing a systemic approach to collaboration and conflict management for employment issues.

- Motorola reported a reduction of outside litigation expenses of up to 75 percent per year over six years by using a systemic approach to conflict management in its legal department, which included a mediation clause in contracts with suppliers.

- NCR reported a reduction in outside litigation expenses of 50 percent and a drop in its number of pending lawsuits from 263 to 28 between 1984 and 1993, following the systemic use of ADR.

- The U.S. Air Force reported that by taking a collaborative approach to conflict management in a construction project involving the Army Corps of Engineers as well as prime and subcontractors, it completed the project 144 days ahead of schedule and $12 million under budget.

- The Defense Mapping Agency reported that systemic conflict management reduced the cost of resolving a particular set of employment disputes by 4200 hours.

- The U.S. Air Force estimated a savings of 50 percent per claim in one hundred equal employment opportunity complaints by using mediation.

[Source: Karl A. Slaikeu and Ralph H. Hasson, *Controlling the Costs of Conflict*, Jossey Bass 1998]
© Kenneth Cloke and Joan Goldsmith

Range of Conflict Resolution Options

Surrender
Avoidance/Denial
Accommodation
Meeting/Retreat
Informal Problem Solving
Strategic Planning
Collaborative Negotiation
Ombudsperson
Conciliation
Mediation
Compromise
Aggressive Negotiation
Mini-Trial

Arbitration
Summary Jury Trial
Litigation
Lobbying
Elections
Demonstrations/Protests
Confrontation
Self-Defense
Revenge
Violence (Aggression)
Murder/Suicide
Genocide/War

© Kenneth Cloke and Joan Goldsmith

Reasons for CR System Design (1)

- Prevent conflicts before they occur
- Reduce the risks and costs of conflict
- Encourage settlement before costs and attorneys' fees accumulate
- Provide a forum for final resolution outside the courts
- Create inexpensive internal mechanisms to prevent, manage and resolve conflict
- Improve participant morale
- Pinpoint and resolve the underlying reasons that created the problem

Reasons for CR Systems Design (2)

- Once conflict is seen as a system it can be addressed in more than one way
- Emphasis in the past has been on discrete dispute resolution procedures, rather than on integrated systems design
- It allows organizations to respond not only to single disputes, but to the *stream* of disputes that arise in all organizations
- Some procedures work better for certain disputes than others
- Systems are needed to encourage negotiation and de-escalation procedures throughout the life of the conflict
- A variety of different professionals can work on the same problem from different perspectives
- A systems approach can promote synergy, in which the whole is seen as greater than the sum of its parts.

Some Questions on Systems Design (1)

A. WHAT IS THE CONFLICT ABOUT?

1. Who are the disputants?
2. What are the issues that are typically in dispute?
3. Are there other important players in these disputes?
4. What types of conflicts do they experience?
5. How frequently do these disputes occur?
6. What is the likely frequency of similar disputes in the future?
7. Have changes in the organization, relationship or wider environment impacted the number or nature of disputes? How?
8. What do people believe is causing these disputes?
9. What do people typically do when these disputes occur?
10. What sources of support, guidance or resolution are typically available for these disputes?
11. What is the attitude of others within the organization to people who are in dispute, or to the issues they are arguing over?
12. What is one thing that might be done to prevent or resolve the dispute?

© Kenneth Cloke

Some Questions on Systems Design (2)

B. HOW ARE DISPUTES HANDLED?

1. What do people do if they have a complaint? With whom, if anyone, do they raise it?
2. How frequently do they avoid conflict? Accommodate to it? Compromise? Engage in it? Collaborate in creating a solution?
3. What happens when disputes are negotiated? What proportion are resolved in this way? Do the parties search for settlements that will satisfy each other's interests? Do they focus chiefly on their respective rights? Are their negotiations dominated by threats, intimidation efforts, or similar power tactics?
4. How frequently do negotiations break down? What happens when they do? Do the parties turn to others -- lawyers, union officials, friends, for help in negotiating? Are disputes turned over to superiors for resolution?
5. Do parties turn to a neutral person for mediation? How often?
6. Are adjudicatory procedures available? What kinds? How often are they used? How long does it take before a decision is reached? Does one party prevail most of the time?
7. How often do power contests erupt? What types of power behaviors are used? What outcomes result? Is there typically a winner, or does the power contest serve no purpose beyond the release of pent-up anger and frustration?

© Kenneth Cloke

Some Questions on Systems Design (3)
C. WHY ARE DISPUTES HANDLED THIS WAY?
1. Why are people resorting to rights and power contests instead of negotiating?
2. Are interests-based procedures available to handle the full range of disputes that occur?
3. Are some disputes being left essentially unresolved simply because no established procedure exists to deal with them?
4. Does a mediation procedure exist that focuses on interests?
5. How satisfied are disputants with the procedures that are available?
6. Does the procedure provide an opportunity for "day in court"? Can disputants air their grievances fully on their own terms? Do disputants have control over the procedure--are they in charge or does someone take it out of their hands? Do disputants participate in shaping the outcome? Do they think the procedure is fair?
7. Does the procedure allow for venting emotions? Is it a way of getting even?
8. How costly do disputants feel the procedure is in terms of time and money?
9. Does the procedure serve the interests of parties other than the disputants?
10. Does the procedure serve purposes other than resolving particular disputes?
11. Do people know what procedures are available and when? Do they know how to use the procedures to generate a satisfactory resolution?
12. How skilled are the disputants and their representatives in problem-solving? Negotiation? Listening? Identifying interests? Exploring creative options?

© Kenneth Cloke

Some Questions on Systems Design (4)
D.   HOW MUCH DOES CONFLICT COST?
1. How long do the various procedures take, and how much money is consumed by them?
2. How satisfied are disputants with the outcomes of disputes? The process?
3. What effect do existing procedures have on personal or organizational relationships?
4. How often do the same disputes recur because they were never resolved?
5. What costs are associated with the continuation of the conflict?

E.   WHAT RESOURCES ARE AVAILABLE FOR RESOLUTION?
1. Are there people to whom the disputants can turn for help--people to represent them, give them advice, or serve as mediators or coaches?
2. How skilled are these representatives, mediators, and coaches? Are they perceived as unbiased?
3. Is negotiation hampered by a lack of norms, precedents, laws, and other standards that could be used to settle disputes, or by a lack of information about the problem?
4 Do the procedures need to be actively administered by a person or an institution? What can be done to provide people with information about resolving conflicts on an ongoing basis?
5. Is the lack of resolution due to insufficient funding? Are alternative low-cost solutions available?

© Kenneth Cloke

Some Questions on Systems Design (5)

F. WHAT ARE THE OBSTACLES TO IMPLEMENTATION?

1. In what ways is conflict resolution impacted by existing decision-making procedures? How centralized are they? Hierarchical? Bureaucratic?
2. How are procedures in use affected by the organization's formal and informal reward systems? What kind of dispute resolution behavior is rewarded by superiors? By peers? By the "culture of conflict?"
3. What impact do other systems like hiring, discipline, feedback, evaluation, compensation and training have on the dispute resolution system?
4. How does the surrounding culture impact the procedures that are used?

G. WHAT SHOULD INFORM THE OVERALL DESIGN?

1. Why are some procedures used and not others? What functions are served by power contests and other high-cost procedures? What hinders the use of interest-based procedures?
2. Is it necessary to have different tracks for different kinds of disputes?
3. What procedures should be built into the system? What should be the sequences?
4. How can people be motivated to use these procedures?
5. How can people be given the necessary skills to use these procedures?
6. What would help disputing parties use these procedures?
7. How can the system be made self-adjusting? What mechanisms need to be set up for learning, feedback and adaptation?

© Kenneth Cloke

Some Questions on Systems Design (6)

H. IS THERE ADEQUATE SUPPORT FOR THE NEW SYSTEM?

1. What are the key problems that need to be overcome?
2. Are there hidden agendas? Is dispute resolution seen as a means of management control, or to conduct power struggles? Is there motivation to implement the system, build coalitions to support them, assure allocation of resources, justify support, develop monitoring and evaluation procedures, and use information from the conflict to create a self-learning system?
3. How much will it cost to build and support the new system? What coalitions can be created to support it?
4. How should opposition be addressed? Or those threatened by the changes or "winning" under the old rules? Or hidden agendas and power struggles?
5. How have you assured the allocation of resources for the system?
6. Have disputants been motivated to use the new procedures? (e.g., demonstrations, using leaders as examples, setting goals, designing incentives, publicizing early successes?)
7. Should the parties be trained or coached in the new procedures?
8. How should the success or failures of the system be evaluated?
9. How can the system be evaluated or improved?
10. Have successful procedures and systems been publicized and propagated?

(Based on work by Chris Moore and William Ury)

© Kenneth Cloke

Elements of CR Systems Design

- Conflict audit and collaborative design process
- Identify predictors of conflict, high conflict areas
- Design preventative measures
- Create safety nets, informal problem solving
- Open outlets for constructive expression of differences
- Provide rich array of procedures for resolution
- Focus on interests, rather than rights or power
- Provide low-cost rights and power back-ups
- Build in "loopbacks" to negotiation
- Provide training before and feedback after
- Arrange procedures in a low-to-high cost sequence
- Offer motivation, skills and resources to make it work

© Kenneth Cloke and Joan Goldsmith

Stages of Problem Solving

1. *Cultivate an Attitude of Curiosity and Excitement around the Discovery of Problems:* The first response to conflict is often one of apathy, denial, avoidance, cynicism and defensiveness.
2. *Listen to the Problem:* Without listening, we may solve the wrong problem.
3. *Form a Diverse Team to Investigate the Problem:* Diverse teams have been shown to produce better solutions than individuals or uniform groups.
4. *Acknowledge and Enlist Emotions in Prioritizing Problems and Solutions:* Problem solving requires us to *integrate* facts and feelings, and without emotions, decisions and prioritization become impossible.
5. *Identify Interests and Paradoxical Elements in the Problem:* Interests help identify what the real problem is, especially where the problem is a paradox, or has multiple, conflicting solutions.
6. *Initiate "Dangerous" Conversations about the Problem:* Discuss the problem honestly and openly.
7. *Collaboratively Negotiate Complex Solutions:* Make the process and the solutions at least as complex as the problem.
8. *Mediate Remaining Differences:* Bring in a third party to help find solutions.
9. *Elicit Feedback and Evaluate the Problem Solving Process:* Examine what worked.
10. *Design Self-Correcting, Preventative Approaches to Problem Solving:* Mine your experiences for preventative opportunities.

© Kenneth Cloke

Two Approaches to Problem Solving

Reductionist	Holistic
Discrete	Continuous
Digital	Analog
Divergent	Convergent
Particle	Wave
Matter	Energy
Position	Momentum
Stability	Change
Difference	Similarity
Analytic	Relational
Linear	Chaotic
Bumpy	Smooth
Rational	Intuitive
Controlled	Free
Sequential	Multiple
Objective	Subjective
Quantitative	Qualitative
Successive	Simultaneous

Effective Systems Design

- Contains options for preventing, identifying and resolving issues
- Promotes a culture that seeks to solve problems at the lowest level through direct negotiation
- Allows multiple access points
- Empowers employees to select from a range of options for addressing conflict
- Contains effective structure and support to maintain options
- Has the support of leadership
- Is run by an oversight body composed of representatives from all key groups
- Uses evaluation processes
- Provides training
- Has a central coordinator
- Aligns the "conflict competency" with mission, vision, values, and policies
- Institutionalizes incentives for effective operation
- Develops a communication strategy
- Provides incentives for early resolution
- Is given adequate resources for the system to function properly
- Emphasizes conflict prevention rather than conflict management
- Increases the ability to understand sources of potential conflict and deal with them before they escalate
- Recognizes existing organizational culture and conflict narratives

Goals of CR Systems Design

- Support core values
- Encourage prevention
- Support early resolution
- Address all varieties of conflict
- Be accessible to all
- Provide choices
- Rank options based on interests, rights, and power
- Centralized coordination and decentralized resolution
- Provide access to a confidential third party
- Championed at all levels
- Stakeholder participation and oversight
- Critical mass training
- Feedback through monitoring and evaluation
- Alignment with goals
- Build in incentives to use processes
- Provide support, both human and financial
- Communicate broadly with consistent messages and terminology
- Flexible and capable of continuous improvement

© Kenneth Cloke and Joan Goldsmith

Some Systems Design Options

1. Agreeing on a common vision, mission, values, and goals
2. Creating empowered self-managing teams
3. Creating fast-forming integrated problem solving teams
4. Training in collaborative negotiation for collective bargaining
5. Electing internal union mediators for disputes between union members
6. Multi-step grievance procedures
7. Expanded Organizational Ombuds offices
8. Expanded counseling through Employee Assistance Programs
9. Elected/ grievant selected Peer Review Boards
10. Peer Mediators
11. Professional Mediators
12. Peer coaching
13. Professional Fact-finders
14. Professional Arbitrators
15. Training supervisors and human relations managers in conflict resolution
16. Training line supervisors in communication and conflict resolution skills
17. Training employees in communication and conflict resolution skills
18. Providing rewards and incentives for using mediation
19. Training in prejudice reduction, diversity, and resolving cross-cultural conflicts
20. Facilitated meetings and retreats to address on-going problems

© Kenneth Cloke and Joan Goldsmith

How to Improve Bargaining (1)

1. Before Bargaining:

- Meet informally with negotiators for your own team, then with teams from the other side to discuss past negotiation experiences, and how to improve on the process.
- Build more trusting relationships through socializing, storytelling and idea sharing.
- Create a common vision of where you would like to go, analyze the barriers to getting there, and take small practical steps to overcome those barriers.
- Obtain joint training in communication, relationship building, conflict resolution, and collaborative negotiation.
- Hire a facilitator to assist throughout the bargaining process.
- Establish a timetable and process rules, including "fail-safe" or "escape clauses".
- Form a bilateral "process team" to set agendas and help things move smoothly.
- Form a joint negotiation advisory committee consisting of leaders and representatives from concerned community groups.
- Try letting the other side pick at least one member of your bargaining team.
- Meet at least once with everyone you represent to get their "wish lists" beforehand.
- Jointly discuss your needs, wishes and interests, and your goals for your relationship with the other side in general terms before starting the bargaining process.

2. During Bargaining:

- Sit in alternate chairs rather than on opposite sides of the table. Use a "round robin" speaking order. Dress informally.
- Brainstorm options for each area of concern or contested section of the agreement, and list these under it before beginning actual negotiation.

© Kenneth Cloke

How to Improve Bargaining (2)

- Form bilateral teams to prioritize each set of options on each outstanding issue and report back on their top recommendations.
- Bargain year-round. Don't wait for conflicts to arise or for the contract to end.
- Work to reach agreement on a single set of facts and financial figures, in order to base economic bargaining on mutually acceptable data.
- Hire an arbitrator or neutral outsider to propose alternate solutions,
- Agree on alternative budgets based on different options for allocating funds.
- At the beginning, exchange realistic minimum and maximum proposals, including figures for salaries, and identify what each is based on. Then be willing to move to accommodate each others' interests.
- Ask questions like: "Why is that important to you?" "How would that work?" "What would it take for you to give that up ?" Look for options that satisfy those interests.
- Agree on a common set of negotiation minutes written by someone acceptable to both sides. Record ideas on flip charts for all to see.
- Agree on common language to describe the process for press releases and statements to constituents and third parties.
- Create a joint negotiation "hot-line."
- Jointly hire a consultant, facilitator or mediator to assist throughout the negotiations.
- If it's not working, change the rules or the process – stop, analyze, and start over again.
- Open negotiations to interested parties from the public or the community.
- At the end of each session, ask each person to briefly identify what worked for them personally, and what did not in that session. Make sure these are included in the minutes and that changes are made in future meetings.

© Kenneth Cloke

How to Improve Bargaining (3)

3. After Bargaining:
- Ask each person to summarize their experiences, and thank everyone from the other side who helped the group work more collaboratively.
- Publicize the results of working collaboratively within your own team and constituency, and in the larger community.
- Acknowledge the legitimacy and cooperation of the other side to *their* constituency. Recognize that some are fearful of collaboration and need to have their self-interests met.
- Keep a list of unresolved problems to come back to later and search for solutions.
- Keep a record of objections or complaints that are expressed to solutions and search later for better solutions. If necessary, reopen negotiations to do so.
- Create a joint evaluation team to report on what worked and what didn't, and make recommendations for the next round of bargaining.
- Form a bilateral implementation team to make sure agreements are being met and fine-tune anything requiring adjustments.
- Identify on-going issues, such as budget, communication, safety, etc. and create teams to solve problems in these areas, and recommend any changes that may be needed.
- Schedule informal problem solving sessions as needed.
- Meet periodically to make certain communications are open, processes are improved, and relationships are working.
- Educate new members about the reasons for collaboration. Don't take anything for granted. Work on continuous improvement in the quality of your relationship.
- Take time out to celebrate what you have accomplished.

(Based partly on work by Smith, Ball and Liotos, in "Working Together")
© Kenneth Cloke

Sample Conflict Audit Questions (1)

1. How much is spent on lawyers, litigation, and human resources time related to conflict?
2. How much time does the average managers spend each week trying to prevent, manage or resolve conflicts? At what salary?
3. What is the cost of stress-related illness and conflict-related turnovers?
4. How much time is spent on rumors, gossip, lost productivity and reduced collaboration due to conflict?
5. What is the impact of conflict on staff morale and motivation?
6. How many conflicts recur because they are never fully resolved?
7. What customers, creativity and opportunities have been lost due to conflict?
8. Where might the organization be now had it not experienced these conflicts?
9. What are the core values of the organization regarding conflict?
10. What are the main messages sent by organizational culture regarding conflict?

© Kenneth Cloke and Joan Goldsmith

Sample Conflict Audit Questions (2)

11. How are negative conflict behaviors rewarded?
12. How do leadership and management typically respond to conflicts? How might they respond better?
13. Have employees been trained in conflict resolution?
14. What do people do when they have conflict? Where do they go for help?
15. Is there an internal mediation process? Who can use it? How often is it used? How many know about it?
16. How satisfied are employees with existing resolution processes?
17. How skilled are managers in using these processes?
18. What hinders the use of existing resolution processes? How can employees be motivated to use them?
19. What skills do employees and managers need to resolve conflicts successfully?
20. What systems changes could prevent, reduce or help resolve conflict?

© Kenneth Cloke and Joan Goldsmith

An Algorithm for System Design (1)

- All interested parties are included and invited to participate fully in designing and implementing content, process, and relationships.
- Decisions are made by consensus wherever possible, and nothing is considered final until everyone is in agreement.
- Diversity and honest differences are viewed as sources of dialogue, leading to better ideas, healthier relationships, and greater unity.
- Stereotypes, prejudices, assumptions of innate superiority, and ideas of intrinsic correctness are considered divisive and discounted as one-sided descriptions of more complex, multi-sided, paradoxical realities.
- Openness, authenticity, appreciation, and empathy are regarded as better foundations for communication and decision-making than secrecy, rhetoric, insult, and demonization.
- Dialogue and open-ended questions are deemed more useful than debate and cross-examination.
- Force, violence, coercion, aggression, humiliation, and domination are rejected, both as methods and as outcomes.

© Kenneth Cloke and Joan Goldsmith

An Algorithm for System Design (2)

- Cooperation and collaboration are ranked as primary, while competition and aggression are considered secondary.
- Everyone's interests are accepted as legitimate, acknowledged, and satisfied wherever possible, consistent with others' interests.
- Processes and relationships are considered at least as important as content, if not more so.
- Attention is paid to emotions, subjectivity, and feelings, as well as to logic, objectivity, and facts.
- Everyone is regarded as responsible for participating in improving content, processes, and relationships, and searching for synergies and transformations.
- People are invited into heartfelt, spiritual communications and inner awareness, and encouraged to reach resolution, forgiveness, and reconciliation.
- Chronic conflicts are traced to their systemic sources, where they can be prevented and redesigned to discourage repetition.
- Victory is regarded as obtainable by everyone, and redirected toward collaborating to solve common problems, so no one feels defeated.

© Kenneth Cloke and Joan Goldsmith

15 Key Roles for Boards of Directors

- Articulating and championing the organization's vision
- Establishing core values and principles
- Developing and monitoring the organization's mission and goals
- Developing strategies and driving change
- Shaping overall direction and clarifying meaning
- Influencing organizational style and culture
- Mobilizing internal morale and external support
- Supporting and encouraging staff and resolving conflicts
- Avoiding micro-managing and management of staff
- Raising funds and guaranteeing survival
- Providing expertise where needed
- Ensuring fiscal and legal oversight
- Evaluating results and identifying needed improvements
- Publicizing successes and accepting responsibility for failures
- Encouraging organizational learning

© Kenneth Cloke and Joan Goldsmith

Roles of Leaders of Boards of Directors

- Provide vision and challenge to the Board
- Empower individual members of the Board
- Assist in solving problems and resolving conflicts
- Help gain membership buy-in
- Provide assistance in formulating strategies
- Review and reward progress
- Coach through difficulties
- Provide honest, timely personal feedback
- Secure resources and support
- Encourage diversity and risk taking
- Hand issues and problems back to the Board
- Give up autocratic management and control
- Encourage creativity, leadership and self-evaluation

Kenneth Cloke and Joan Goldsmith

Options for Boards of Directors (1)

1. Don't wait until crises occur to discuss problems or formulate solutions. Give on-going issues to problem-solving teams that meet on a year-round basis with full authority to act.
2. Form small bilateral teams of two to four members to meet at least once a year to formulate and recommend long and short term organizational changes.
3. Create fast-forming teams of two to three members to respond quickly with interim or temporary solutions.
4. Make changes in process, organizational policy, board/staff relationships, budget and bylaws continuously.
5. Create two sets of procedures or rules: one for short-term operational issues that change frequently and another for long-term problems.
6. Create a By-Laws committee, where changes in long-term agreements or organizational policy are proposed, debated, reviewed and recommended.
7. Consider what really needs to be in your bylaws, including:
    - A Preamble in the form of a mission statement everyone can agree on
    - A Bill of Rights
    - A decision-making structure
    - A system for delegating authority
    - A list of expectations of board members and staff
    - A mechanism for resolving disputes such as mediation, with a back-up in case mediation fails.

© Kenneth Cloke and Joan Goldsmith

Options for Boards of Directors (2)

8. Take issues outside board meetings for joint study, experimental solutions, brainstorming options, preparation of reports, or consultation with experts.
9. Critiques of committee actions should take place first in the committee rather than before the board, and be done respectfully, positively and constructively.
10. Instead of moving forward when there is conflict or deep division, meet to agree on goals and processes for resolving it, or on temporary, interim solutions.
11. Make sure leadership regularly receives training in leadership, communication, collaborative negotiation, problem solving, and conflict resolution.
12. Use role reversal in difficult meetings. Give each side responsibility for presenting or summarizing the other side's arguments. Allow each side to say what's wrong.
13. Decentralize decision-making over routine issues. Let committees create their own rules and procedures and report to the board afterwards.
14. Eliminate By-laws and formal rules wherever possible and instead reach interim agreements to satisfy interests.
15. Conduct periodic "conflict audits" to determine the source of chronic disputes and lead into group problem solving.
16. When conflicts arise, stop to discuss them, or schedule a special session to listen fully and try to reach accommodation. Do not sweep them under the rug.
17. If conflict is dysfunctional, bring in a mediator to facilitate group discussion.
18. Train board members in mediation, collaborative negotiation and communication skills, without waiting for things to fall apart.

© Kenneth Cloke and Joan Goldsmith

Consequences of System Design (1)

- Shift from hierarchy, bureaucracy, and autocracy to heterarchy, participation, and democracy

- Reduce inequalities in status, inequities in wealth, and autocracies in power

- Foreswear the use of military options except in the decreasing likelihood of self-defense when under attack

- Invite direct public participation in all significant decision-making

- Substitute dialogue for debate

- Reach consensus whenever possible and vote only as a last resort

- Shift from exercising power and defending rights to satisfying interests

- Commit to open, honest, authentic communication and elimination of government secrecy

© Kenneth Cloke and Joan Goldsmith

Consequences of System Design (2)

- Conduct internal and external operations based on collaboration and partnership rather than antagonism and hyper-competition
- Celebrate diversity in race, gender, sexual orientation, culture, and individual personality on all levels
- Flatten hierarchical agencies by reducing the ranks of middle management and leveling pay differentials
- Treat employees as equals and reorganize internally into self-managing teams
- Bridge organizational silos and institutional specializations
- Implement continuous feedback and 360-degree performance improvement processes
- Reward disagreement and dissent, and invite organizational learning
- Encourage self-assessment, organizational learning, evolution, and transformational change

© Kenneth Cloke and Joan Goldsmith

10 Questions on Organizational Design

1. Who makes the decision to hire?
2. Who allocates work and assigns tasks?
3. How is work evaluated and improved?
4. Who selects leaders?
5. Who gets promoted, how, and by what criteria?
6. Who gets trained in what?
7. Who determines and enforces rules?
8. Who resolves conflicts and how?
9. How is compensation determined?
10. How are profits and losses divided?

[Excerpted from Kenneth Cloke and Joan Goldsmith, *The End of Management and the Rise of Organizational Democracy*]

10 Questions for Organizations (1)

1. *Who makes the decision to hire?* Hiring has traditionally been a unilateral activity engaged in by managers based on criteria they alone select. Yet better results can be achieved when hiring becomes a collaborative, peer-based responsibility of self-managing teams.
2. *Who allocates work and assigns tasks?* Self-management and task selection by self-managing teams can dramatically increase productivity by improving motivation, limiting unproductive behavior, and reducing managerial expenses through reverse economies of scale. Teamwork makes assignment flexible and dynamic rather than bureaucratic and static, and oversight becomes a responsibility of everyone on the team.
3. *How is work evaluated and improved?* Feedback, evaluation, self-correction, learning, and improvement ought to be the responsibility of all team members. Contributions to personal and organizational improvement become far more powerful when feedback is received from everyone affected by the work.
4. *Who selects leaders?* Management is a title, a set of involuntary roles assigned to people selected from above; leadership is a voluntary relationship informed by vision and maintained by skill with people who freely choose to follow. To establish a mandate, leaders should be selected, even elected, by those they lead.

10 Questions for Organizations (2)

5. *Who gets promoted, how, and by what criteria?* In hierarchical organizations, promotions are often based on having done a lower-level job well, that is, on technical ability; some guessed-at capacity to succeed in meeting a set of abstract, objective criteria; or purely subjective, intuitive feelings about the personality of the candidate.
6. *Who gets trained in what?* Training should be organized from the bottom up rather than the top down, and focus on team skills rather than those of individual managers. It should improve practical skills in facilitating, coaching, communicating, negotiating, building ownership, giving honest feedback, building better relationships, resolving interpersonal conflicts, and negotiating collaboratively.
7. *Who determines and enforces rules?* Every employee in a team environment has a vested interest in increasing productivity and client satisfaction and is capable of setting rules that advance common interests and result in shared responsibility for preventing future violations. Employee-generated rules counteract the dynamic created by externally imposed rules, which lead to blind obedience rather than creativity and result in resistance, unequal enforcement, cynicism, coercion, and duress.

10 Questions for Organizations (3)

8. *Who resolves conflicts and how?* Conflicts provide teams with rich opportunities to reveal the inconsistencies between expressed values and actual behaviors. They offer openings for growth, personal improvement, and increased team effectiveness. When teams own their conflicts and become responsible for resolving them, the entire paradigm of conflict shifts from one of avoidance or confrontation to one of learning.
9. *How is compensation determined?* When employees make compensation decisions, productivity increases enormously. Several studies have shown that when employees are permitted to decide what to pay themselves, they not only set aside adequate sums for investment but make their products and services more competitive. Experience in employee-owned firms demonstrates that pay cuts and reductions in benefits are more readily agreed to in employee-owned firms than in hierarchies.
10. *How are profits and losses divided?* As self-managing teams become adept at making strategic financial decisions, dividing profits, covering losses, budgeting, allocating resources, and making investments, they should be permitted to share in the profits and losses that flow from their work.

© Kenneth Cloke and Joan Goldsmith   230

How to Rebuild Trust

- Honesty about yourself
- Openness about problems
- Unconditional respect
- Clarity about boundaries
- Consistency over time
- Actions based on vision or values
- Collaboration and joint action
- Empowerment of others
- Teamwork, joint participation
- Listening, empathizing
- Dependability in crises and hard times
- Congruency between words and actions
- Social interactions
- Curiosity and asking open-ended questions
- Personal sharing, especially about mistakes
- Willingness to sacrifice something important
- Sincere apologies

231

CHAPTER 7

USING DIALOGUE, MEDIATION & SYSTEMS DESIGN TO PREVENT AND RESOLVE POLITICAL CONFLICTS

Politics and Organizational Conflict (Ken)

Our last topic concerns politics as a source of organizational and institutional conflict. This raises a question: Why talk about politics in the context of organizational conflict? There are two reasons. First, political organizations are still organizations, and how they handle conflict can reveal a great deal about the nature of organizations in general. Second, politics is about the exercise of power, and organizations are places where power is organized and used in a variety of ways, many of which result in conflict.

So we want to look at how power is exercised inside organizations, but we also want to look at the nature of political conflicts themselves, because these conflicts have a direct impact on how other kinds of conflicts are resolved throughout society, in organizations, and in families and couples. Moreover, they have an immediate impact on organizational systems, revealing a direct relationship between democracy and autocracy.

There is another reason for discussing this issue. We are going through significant political conflicts at the present time, and these conflicts are becoming more serious, and if we can bring some of what we have learned about organizations and how they resolve their conflicts into the political arena, we may have an impact on political organizations, and on our lives in general.

Here are three nice quotations to open this discussion. Amos Oz, an Israeli novelist, wrote:

> The fact is that all the power in the world cannot transform someone who hates you into someone who likes you. It can turn a foe into a slave, but not into a friend. All the power in the world cannot transform a fanatic into an enlightened man. All the power in the world cannot transform someone thirsting for vengeance into a lover." And this is as true in the political arena as it is in the organizational arenas that most of us work in.

Archbishop Desmond Tutu from South Africa, who helped create the Truth and Reconciliation Commission that ended apartheid pointed out:

> If you are neutral in situations of injustice, you have chosen the side of the oppressor. If an elephant has its foot on the tail of a mouse and you say that you are neutral, the mouse will not appreciate your neutrality.

And finally, Martin Luther King, Jr. reminded us,

> Our lives begin to end the day we become silent about things that matter.

We have all watched political conversations degenerate into angry quarrels and people sink into screaming matches over political issues, and these can easily transform into violence and appalling acts of brutality. The question then becomes, how might we prevent these brutal acts from taking place?

A similar dynamic occurs within the political arena occurs within the organizational arena, when people feel passionately about some issue and find it difficult to discuss it. And, political conversations matter. They concern our future, our values, our integrity, and our ethics, morality, beliefs, and behaviors — as individuals, as nation states, as organizations, and as human beings who are responsible for the world our children and grandchildren will inherit.

In order to make intelligent decisions, we require neither silence nor pointless rage, but dialogue, engagement, and conversation. The point of conflict resolution is that it is possible, using a variety of skills, methods and techniques, to bring fundamental communication principles into organizational and institutional settings. And we would not be complete in our work if we did not try to bring these same principles into politics, the most difficult arena of all for conversation, the arena in which people feel most passionately and deeply about things that matter.

Yet mediators have largely been silent about political events, partly because we have lacked the skills in being able to handle these conversations, partly because we have not really understood what politics *is*, as a conversation, and partly because the culture of politics is one in which denunciation and personal attacks are commonplace, far more commonplace than they are, for example, in discussing other organizational issues.

Many people also think of themselves as uninterested in politics. Yet, as the Greek statesman Pericles declared about 2,500 years ago, "You may not be interested in politics, but politics is interested in you." So whatever our justifications for treating each other as enemies, or remaining silent when difficult issues are discussed, we have to improve our ability to talk about these topics in order to create an arena in which problem solving can be effective with regard to important social issues.

Politics has been referred to as the art of compromise. But what if, instead, we think of politics as the art of *conflict resolution*, in which compromise is simply one of many possible outcomes, and perhaps a lesser outcome at that?

Earlier in these lectures, we described the difference between power, rights, and interests. So what would an interest-based, collaborative form of politics look like? What would be required, as a set of skills, for democracy to work more effectively and incorporate interest-based solutions into our social lives?

The very first person to write intelligently and at length about politics was Aristotle, who wrote a book called *Politics,* in which he defined politics as "a search for the highest common good." That sounds pretty worthwhile. The only difficulty is, it doesn't predict the kind of politics we experience today. But if we read Aristotle just a little further, we discover him arguing that none of this applies to women, children, slaves, or barbarians, who are all excluded from political conversations, yet constituted the overwhelming majority of the Athenian population.

So we have now two definitions of politics, whose contrasting orientations give rise to conflict. First, politics is a *social problem solving process*; and second, it is a *method of domination*, a form of decision-making that excludes those who are thought unworthy of participating in social decision making, generating chronic conflicts.

So what is wrong with politics as it is commonly practiced? First, it is unnecessarily divisive and adversarial — meaning that it is possible to have intelligent conversations, even about divisive issues, without slipping into name-calling, personal attacks, and other behaviors that ultimately encourage violence.

Second, politics is nearly always thought of as a win-lose process, in which the winner takes all. It's power-based — yet, as Lord Acton reminds us, "all power corrupts, and absolute power corrupts absolutely." But politics is also often rights-based, meaning that it *can* be governed by law. Yet, law is controlled by power, so ultimately, we are drawn back to power and a set of adversarial, zero sum solutions.

Third, politics takes too long, costs too much, and is exercised too personally. Here are a few others: It's increasingly ineffective in solving large-scale global problems. It is controlled by wealthy individuals, military and industrial elites, corporations, and special interests. And this is true not just in the United States, but around the world, especially true in countries where we can see very clearly how it operates, without any of the usual idealistic assumptions surrounding democracy and elections. Global political collaborations are perceived by those in power as reducing their sovereignty and imposing ideas that are alien to their goals and culture, even through institutions like the United Nations.

Politics is therefore grounded *both* in social problem solving and in domination, inequality, and disrespect, and as a result, as Aristotle pointed out, there is little interest among elites in encouraging political openness or direct democracy, and considerable interest in promoting secrecy and amassing power. Governments therefore easily slip into political autocracy, defend economic inequity and boost social inequality. They also generate bureaucracy to defend themselves against change, foster corruption, and produce chronic, systemic conflicts.

We can now see that many of the problems with "politics as usual" are also problems in organizational settings. There is a "politics" of organizational life that can have a very powerful impact on how people live inside organizational settings.

Aristotle developed a number of additional logical principles that impact political conflicts, and perhaps the most important of these for mediators is the "Law of the Excluded Middle," which holds that a statement is either true or false, and can't be true and false at the same time. Yet we know that there are times when, in politics as in life, statements are both true and false at the same time. Conflict stories are a good example, as discussed earlier.

We can also consider different forms of argument, or what Aristotle called rhetoric, which are forms of persuasion consisting principally of arguments based either on *logos* or *logic*, *ethos* or *ethics* (or character), and *pathos* or *emotions*. The difficulty is that each of these forms can be used in ways that are divisive and adversarial; that castigate those on the other side — as the enemy, even as traitors who can be eliminated without difficulty.

Here are five alternative forms of political persuasion Aristotle did not mention that are more common in mediation:

1. Personal experience and empathy building through storytelling, dialogue, and listening;
2. Vision and values through leadership, strategic planning and modeling;
3. Synergy and syntheses through conflict resolution and the integration of competing ideas;
4. Beauty and symmetry through the arts, sciences, and mathematical equations;
5. Love and caring, through kindness, heartfelt interactions, shared intimacy, and relationships.

It is possible for us to organize dialogues and efforts at political persuasion using any of these forms. And the more we use this second set or arguments, the less adversarial the outcomes are likely to be.

If we assume that there is only one solution to a social problem, one outcome that is correct, then tolerance, plurality, democracy, and dialogue are not especially useful. The only issue then is how to make the single correct outcome happen. But if there are multiple correct outcomes, then tolerance, plurality, democracy, and dialogue become values and virtues, and our project is to figure out how to assist these different forms of truth and multiple possible outcomes in interacting and combining with each other in creative ways.

As a consequence, there are many alternative ways of defining politics, which are simply a set of conversations about what should be done and why. If we think of politics in this way, the adversarial parts that demonize our opponents or victimize ourselves make these conversations ineffective as a form of problem solving. Politics, in the end, is then just a diverse group of people trying to agree on common goals; it is a living, evolving, adapting expression of national or organizational identity; a continually changing set of values and purposes; a way of resolving conflicts; and a mediation between diverse interests.

Here are three ways we can define politics based on *interests* rather than on power or rights. First, as suggested, we can define politics as *a social problem solving process*. If that Is the case, we will want to encourage a diversity of views about the problem and alternative ways of solving it so we can create a rich set of alternatives and better solutions.

Second, we can define politics as *a large group decision-making process*. If that is the case, we will try to build consensus, and the greater the consensus, the stronger the democracy; i.e., the more people who agree with the decision, the more likely it is to be effective and implemented without resistance.

Finally, as mentioned earlier, we can think of politics as *a conflict resolution process*. If that is the case, we can reduce the amount, length, and cost of conflicts by looking for multiple correct answers and developing interest-based methods through systems design that bring these diverse interests and perspectives into conversation with each other.

If we ask, "What are the elements of political conflict?" we can see that there are actually, fundamentally, just three: first, there has to be *diversity*, because without diversity, there is no conflict – that is, a diversity of views of what we should do, or a diversity of beliefs about what's right. Second, there has to be *inequality* in terms of whose views and beliefs are going to be implemented and whose are not. Third, there has to be *an adversarial win-lose process* for deciding whose beliefs and views will get implemented, and whose will not.

In reflecting on the nature of political conflicts, Vaclav Havel, a writer and first president of a newly independent Czechoslovakia, wrote:

> Genuine politics — politics worthy of the name, and the only politics I am willing to devote myself to — is simply a matter of serving those around us, serving the community, and serving those who will come after us. Its deepest roots are moral, because it is a responsibility. There is only one way to strive for decency, reason, responsibility, sincerity, civility, and tolerance. And that is decently,

responsibly, reasonably, responsibly, sincerely, civilly, and tolerantly. I'm aware that, in everyday politics, this is not seen as the most practical way of going about it.

Indeed, we have discovered, through conflict resolution, that the costs of conflict are so enormous that acting decently is, in fact, the most practical way of going about any joint activity. To operate in a collaborative way and attempt to understand our differences ends up costing us a great deal less than assuming we are enemies and proceeding as though we have nothing in common.

The Language of Power, Rights, and Interests (Ken)

Not only in political institutions, but and families as well, there are languages that reinforce relationships based on *power*, or relationships based on rights, or relationships based on interests. Our purpose in this section is to look more closely at the nature of languages of power, rights, and interests.

Mexican Novelist and Nobel Prize winner Octavio Paz wrote,

> When a society decays, it is language that is first to become gangrenous. Although moralists are scandalized by the fortunes amassed by the revolutionaries — rights in Mexico under the ruling party— they have failed to observe that this material flowering has a verbal parallel; oratory has become the favorite literary genre of the prosperous. And alongside oratory, with its plastic flowers, there is the barbarous syntax in many of our newspapers, the foolishness of language on loudspeakers and the radio the loathsome vulgarities of advertising — all that asphyxiating rhetoric.

The asphyxiating rhetoric he describes can be found on many levels in many different environments. It parallels the loss of authenticity and groundedness that takes place in relationships between individual people, and in bureaucratic organizations that have adopted false languages that make it difficult for people to live naturally.

When can then see that the language favored by power-based organizations, like military, police, and monarchical states, requires clarity and simplicity, and uniform interpretation in order to encourage unthinking obedience, which is the primary goal of the language of power. The communications that emanate from these institutions and organizations therefore take the form of declarations, propaganda, pronouncements, and orders that reinforce hierarchy and command, and imply punishment and contempt to those who disobey.

The language of rights, on the other hand, is favored by legal institutions, bureaucracies, and *formally* democratic organizations and states, and requires narrow distinctions, exceptions, and adjudicated interpretations in order to maintain control by permitting some behaviors and forbidding others. The communications that emanate from these institutions therefore take the form of rules and regulations, policies and procedures, legislative definitions, adversarial arguments, and legal interpretations that reinforce bureaucracy and control, and imply coercion and censure for those who do not fit in.

The language of interests is fundamentally different. This is the language of teams, civil society, and *substantively* democratic states. These require diversity, dissent, and dialogue in order to encourage collaboration and participation by diverse groups of people, so the communications that emanate from these institutions take the form of open-ended questions, dialogues, value-driven rules (as opposed to rule-driven values), conversations, consensus building, and joint decision making, all of which reinforce social equality, economic equity, and political democracy.

Thus, an evolution can be seen to be taking place from power to rights to interests, that is reflected in language. Even, for example, between children in a sandbox, there are three options. If you want to use power, grab the toy, hit, scream, or get someone in authority to solve it for you by taking the toy away from one and giving it to another. If you want to use a rights-based process, create rules like, first come, first served, which requires a language in which anyone can identify what the rule is, what it means, how it applies, and enforce it. Someone can then decide to try and manipulate the rules, or cite technical reasons why they're right, or appeal to a higher authority, or perhaps even vote, which is a rights-based process. But with interests, the children ask each other questions to find out what each of them wants and why, and helping them learn how to play together. This is a simple way of defining these terms.

Here is another example that can be found in the language used by any couple or family. Power-based language includes phrases such as: "you must," "you shall," "you will, or else," or "because I said so, that's why." Rights-based language includes phrases such as: "you should," "you ought to," "you need to," "you have a right to," or "you are entitled to." And interest-based language includes phrases such as: "you could," "you might consider," "what would happen if you," "what would you like to have happen," "why," or "what do you think would happen if you," etc. These examples show that we can shift entire relationships from power to rights to interests simply by changing the way we use language to communicate what we want.

Every time we use the words "you must" or "you shall," we revert in language to power-based relationships, that are reinforced by the use of this language, but begin to evolve and move in a different direction when we use different phrases, like interest-based ones in which we *actually* show respect for what other people think and want.

This fundamental dependence of politics on language makes it interesting and worthwhile as a topic for conversation, as it is relatively easy to draw people into interest-based conversations when we dismantle our desire for victory over others, and search instead for ways we can each walk away feeling we have won.

Facilitating Community Dialogues (Joan)

Mediators can play significant and powerful roles in facilitating community dialogues. Ken and I have had years of satisfying experiences facilitating dialogues, worldwide. For example, we were invited by a group of mediators to Athens, Greece, to work on designing and facilitating dialogues between Greek citizens and immigrants who were fleeing persecution in Africa and elsewhere. We worked for several weeks with Greek mediators, immigrants, and citizens, and included members of the Coast Guard and police, to train them to facilitate dialogues so citizens and immigrants could talk with each other and begin to work together as a community to solve any problems that resulted.

We also worked in a community in the southern part of the United States where there were conflicts between conservationists who wanted to maintain a dam to promote natural energy, and others who wanted the dam removed so the original river could be returned to its natural state.. We trained city council members, mediators, and community leaders to facilitate dialogues between people on all sides in the conflict, and they were able to come to an agreement.

I had an opportunity, when I was a graduate student at the University of Chicago in 1965, to march with Dr. Martin Luther King Jr. in an all-white community where residents had initiated violent attacks against African-Americans who had begun moving into that community. When we marched through the community, we did so, not with big signs or aggressive actions, but inviting people who were standing on the side-lines, or watching the march, or in their yards, or on their porches, to join us, to talk with us. Some of us who were Caucasian, went from the march to speak with people who were standing and watching. We invited them to feel part of our effort to integrate the community. Dr. King wrote, about these efforts to bring about dialogue:

> In a real sense, all life is interrelated. All men are caught in an inescapable network of mutuality, tied in a single garment of destiny. Whatever affects one directly affects all indirectly. I can never be what I ought to be until you are what you ought to be, and you can never be what you ought to be until I am what I ought to be. This is the interrelated structure of reality.

Remembering this interrelated structure of reality helps us work in communities where there is conflict, tension, and stress. Mediators may ask the question: "How can we relate to one another?" Or:

"How can we solve problems and become interconnected?" In doing so, we start to create dialogue and conversation.

We facilitated a community dialogue several years ago in Santa Monica, when three boys were shot to death at a local high school in a gang war. They all came from the same community, a poor community where most of the residents were African-American or Latino. The community was grieving and angry with the police for not stopping the gangs, angry with the city government for not making their community safe, and angry with the way they were treated.

The city asked us to help end the turmoil and we convened a community dialogue. . When participants came to the sessions, some were crying or angry or hurt because of the death of these kids, and we shared those feelings. When we convened the dialogue, we not only reached out to the members of the community, but included church leaders, police, and city staff, inviting everyone who was touched by this crisis. So when you convene a dialogue, consider who ought to be included, and that may mean inviting outsiders, in addition to those who are directly implicated. This means including even those that have been blamed for the problem, or considered criminals.

At the beginning of this dialogue process in Santa Monica,, participants were upset and everybody wanted to speak at once. We wanted to get everybody's attention so we could describe how we were going to work together and create ground rules for talking and listening to each other. In desperation, I stood on a table in the middle of the room to get everyone's attention so they would stop talking, crying, screaming, and decide how they were going to work together to come up with solutions to this crisis.

We began by asking everyone to number off and form randomly organized small groups. All groups had participants who were community members, members of the police, city staff, and people from local church or community college. We recommended ground rules, the first of which was that everybody was there voluntarily; the second was that everybody would listen, and the third was that everyone would participate and speak up if they had something to say.

We then asked if anyone had any other ground rule to suggest and somebody said, "Yes, I think we should not have any name-calling and try to be civil with each other." We asked if anybody objected to any of the ground rules, and everyone agreed to abide by all of them.

Any issues can be raised in a community dialogue, and as a facilitator you have to be prepared to be welcoming and permit all issues to surface.. By listening in a committed, empathetic way, facilitators model asking open an honest questions, and intervene so participants can listen to each other and resolve their conflicts. And after each session, we asked for feedback to evaluate the process and improve.

In small groups, we often ask one person to volunteer to act as the facilitator of the small group, one to record all the ideas, one to be a timekeeper, one to be a presenter, and one to be a process observer who will offer feedback and an evaluation at the end of the small group discussion.

At the end of the Santa Monica dialogue, recommendations for change were reported from discussions in the small groups. They included the observation that, in their neighborhood, where these kids grew up, there were no trees planted by the city, and no dividers in the roads. Some groups noted that in the more affluent neighborhoods, the city had created landscaping, and there was a feeling that the people who lived in those places felt more valued by the city. . The city representatives agreed to plant trees and build dividers, and create a big park for the community that included a youth center with trained staff who would work with the kids so they could chose to leave gangs ,and offer tutoring so they could develop better academic skills, improve in school and perhaps attend the local college. The police came up with a plan to walk and bicycle through the neighborhood, rather than just drive by in cars with sirens going.

Many people from the neighborhood did not come to the dialogues, did not believe in them, and did not want any part of the process.

Afterwards, one person who had been in the session had T-shirts made with the message: "Community Together," and all the participants, including Ken and I, wore the T-shirts and went door-to-door interviewing people in the community to get their ideas about what should happen next.

Most of the people we interviewed had not been at the dialogues, but when we asked for their ideas, they willingly joined the process. We live adjacent to they community that was involved in the process and after 25 years later, we smile noticing that the trees have matured, the plants on the traffic islands have blossomed, and the community center and city managed park are often crowded with high school students who have turned away from gang activities.

Organizational Dialogue (Ken)

Based on the experience of community dialogue over many years, we can see that it is also possible for people in organizations to speak to each other using dialogue as a technique. So in this section, we will look briefly at what organizational dialogue looks like, how it is defined, and some of the ways you can organize dialogues that are effective.

A physicist whose name is David Bohm, who is among the top ranks of physicists in the world, began to study dialogue in the later years of his life and wrote an interesting book, *On Dialogue,* in which he defined dialogue as, "the stream of meaning that flows between us." The essence of dialogue is that flow of communication regarding what things mean to us. Their real meanings can be hidden, or can shift from one moment to the next, but the essence of dialogue is one of jointly discovering and sharing the meaning of things to each of us.

There are three varieties of dialogue that we want to define a bit more carefully. The first variety encourages empathy and understanding on a personal level between people who are opponents. The second is oriented to problem solving and has, as its fundamental purpose, the discovery of alternative solutions and narrowing them down into recommendations through a consensus building process.

The third is to combine these techniques in different degrees depending on the needs of the parties. We want to begin, of course, with empathy, and then transition into problem solving. These then become two phases of the dialogue process.

Another definition of dialogue is that it is any conversation that is not superficial, but is directed at deepening insight, learning, and mutual understanding between people who are different from each other. It's a very common experience, for example, to take groups inside an organization, separate them, ask them to perform some kind of exercise, bring them together to exchange their views, and then talk about what they learned from each other.

Dialogue can also be defined as the flow of empathy and caring between people, or as a field of relational energy in motion, or a DNA-like double helix of evolving understanding and synthesis of diverse truths. Instead of being static, or even dual (in the sense of symmetrically opposed), it is an evolving conversation that may take different forms in every moment. We want to encourage that evolutionary process so the process can track the evolving understanding of meaning between different people or groups.

A simpler definition of dialogue is that it is what takes place between opposite poles as one approaches the equator, so that it is not *polarized* in the traditional sense. Instead, it searches for ways of *migrating* information from one pole to the other, and both toward the center. It is thus a place where insight, connection, learning, change, and magic can happen.

We have had direct experience of this magic. and have facilitated dialogues between Israelis and Palestinians, Azerbaijanis and Armenians, Russians and Ukrainians, Russians and Georgians, Contras and Sandinistas, etc. and have had lots of experience, not just in community settings, but as we mentioned, in Athens creating dialogues between Greek citizens and immigrants, where there was an enormous amount of emotion, many diverse experiences, and intense polarization.

Out of these dialogues emerged not only deeper empathy and a better understanding of what happened to people and group they didn't understand well to begin with, but joint problem solving that tackled conflicts and difficulties as *common* issues, rather than personalizing them or blaming them on others.

Many of these dialogue techniques are applicable in organizational settings as well, and it is possible to set up dialogues in organizations in many different ways. For example, we worked with a large entertainment industry company, a Fortune 100 company in film production. We brought together all the departments that produced these films, and asked them to describe how they thought others in the organization saw them, what they felt were the stereotypes of their group, and what they most wanted others to understand about what they actually did.

It sounds simple, but it was a very powerful exercise. The dialogue took all day and it was very deep and useful and moving. So what makes dialogues deep and useful and moving? We believe the answer is the *design* — not merely of the process and how people come together, but of the *questions* we ask once they do. Here are some questions that can encourage dialogue. There are hundreds and hundreds of these, but here are some we find helpful.

The first is especially useful in political dialogues where people get into difficulties with ideas one side believes are true and the other believes are false. What do we do in that situation? One question we often ask is, "What life experiences have you had that have led you to feel so deeply and passionately about this issue?" Now, we are not discussing the issue any longer, we are discussing people's life experiences, what has happened to them. Another similar question is: "What's at the heart of this issue for you as an individual, not as a spokesperson for a group, not as a manager or employee or representative of HR, but just for you as an individual? How do you see it, and why?"

Here are a few others: "What made you willing to participate in this dialogue?" "What brought you here?" "Why do you care so much about this issue?" There are many questions like this that are inherently respectful and designed to encourage people to come forward with conversations they might otherwise keep to themselves, or take to outsiders.

Here are a few more: "Do you see any gray areas in the issue that we are talking about, or ideas that you find it difficult to define?" In other words, "Can we agree that there are certain areas that are ambiguous and nobody knows the complete answer, and can we talk about those?" Or, "Do you have any mixed feelings, any uncertainties, any discomforts regarding this issue that you would be willing to share?" "Are there any parts of this issue that you're not 100 percent sure of or would be willing to discuss or talk about it?" "Even though you hold widely differing views, are there any concerns or ideas that you think you may have in common?" "What underlying values or ethical beliefs have led you to your current political beliefs?"

Part of what makes dialogue useful is designing questions that elicit a deeper understanding of what it might feel like to be in the other side's shoes. For example, in the dialogue we designed for Greek citizens and immigrants, we began with two basic questions for everyone in the room, immigrants and Greek citizens. Question one, "Have you ever, in your life — in a family or neighborhood or school or workplace — been the new one, and everyone else has been there for a while?" "What did that feel like?" "What experiences did you have that you would be willing to share?" And people then start to talk about experiences in their lives that had real meaning, specific events or circumstances they recall and get in touch with.

Question two: "Have you ever, in your life — in a family or neighborhood or school or workplace — been the one who has been there for a while, and now new people are coming in and changing everything?" "What did that feel like?" "What experiences did you have that you would be willing to share with others?"

And in these two sets of simple questions, people start to understand what it might feel like to be an immigrant or a Greek citizen, to be the new one who is coming in, or the one who has been there for a while. And now we can open the issues up for real conversation.

It is important to understand the difference between large and small group conversations. You can see this in some of the examples we have related regarding community dialogues, but we also see it in organizations. If you are working with an organization with, 150 people, or 250, or several thousand, it will be difficult to bring that many people together in a single conversation. Even if it is just 50 people, or 30, it can still be difficult to create a single conversation without bypassing some people who will not speak, or having some people speak more than their turn, or keep the issue from becoming abstract and impersonal.

What we do then is break the large group into small group session and assign various tasks, so everyone is participating. We also ask questions that invite people to have more intimate conversations than would otherwise be possible in a large group setting. Also, in small groups, it almost never happens that somebody stands up and yells or gets into interpersonal conflicts.

If you ask for volunteer facilitators, not only in small group, but ask more experienced facilitators to watch the small groups and be ready to step in if they get out of hand, you will create a setting in which people can feel secure enough to come forward with issues that are deeply personal or difficult or complex, which by itself can induce empathy and understanding. A typical way to do this is to simply number off and put people into separate small groups, and then ask the small groups to present to the larger group as a whole on a common topic.

We encourage you to try dialogue techniques in your organization. If you would like more information about how to organize dialogues, look at my books, *The Dance of Opposites* and *Politics, Dialogue, and the Evolution of Democracy*, where there are chapters about how to organize and conduct dialogues on difficult and dangerous issues.

Failed Mediations, and an Algorithm for How to Disagree (Ken)

In discussing political conflicts, it is useful to look at some famous failed mediations in history that took place when mediators tried to intervene in political conflicts. This is important because there have been failed mediations in organizations over what are essentially political issues — that is, issues that concern the exercise of power, or the distribution of power within the organization. So it will be instructive to look at an example or two of how efforts to reduce political conflict can fail.

A perfect example was efforts to mediate slavery in the U.S. before the Civil War. As we know, slavery led to a lengthy period of conflict between slave states and free states in the U.S., and Henry Clay, the "Great Compromiser," was one of the principal mediators between southern slave states and northern free states. The Constitution of the U.S. had a fugitive slave provision, which provided that if slave ran away from the South to the North, the Constitution required that they be returned to their owners.

With the rise of abolitionism and the "underground railroad," this provision was becoming increasingly ineffective. The U.S. became increasingly divided, and for years before the Civil War, the Senate was divided 50-50, slave and free, while the House of Representatives, which was based on population, became more representative of the free states that were far more populous – and in the Constitution, slaves only counted as 3/5ths of a person for representation purposes.

Also at this time, the Supreme Court of the United States was divided with a 5 to 4 majority in favor of slavery. Anti-slavery sentiment was increasing rapidly in the period leading up to, and during the 1850s. The publication of *Uncle Tom's Cabin* had an enormous impact. The emergence of Frederick Douglass as a brilliant spokesperson for abolition, and expansion into the West created the possibility that Western states would petition to join the U.S. as slave or free states.

The Compromise of 1850, mediated by Henry Clay, allowed some states to join as free and others as slave, but as a price for this compromise, the Congress was required to pass a Fugitive Slave Act, which it did. This Fugitive Slave Act required not only that fugitive slaves be returned from the North, where they had become free, to the South where they would again become slaves, it required every

US citizen in the North to support the return of those slaves to the South, and not stand in the way of their forcible return. It also created a mechanism for returning the slave to the South, in which the slave was brought into federal court, and in federal court, through a seemingly simple procedural rule, the slave had no right to speak.

Today we can recognize that if the slave had no right to speak in federal court, not only would slavery continue to exist in the South, it would exist in the North, as well, so the entire country would be required to accept slavery. On the other hand, if, as a procedural rule, the slave *had* a right to speak in federal court, slavery would be abolished procedurally, not only in the northern states but in the South as well.

The issue of the constitutionality of the Fugitive Slave Act came to the United States Supreme Court in the *Dred Scott* case, which held that Scott, a slave who had been taken into a northern free state and then returned to a slave state, did *not* acquire freedom as a result, and to quote U.S. Supreme Court Chief Justice Taney for the majority of the Court, that "A black man has no rights which a white man need respect." That was the decision that led directly to the Civil War.

A number of mediation efforts had taken place, from the 1820s through the 1850s, and every one of those efforts was directed at trying to reduce the conflict between slave states and free states, but each did so by recognizing the validity of slavery and permitting it to continue.

Yet if we consider slavery a source of chronic conflict, we have to recognize that as long as it exists in *any* area and in any form, there will be chronic conflicts, and the bitterness and difficulties will continue, as they have indeed, in different forms, up to the present day.

Similarly, we can consider the failed mediation that took place in Munich, when Chamberlain from England and Daladier from France met with Hitler from Germany and Mussolini from Italy over the fate of Czechoslovakia. What ensued was regarded by many at the time as a successful mediation, while others considered it a betrayal. Interestingly, the mediator was Benito Mussolini. Today, this would be recognized as a clear example of a biased mediator with a clear conflict of interest, and a failed mediation — in part, because Hitler had no intention of giving up Czechoslovakia; in part, because Czechoslovakia, Poland and others were not represented at the mediation; in part, because the mediator had already chosen sides; and in part, because the chronic, underlying issues of expansionism, anti-Semitism, political autocracy, etc., were not addressed, leading directly to World War II.

There are many examples where mediation efforts have failed because those whose lives were impacted, or who were directly concerned with the issue were not invited to participate in the conversation, or their rights to free speech, or to be recognized as individuals were not acknowledged, or the mediation did not address the deeper underlying issues, or end chronic and systemic conflicts at their source through a systems design approach.

This leads us to what we think of as an *algorithm* on how to go about creating dialogues and mediating disagreements. We want to begin by creating an atmosphere, an attitude, and a *context* of unconditional respect for each other, regardless of our opinions or positions on the issues — that is, of respectful behaviors without conditions. And if we are able to create this context, we will have much more successful conversations. Here, again, we are not looking at specific political or organizational issues. We are simply looking at the process and relationships, and the nature of the conversation that has to take place for conflicted parties to be able to address their issues.

We therefore need to be sure to include people who do not agree with each other. This is difficult because it initially looks like the conversation is being set up to fail, but on the other hand, those are exactly the people who have to come together and talk to each other for the conflict to end.

To improve our chances of success, we can reach consensus on a set of ground rules or shared values that will guide our conversation.

We can use skilled facilitators to keep conversations on track, not suppress anyone's experiences, reflections, ideas, beliefs, passions, and focus on the problem as an it, rather than as a you.

We can ask questions that do not have a single correct answer, but invite people to offer their own unique answers — that is, not simple yes or no answers of the kind lawyers ask in court, but questions like, "What does that mean to you?" Or, "Why do you feel so deeply about this" We can come from a place of curiosity and learning, acknowledge and validate everyone's deepest interests, express gratitude and thank people for their dissent, for their diversity, for their courage, and their willingness to learn.

The true goal of mediation and dialogue is not for people to give in, or concede when they are right and others are wrong — the goal is to deepen their conversation in order to find out what is taking place beneath the surface that led someone to insist on an idea that is wrong. When we get there, we discover *something* that is right immediately beneath the thing that is wrong. For example, beneath race or gender prejudice, which we may believe as wrong, there often lies a fear of loss of status, wealth, and power — i.e., of one's position in a hierarchy; or perhaps a lack of skill at being able to talk to someone who is different; or even self-loathing that has been shifted onto others — all of which are *true*. Yet there is a resistance to the truth and a need to defend the falsehood because the *consequences* of telling the truth are perceived to be too great. The trick of conflict resolution is to design conversations that invite these deeper truths to emerge and directly engage with one another — not an easy task to be sure, but one that can is magical when it happens.

In the end, it is not just designing questions that draw people into dialogue with each other, or working in small groups, or any other techniques, but the commitment to seeking ways that those on opposite sides of an issue can agree on specific, practical steps to improve their communications and relationships in the future, elicit honest feedback, jointly evaluate the process, and make improvements as we go.

In the end, we are left with a profound idea that was quite beautifully expressed by Martin Luther King, Jr., with which we end this course:

> We will have to repent in this generation not merely for the vitriolic words or actions of the bad people, but for the appalling silence of the good people. We must come to see that human progress never rolls in on wheels of inevitability. It comes through the tireless efforts and persistent work of men. And without this hard work, time itself becomes an ally of the forces of social stagnation. We must use time creatively and forever realize that the time is always ripe to do right.

SESSION 7 LECTURE SLIDES

The fact is that all the power in the world cannot transform someone who hates you into someone who likes you. It can turn a foe into a slave, but not into a friend. All the power in the world cannot transform a fanatic into an enlightened man. All the power in the world cannot transform someone thirsting for vengeance into a lover.

AMOS OZ

If you are neutral in situations of injustice, you have chosen the side of the oppressor. If an elephant has its foot on the tail of a mouse and you say that you are neutral, the mouse will not appreciate your neutrality.

DESMOND TUTU

Our lives begin to end the day we become silent about things that matter.

MARTIN LUTHER KING, JR.

Mediators and Politics – Introduction (1)

- We have all watched political conversations degenerate into angry quarrels, pointless personal attacks and antagonistic power contests. We have all seen people sink into screaming matches, shaming and blaming, and personal viciousness, often over the loftiest ideas, deepest passions and most profound political principles. We all know that these tirades can easily descend into senseless violence and appalling acts of brutality. And we have all participated in them, fanned the flames, or stood passively by and done nothing.
- Yet political conversations matter; they concern our future, our values and integrity, our ethics and morality, our beliefs and behaviors, not only as individuals and nation states, but as *human beings* who are responsible for the world our grandchildren, and our grandchildren's grandchildren, will inherit.
- Successful political decision-making requires not silence or pointless rage, but dialogue; not apathy or aggression, but collaborative negotiation; not passivity or accommodation, but courageous, constructive, *creative* contention. Silence in the face of critical issues signifies not merely the absence of speech, but the loss of learning and *integrity*, and therefore of self, of values, of citizenship, of democracy, of community, of humanity.

Mediators and Politics – Introduction (2)

- As mediators, we have largely been silent about political events. In part this may be because we do not know how to express our political views without slipping into adversarial attitudes and assumptions that define most political communications -- yet we know from practice that both can be transformed and overcome.
- Many of us think of ourselves as "not interested in politics." Yet, as Pericles declared over two millennia ago, "You may not be interested in politics, but politics is interested in you."
- Whatever our justifications for treating each other as enemies or remaining silent when political ideas are discussed, our ability to address the highly complex, increasingly challenging issues that characterize modern political life is no longer optional. What happens in the world politically has an impact on our work in conflict resolution, expanding or contracting the willingness to seek peaceful options. Is it possible that the opposite might also be true? Could mediation have an impact on politics?
- Politics has been called the art of *compromise*, but what if we think of it as the art of *conflict resolution*, in which compromise, as in mediation, is merely one of many possible outcomes?
- What, then, would a *mediative*, interest-based, collaborative form of politics look like? What skills are required for democracy to work?

Why Politics Matters to Mediators

- If couples, families or opposing parties engaged in these behaviors during a typical mediation, it would predictably result in a downward cycle of defensiveness, escalation, mutual retaliation, resistance to settlement, loss of trust in the other side (and perhaps the mediator); increased costs, time and effort required to resolve the dispute; decreased effectiveness and listening, fractured relationships, heightened aggression and less willingness to use mediation again.
- The persistence of these behaviors will predictably impact all of us professionally, encouraging the creation of a *culture* of conflict that is openly aggressive, biased, and hostile toward others -- rather than one that encourages conflicted parties to negotiate collaboratively for mutual gain, act respectfully, and seek to satisfy each others' interests.
- Even if some of us agree with the political beliefs that promote these actions, it is important for us *as mediators* to articulate the reasons why they are *professionally* counter-productive, and advocate conflict resolution practices we know from decades of experience are likely to produce better outcomes. Silence, in this case, becomes capitulation, condonation, and a loss of opportunities and professional integrity.

Some Classical Purposes of Politics

- Search for the highest common good (Aristotle)
- Provide for the general welfare (Aristotle)
- Make sure that laws are fairly conceived, wisely interpreted and justly enforced (Aristotle)
- Make the citizen "as good as possible." (Socrates)
- Search for justice (Plato)
- Support "… not the disproportionate happiness of any one class, but the greatest happiness of the whole." (Plato)
- Promote democracy (Democritus)

Every state is a community of some kind, and every community is established with a view to some good, for mankind always act in order to obtain that which they think good. But, if all communities aim at some good, the state or political community, which is the highest of all, and which embraces all the rest, aims, and in a greater degree than any other, at the highest good.

ARISTOTLE

What's Wrong with Politics as Usual

- It is unnecessarily divisive and adversarial
- It is nearly always win/lose and winner take all
- It is power-based, yet "all power corrupts and absolute power corrupts absolutely;" or rights-based, yet controlled by power
- It takes too long, costs too much, and is exercised too personally
- It is increasingly ineffective in solving global problems
- It is controlled by wealthy individuals, military and industrial elites, corporations and special interests
- Global political collaborations, as in the United Nations, are perceived as reducing sovereignty and imposing alien ideas
- It is grounded in domination, inequality and disrespect
- There is little interest among elites in openness or direct democracy, and great interest in secrecy and amassing power
- It easily slips into autocracy and boosts social inequality
- It generates bureaucracy and corruption, stifles change and increases chronic conflict

Spectrum of Responses to Opposition

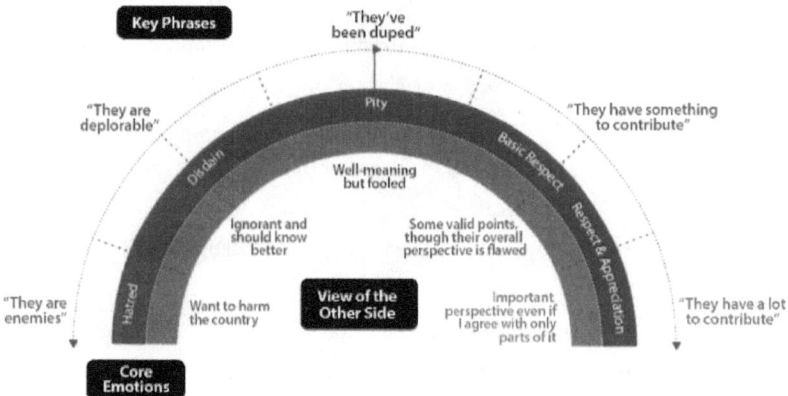

Aristotelian Logic and Politics

1. *The Law of Identity:* A statement is what it is. A is identical to A. Yet we know there are times when A is not entirely A. For example, political calls to "support our soldiers" or "be tough on criminals" may mask calls to war or discriminatory social policies.
2. *The Law of Non-contradiction:* A statement and its contradiction cannot both be true. If A is true and B is the opposite of A, both A and B cannot be true. Yet we know there are times in politics when A and B are both true and opposites. For example, political parties frequently assert opposing claims and principles about complex issues that cannot be reduced to single truths. Physicist Neils Bohr called these "complementarities," which are "great truths whose opposites are also great truths."
3. *The Law of the Excluded Middle:* A statement is either true or false, and cannot be both true and false at the same time. Yet we know there are times when political statements are both true and false at the same time. For example, the stories political opponents tell about themselves and each other may be true and false at the same time.

Aristotle's Forms of Political Persuasion, Advocacy, or Rhetoric

1. *Logos*: Arguments based on logic or reason, or on evidence such as facts or figures. Yet is it common for political candidates to play fast-and-loose with facts and figures, and for fact checking and corrections to go unnoticed.
2. *Ethos*: Arguments based on character or ethics, or on credibility or expertise. Yet political debates often place a premium on character assassination, ignore ethical violations, and discount both credibility and expertise.
3. *Pathos*: Arguments based on emotion or feelings. Yet powerful negative feelings like fear and anger can be stirred up by political debates, and easily overwhelm rationality.

Five Other Forms of Political Persuasion

1. *Personal Experience and Empathy*, chiefly through storytelling, dialogue and empathetic listening
2. *Vision and Values*, chiefly through leadership, commitment and modeling
3. *Synergy and Syntheses*, chiefly through conflict resolution and the integration of competing ideas
4. *Beauty and Symmetry*, chiefly through the arts, sciences and mathematical equations
5. *Love and Caring*, chiefly through kindness, heartfelt interactions, shared intimacy and relationships

So long as only one ideal is the true goal, it will always seem to men that no means can be too difficult, no price too high, to do whatever is required to realize the ultimate goal. Such certainty is one of the great justifications of fanaticism, compulsion, persecution .... If there is only one solution to the puzzle, then the only problems are first how to find it, then how to realize it, and finally how to convert others to the solution by persuasion or by force. But if this is not so ..., then the path is open to empiricism, pluralism, tolerance, compromise. Tolerance is historically the product of the realization of the irreconcilability of equally dogmatic faiths, and the practical improbability of complete victory of one over the other. Those who wished to survive realized that they had to tolerate error. They gradually came to see the merits of diversity, and so became skeptical about definitive solutions in human affairs.

ISAIAH BERLIN

Alternative Ways of Defining Politics

- A process of social problem solving that can be adversarial or collaborative
- A collection of ideas, beliefs, interests and desires for the future
- A group of conversations about what should be done and why
- A set of stories and beliefs about the past that shape the future
- A set of relationships and processes organized around power
- A diverse group of people trying to agree on a common goal
- A system for making decisions that bind everyone
- A living, evolving, adapting expression of national identity
- A variety of interlocking activities and processes
- A culture or mind-set about people, power and privilege
- A way of fixing and diffusing responsibility
- A compact, agreement, or contract reconciling competing interests
- A mix of unspoken expectations and desires
- A continually evolving set of values and purposes
- A way of resolving conflicts, a mediation between diverse interests [245]

© Kenneth Cloke

Three Simple *Interest-Based* Ways of Defining Politics

1. *Politics is a social problem-solving process.* As a result, a diversity of views about the nature of the problem and multiple alternative ways of solving it will predictably result in better, more sustainable solutions.

2. *Politics is a large group decision-making process.* As a result, the greater the consensus, the stronger the democracy, and the more people agree with a decision, the more likely it is to be effective.

3. *Politics is a conflict resolution process.* As a result, the amount of chronic, on-going, systemic conflict can be dramatically reduced by assuming there is more than one correct answer and a complex, egalitarian, interest-based approach can result in no one having to lose so that that others are able to win.

Three Elements of Political Conflict (1)

1. *Diversity*: In the first place, there must be two or more distinct individuals or groups of people, each with diverse beliefs, ideas, opinions, needs, and interests. Without this, there cannot be conflict.

2. *Inequality*: In the second place, there must be an inequality in power between these individuals or groups, reflecting their ability to implement their diverse beliefs, ideas, opinions, etc. Without this, the conflict will not take a political form.

3. *Adversarial, win/lose process*: In the third place, there must be an adversarial, win/lose process for problem solving or decision-making that pits diverse groups against each other, allowing only one to win. Without this, the conflict will not become polarizing.

Three Elements of Political Conflict (2)

1. *Conservatives* and the right commonly seek to reduce the level of political conflict by decreasing diversity, boosting respect for accepted, conventional ideas, and buttressing established authority.

2. *Liberals* and the left commonly seek to do so by increasing equality, drawing attention to new and diverse ideas, and championing the freedom to articulate, argue for and implement them.

3. *Neither*, however, focuses much attention on the adversarial win/lose nature of the political process, without which diversity and inequality do not routinely result in political polarization. 248

© Kenneth Cloke

Genuine politics politics worthy of the name, and the only politics I am willing to devote myself to — is simply a matter of serving those around us: serving the community, and serving those who will come after us. It's deepest roots are moral because it is a responsibility ... [T]here is only one way to strive for decency, reason, responsibility, sincerity, civility, and tolerance, and that is decently, reasonably, responsibly, sincerely, civilly, and tolerantly. I'm aware that, in everyday politics, this is not seen as the most practical way of going about it.

VACLAV HAVEL

The Language of Power, Rights and Interests

When a society decays, it is language that is first to become gangrenous ... Although moralists are scandalized by the fortunes amassed by the revolutionaries [in Mexico under the ruling party], they have failed to observe that this material flowering has a verbal parallel; oratory has become the favorite literary genre of the prosperous ... and alongside oratory, with its plastic flowers, there is the barbarous syntax in many of our newspapers, the foolishness of language on loudspeakers and the radio, the loathsome vulgarities of advertising — all that asphyxiating rhetoric.

OCTAVIO PAZ

Power, Rights and Interests

Power
Dictatorship, Autocracy and Hierarchy, Command and Control
Violence, Orders, Pronouncements, Negotiation by Force

↓

Rights
Legal Institutions, Rules and Regulations, Coercion and Restricted Voting
Adjudication, Arbitration, Decision, Positional Negotiation

↓

Interests
Community or Civil Society, Needs and Desires, Consensus and Full Participation
Informal Problem Solving, Mediation, Dialogue, Collaborative Negotiation

252

© Kenneth Cloke and Joan Goldsmith

The Language of *Power*

The language favored by power-based organizations such as the military, police, and monarchical states requires clarity, simplicity, and uniform interpretation in order to encourage unthinking obedience.

The communications that emanate from these institutions therefore take the form of declarations, propaganda, pronouncements, and orders, which reinforce hierarchy and command, and imply punishment and contempt for those who disobey.

© Kenneth Cloke

The Language of *Rights*

The language favored by rights-based organizations such as legal institutions, bureaucracies, and formally democratic states, requires narrow distinctions, exceptions, and adjudicated interpretations in order to maintain control by permitting some behaviors and forbidding others.

The communications that emanate from these institutions take the form of rules and regulations, policies and procedures, legislative definitions, adversarial arguments, and legal interpretations, which reinforce bureaucracy and control and imply coercion and censure for those who do not fit in.

© Kenneth Cloke

The Language of *Interests*

The language favored by interest-based organizations such as teams, civil society, and radically democratic states, requires affirmation of diversity, dissent, and dialogue in order to encourage collaboration and participation.

The communications that emanate from these institutions take the form of open-ended questions, open dialogues, value-driven rules, conversations, and consensus decision making, which reinforce social equality, economic equity, and political democracy.

© Kenneth Cloke

Conflict Evolution in the Sandbox

Power:
- Grab the toy, hit and scream.
- Get someone in authority to solve it for you.

Rights:
- Create rules like "first come, first served."
- Manipulate the rules, cite technical reasons why you are right, and appeal to a higher authority.

Interests:
- Offer them questions they can ask each other to find out what they want and resolve it themselves.
- Help them learn how to play together.

© Kenneth Cloke

Some Trivial Examples

Power: "You must ..." "You shall ..." "You will ..." "... or else." "... because I said so, that's why."

Rights: "You should ..." "You ought to ..." "You need to ..." "You have a right to ..." "You are entitled to ..."

Interests: "You could ..." "You might consider ..." "What would happen if you ..." "What would you like to have happen?" "Why?" "What do you think will happen if you ..."

Distortions of Language in Politics (1)

- Broad statements that are so abstract and meaningless they cannot be opposed
- Excessive personalization of issues so they can only be addressed individually
- Negative frameworks that reinforce pessimistic images of the world
- Inculcation of a "learned helplessness" that assumes change is impossible
- Adversarial assumptions that undermine trust
- Strangled or suppressed expression of intense emotions, glorification of abstract symbols, and romanticization of virtues, destiny, and ideals
- Stories of demonization and victimization
- All or nothing assumptions that eliminate common ground
- Demonization of all critics and independent actors

Distortions of Language in Politics (2)

- Repeated references in noble, *basso profundo* tones, to "the country," "the fatherland," or "the people"
- Crass manipulations of maudlin sentimentality, particularly regarding children, struggling families, religious figures, the nation's history, and recently departed political leaders
- Facades of personal outrage and affront about others
- Loud protestations and harsh denunciations of moral transgressions committed by others
- Simplistic claims of uncompromising toughness, formulaic responses, and unyielding principles regarding complex, multilayered, shifting problems
- Demands for punishment of opponents
- Crass use of religious sentiment and God's support for one nation
- Sanctimony and self-righteousness combined with false humility

Conflict, Language and Fascism

- Repetitive stereotyping, emotional superlatives, and use of romantic adjectives and personal insults
- Hijacking or poisoning formerly positive terms such as "collective," "followers," and "faith"
- Transforming formerly negative words into positives, such as "domination," "fanatical," and "obedient"
- Militarizing and brutalizing common speech
- Promoting fear and disgust toward immigrants and foreigners
- Discounting reason and elevating feelings
- Using "big lies" and doublespeak
- Generally debasing and "dumbing down" ordinary language
- Legitimizing hatred toward religious, racial, sexual or ethnic groups such as Jews, Blacks, Gypsies, Gays, and others
- "Dumbing down" language to the level that is used by children to ostracize others

(Based partly on work by Victor Klemperer)

Propaganda must not serve the truth ... All propaganda must be so popular and on such an intellectual level, that even the most stupid of those toward whom it is directed will understand it. Therefore, the intellectual level of the propaganda must be lower the larger the number of people who are to be influenced by it ... The size of the lie is a definite factor in causing it to be believed, for the vast masses of a nation are in the depths of their hearts more easily deceived than they are consciously and intentionally bad.

ADOLF HITLER

If you tell a lie big enough and keep repeating it, people will eventually come to believe it. The lie can be maintained only for such time as the State can shield the people from the political, economic and/or military consequences of the lie. It thus becomes vitally important for the State to use all of its powers to repress dissent, for the truth is the mortal enemy of the lie, and thus by extension, the truth is the greatest enemy of the State.

JOSEPH GOEBBELS

Voice or no voice, the people can always be brought to the bidding of the leaders. That is easy. All you have to do is tell them they are being attacked, and denounce the peacemakers for lack of patriotism and exposing the country to danger. It works the same in any country.

HERMANN GOERING

Democracy and Elections

Democracy must be something more than two wolves and a sheep voting on what to have for dinner.

JAMES BOVARD

Words like 'freedom,' 'justice,' and 'democracy' are not common concepts; on the contrary, they are rare. People are not born knowing what these are. It takes enormous, and above all, individual effort to arrive at the respect for other people that these words imply.

JAMES BALDWIN

If voting made any difference they wouldn't let us do it." Mark Twain

The fire, the energy, and the life of democracy is popular pressure. Democracy itself is a government constantly responding to continuous pressures of its people. The only hope for democracy is that more people and more groups will become articulate and exert pressure upon their government ... Can man envisage a more sublime program on earth than the people having faith in their fellow men and themselves? A program of co-operation instead of competition? This, then, is the job ahead ...

SAUL ALINSKY

We may have democracy, or we may have wealth concentrated in the hands of a few, but we can't have both.

JUSTICE LOUIS BRANDEIS

Deep democracy is what justice looks like in practice.

CORNEL WEST

Direct government as at present generally understood is a mere phantom of democracy. Democracy is not a sum in addition. Democracy is not brute numbers; it is a genuine union of true individuals.

MARY PARKER FOLLETT

Five Kinds of Democracy

1. **Representative Democracy:** Citizens vote for representatives who make decisions on their behalf. This approach is used in most countries today.
2. **Liquid Democracy:** Citizens can either vote directly or delegate their right to vote to someone on particular issues. These delegates can also delegate their right to vote. Everyone can withdraw their delegation at any time and vote themselves.
3. **Direct Democracy:** Citizens vote on policy decisions directly. This was used in ancient Athens, and is still used in parts of Switzerland today, and in referendum voting.
4. **Deliberative Democracy:** Citizens participate in learning about and discussing policy issues in dialogues and debates that are part of a consensus building process.
5. **Participatory Democracy:** Citizens become organizers who seek to draw others into action around issues that impact their lives.

Some Requirements for Democracy

- The rule of law – that is, voting is fair, votes are counted, and if there are disputes, a politically independent judiciary is available to resolve it. This requires that judges be appointed not just from the wealthy or dominant political factions, but independently, from diverse groups, populations and political backgrounds.
- One person, one vote – that is, every citizen is allowed to vote and wealthy or powerful individuals do not have extra votes or unequal ability to influence them. This requires the prohibition of secret campaign contributions and advertising by the wealthy.
- Laws and enforcement mechanisms to halt graft and corruption.
- Legal protection for political dissent and minority views.
- Freedom of the press and an independent media.
- Freedom of speech and assembly, including the right to dissent from government decisions and actions and protest them.
- Widespread opportunities for discussion, debate and dialogue on political issues by people of all political persuasions.
- Citizen participation and direct involvement in decision making.

15 Ways of Undermining Democracy

1. Installation of a semi-permanent autocratic leadership
2. Illusion of objectively correct political beliefs and exclusive truths
3. Excessive reliance on command and control
4. Support for managers and bureaucrats and punishment of leaders
5. Manipulation of popular desire for security to suppress criticism
6. Elevation of bureaucracy over art and science
7. Restriction of freedom to speak, publish, assemble, and dissent
8. Limitation of culture and language to artificiality and superficiality
9. Constriction of civil society by police and informers
10. Excessive competition and corruption of economic power
11. Autocratic organization of political power
12. Conversion of unity into conformity, subordination, and obedience
13. Identification of criticism with opposition and treason
14. Use of slogans and promises to mask regimentation and fear
15. Avoidance, suppression, and coerced settlement of conflicts

© Kenneth Cloke

Elections as a Source of Chronic Conflict

- Elections are highly adversarial, power- and rights-based, most often winner- take-all processes.
- Electoral processes usually start with debates, where a premium is placed on character assassination, negativity and personal attacks.
- No one in electoral debates is interested in collaboration, learning, consensus building, or problem solving.
- Each candidate makes promises they know in advance they can't possibly keep.
- Each candidate has to curry favor with so many diverse constituencies that they can't really represent any of them.
- Elections are so expensive that candidates have to cater to wealthy donors and lobbyists, undermining democracy and increasing social and class conflict.
- Whoever wins as a result is distrusted, even despised, by nearly half the population.
- As a result, people are divided and leadership, commonality and problem solving are severely compromised.

© Kenneth Cloke

Game Theory and Elections (1)

- Game theory has been used to select optimal voting procedures. Thus, out of 3 candidates, it is possible for the winner to be the *least* favored by almost 2/3rds of the voters. Yet if elections occur in two stages, the least-preferred candidate can be eliminated in the first round. While voters can still cross over and create disparities, encouraging votes for the "lesser of two evils," it is possible to design alternative approaches that minimize these problems.
- Mathematician Lloyd S. Shapley developed a method to calculate voting power based on the frequency with which someone is a swing voter. This "Shapley value" has been used to calculate, for example, that the 5 permanent members of the UN Security Council have 98 percent of the voting power. This method has led to successful legal challenges against weighted systems of voting that disenfranchise parts of the electorate.
- It is possible to organize elections as non-zero-sum, cooperative, perfect information games that maximize early communication and collaboration, use voting procedures in staged choices and optimize democratic, interest-based, mediative outcomes.

© Kenneth Cloke

Game Theory and Elections (2)

Thus, games of imperfect information allow each player to select an optimal strategy no matter what the other player does, as in the Prisoner's Dilemma. Professor Morton D. Davis offers this example:

> "Two campaigning political parties, A and B, must each decide how to handle an issue in a certain town. They can support the issue, oppose it or evade it. Each party must make its decision without knowing what its rival will do. Every pair of decisions determines the percentage of the vote that each party receives in the town, and each party wants to maximize its own percentage of the vote... [I]f, for example, A supports the issue and B evades it, A gets 80 percent (and B, 20 percent) of the vote.
>
> A's decision seems difficult at first because it depends upon B's strategy. A does best to oppose if B supports, evade if B opposes, and support if B evades. A must therefore consider B's decision before making its own. No matter what A does, B gains the largest percentage of votes by opposing the issue. Once A recognizes this, its strategy should clearly be to evade and settle for 30 percent of the vote."

© Kenneth Cloke

Arrow's Impossibility Theorem (1)

- It has been demonstrated mathematically by Nobel Prize winning economist Kenneth Arrow, in what is known as "Arrow's impossibility theorem," that no voting system is perfect.
- Or, more precisely, that no "rank order" voting system in which there are three or more choices can be designed so as to meet the following seemingly unremarkable axioms, or criteria for fairness, from which he is able to prove that no voting system can satisfy them all:
    - If every voter prefers candidate A over candidate B, then the group prefers A over B
    - If every voter's preference between A and B remains unchanged, then the group's preference between A and B will also remain unchanged (even if voters' preferences between other pairs like A and C, B and C or C and D change)
    - There is no "dictator": no single voter possesses the power to always determine the group's preference

Arrow's Impossibility Theorem (2)

For example, assume there are three candidates, A, B and C, that A and C each have the support of 35 percent of the voters but are hated by all the others.

Assume also that B has 30 percent of voter support, but would have 65 percent if the election were only between B and A, or between B and C.

If all three candidates run for office, in most cases B will be eliminated in the first round, even though B would win in a two-way race against either A or C.

However, B would win the election if the candidates were ranked in preference with the "least preferred" candidate(s) eliminated, but this method will often result in a "lesser of two evils," mediocre, "do-nothing" candidate being elected.

There are, in other words, trade-offs and disadvantages no matter which option is selected.

Alternatives to Arrow's Theorem

- Voting systems that use rated or *"cardinal" voting,* such as "range voting," in which each candidate receives, for example, a number between zero and 10; or *"approval voting,"* in which there are votes either for or against each candidate; and *"majority judgment,"* in which each candidate is assigned a grade or judgment in repeated rounds of voting, do not succumb to the impossibility theorem because they take "intensity of preferences" into consideration.
- Each of these methods of voting, however, also assumes there is a single winner — in other words, that it is a zero-sum game. Arrow's impossibility theorem does not hold if elections are conducted as interest-based, non-zero-sum, cooperative games, as by allowing *all* candidates to win, but with fractional representation that reflects the percentage of votes they received. A variation allows proportional representation with numerous small parties, but they can become unable to make decisions and dilute responsibility for outcomes.
- While no single voting system may be able to satisfy all of Arrow's criteria or axioms of fairness, or prevent strategic choices that allow people to "game" the system, the electoral process can be improved through an application of collaborative interest-based principles. [273]

Alternative Ways of Voting

Legislative election methods generally fall into four families:

- With **Majoritarian** methods, used in the United States and Canada, all or most legislators represent majority views while minority groups do not have fair representation. Usually, two major parties representing the social or political majority dominate the legislature.
- With **Proportional** methods, used in most developed countries, legislators more fairly represent the diversity of voters. Usually, several parties representing a diversity of social and political views win seats in proportion to the votes they receive.
- With **Semi-proportional** methods, used in local elections across the United States, minority social or political groups have a chance to win seats.
- **Potentially Proportional** methods have not been used in any public elections, but might achieve proportional results. [274]

Single Transferable Voting

Single Transferable Voting Ballot

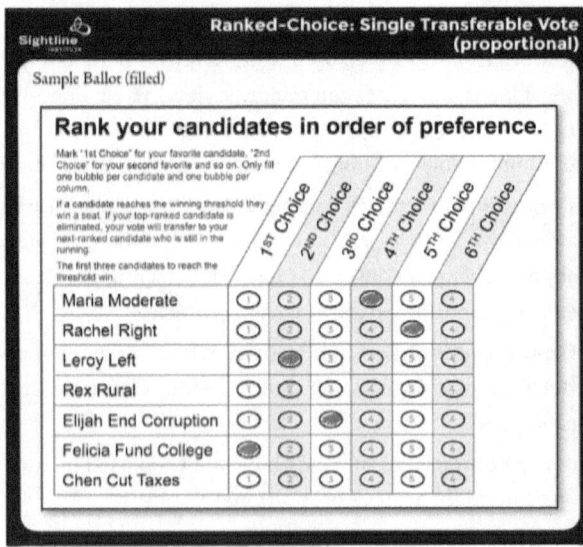

Some Election Reforms (1)

- Approach elections as consensus building efforts that identify potential solutions to important public problems and begin with discussions of shared values, common visions, problem solving, or strategic planning
- Organize facilitated community dialogues in advance of elections to discuss key questions, explore disagreements, unite around common strategies, and build relationships between diverse communities
- Restructure and democratize the electoral system to increase respect for diversity, maximize participation and elicit broader representation of interests among groups seeking change
- Provide public campaign financing for all candidates, remove soft money bribery from politics, and reduce incentives for graft, corruption, and financially motivated appointments
- Prohibit campaign contributions and expenditures in excess of minimal amounts and impose fines or disqualify candidates, contributors or lobbyists who exceed these limits, overturning the USSC's Citizen's United decision
- Equalize access to media and provide free government sponsored television discussions, with fines or disqualification for slanderous and dishonest ads
- Create a Voter Bill of Rights, or alternatively, a Constitutional right to vote
- Establish minimum standards for negativity in local and national elections
- Establish a shorter number of days for primaries to reduce costs, media hype, exhaustion, and opportunistic appeals to narrow sectional interests

Some Election Reforms (2)

- Create nonpartisan election management/conflict resolution teams
- Provide for automatic, universal, lifetime voter registration linked to social security numbers, or create opportunities for election day registration
- Establish an election day work holiday, as is done in Puerto Rico
- Extend the right to vote to everyone who is taxed, including recent immigrants and former felons
- Prohibit removal of voters from voting lists without advance notice, opportunities to appeal, and penalties for partisan elimination of voters
- Require voting machines to be reliable, publicly owned and tamper proof, with an easily accessible paper trail to confirm results
- Formulate party platforms as vision statements, drafted by facilitated local citizen assemblies and agreed upon wherever possible by consensus
- Focus on issues rather than personalities by scheduling sustained, meaningful, long-term public dialogues regarding important issues
- Require candidates to mediate ground rules for debates and campaigns in advance, and to publicly indicate the kind of campaign they intend to run
- Arrange for multiple, facilitated public dialogues; include independent candidates, write-ins, and "fringe" political parties; eliminate "stacking" of audiences; and encourage public participation in dialogue sessions

© Kenneth Cloke

Some Election Reforms (3)

- Schedule discussions of divisive political issues in mediated forums and televised town hall meetings, facilitated by professional mediators
- Eliminate gerrymandering of electoral boundaries and use nonpartisan officials, and community-based citizen commissions to draw nonpartisan voting boundaries that give diverse and minority constituencies a voice
- Seek alternatives to winner-take-all elections, such as proportional representation, instant runoff voting, single transferable voting and fusion voting (i.e., allowing two or more parties to nominate the same candidate)
- Allow people to vote electronically from homes, workplaces, and publicly accessible computers with passwords or social security numbers
- Publicly mediate and arbitrate disputes between candidates who violate ground rules, and censure, fine or disqualify those who are responsible
- Require multilingual ballots and poll workers fluent in local languages
- Require polling places to be wheelchair accessible and ballots to be printed in Braille, large print, and available in audio
- Eliminate the Electoral College and make the popular vote conclusive
- In the event of close outcomes, recount or repeat the process
- Continue to conduct dialogues on issues after elections regardless of who wins, and include losing candidates in newly elected governments
- Publicly evaluate the process afterwards and agree on better procedures for next time

© Kenneth Cloke

Potential Political Pitfalls in Mediation

1. *False Assumption of Symmetry:* It is mistaken to assume that oppressor and oppressed, occupier and occupied, powerful and weak are the same or that they can be treated as equally aggrieved.
2. *Tendency to Ignore Underlying Conflicts:* People in mediation often behave reasonably and want to reach agreements, and may ignore or avoid issues that could be disruptive.
3. *Acceptance of the Status Quo:* There is a tendency in mediation to accept and take for granted what is or have been the case for years, even when this is perceived by some to be wrong.
4. *Pressure to Compromise Principles:* People in mediation often feel pressured to surrender or compromise on points of principle in order to reach agreement, even when there are moral reasons not to.
5. *Dialogue as a Substitute for Action:* There is a tendency to substitute talk for action, especially for those who seek to change the status quo. Many see mediation as an end in itself, rather than as an effort to secure justice.
6. *Pressure to Renounce Allies and Practices:* Members of out-group and oppressed groups are often pressured to renounce violence, yet in-groups and oppressors are permitted to continue.
7. *Danger of Co-Optation:* Government authorities can misuse and co-opt mediation for their own purposes.

[Based on work by Palestinian Attorney Jonathan Kuttab.]

© Kenneth Cloke

Some Examples of Failed Mediations in Political Conflicts

- Slavery, the Compromise of 1820, the Compromise of 1850, the Fugitive Slave Act, and the Dred Scott decision
- The Kerensky government, the Bolsheviks, the British, and Russian participation in World War I
- Munich, Mussolini, Chamberlin, and the Mediation over Czechoslovakia
- "Go slow" advocates, Martin Luther King, Jr., and the Civil Rights Movement

How to Disagree – An Algorithm (1)

1. By creating an atmosphere, attitude and context of unconditional respect for each other, regardless of our opinions or positions on the issues
2. By being sure to include people who do *not* agree with each other
3. By reaching consensus on a set of ground rules or shared values that will guide our conversations
4. By agreeing to use skilled facilitators to keep conversations on track, and skilled mediators to intervene if necessary
5. By agreeing not to suppress anyone's experiences, reflections, ideas, beliefs, passions, or emotions, while at the same time focusing on the problem as an "it" rather than a "you," and doing our best not to personalize the problem
6. By asking questions that do not have a single correct answer, but invite people to offer their own unique answers
7. By consistently coming from a place of curiosity and learning, and probing to discover the deeper meaning of the issues to each person

How to Disagree – An Algorithm (2)

8. By acknowledging and validating everyone's deepest interests and concerns, intentions and experiences
9. By expressing gratitude and thanking people for their dissent and diversity, their courage and willingness to learn
10. By breaking large groups up into smaller groups where everyone can participate
11. By sharing responsibility for group process, and modeling openness and honesty, empathy and compassion, listening and acknowledgement
12. By asking each small group to select volunteers to perform important tasks, such as facilitation, recording, process observation, critique of content, presentation to other groups, time-keeping, etc.
13. By stopping the process when it isn't working, talking openly about what is not working, and agreeing on what can be done to improve it

© Kenneth Cloke

How to Disagree – An Algorithm (3)

14. By designing questions that will draw people on opposite sides into dialogue with each other
15. By asking people in small groups to brainstorm possible solutions and present them to each other
16. By reaching consensus on recommendations for action, and setting aside for future discussion all points on which there is no consensus
17. By seeking ways for those on opposite sides of an issue to agree on specific, practical steps that could improve their communications and relationships in the future
18. By inviting people to consider how they might continue and expand the dialogue
19. By applauding everyone's efforts and acknowledging their contributions
20. By eliciting feedback, jointly evaluating the process, and making improvements

© Kenneth Cloke

We will have to repent in this generation not merely for the vitriolic words or actions of the bad people, but for the appalling silence of the good people. We must come to see that human progress never rolls in on wheels of inevitability. It comes through the tireless efforts and persistent work of men … and without this hard work time itself becomes an ally of the forces of social stagnation. We must use time creatively, and forever realize that the time is always ripe to do right.

MARTIN LUTHER KING, JR.

ACKNOWLEDGMENTS

Our deepest thanks go to the generous staff and leadership at the Straus Institute for Dispute Resolution at Pepperdine University School of Law, in particular to Dean Sukhsimranjit Singh, who invited us to teach this course; and to the staff at 2U for their support and encouragement in videotaping and transcribing it.

We are also grateful to the many conflict resolution and consulting clients with whom we worked closely over four decades as consultants, mediators, facilitators, coaches, and external change agents. The problems and conflicts we encountered while working with them taught us many of the lessons we share in these materials.

Most importantly, we are immensely grateful to our inspiring students, from whom we learned each time we taught. We bow to you, and are hopeful that your curiosity and courage, your creativity and kindness, hard work and feedback, have made the course more exciting and useful for others.

ABOUT THE AUTHORS

Kenneth Cloke

Kenneth Cloke is Director of the Center for Dispute Resolution and for over forty years has been a mediator, arbitrator, facilitator, coach, consultant and trainer, specializing in communication, negotiation, and resolving complex multi-party disputes, including marital, divorce, family, community, grievance and workplace disputes, collective bargaining negotiations, organizational and school conflicts, sexual harassment, discrimination, and public policy disputes; and designing preventative conflict resolution systems.

His facilitation, coaching, consulting, and training practice includes work with leaders of public, private and non-profit organizations on effective communications, dialogue, collaborative negotiation, relationship and team building, conflict resolution, leadership development, strategic planning, designing systems, culture and organizational change.

His university teaching includes mediation, law, history, political science, conflict studies, urban studies, and other topics at several colleges and universities. He is or has recently been an Adjunct Professor at Pepperdine University School of Law; Southern Methodist University; USC, Global Negotiation Insight Institute at Harvard Law School; Omega Institute; Albert Einstein College of Medicine, Cape Cod Institute; University of Amsterdam ADR Institute; Saybrook University; Massey University (New Zealand).

He has done conflict resolution work in Armenia, Australia, Austria, Bahamas, Brazil, Canada, China, Cuba, Denmark, England, Georgia, Greece, India, Ireland, Japan, Mexico, Netherlands, New Zealand, Nicaragua, Pakistan, Puerto Rico, Scotland, Slovenia, Spain, Thailand, Turkey, Ukraine, USSR, and Zimbabwe. He is founder and first President of Mediators Beyond Borders.

He served as an Administrative Law Judge for the California Agricultural Labor Relations Board and the Public Employment Relations Board, a Factfinder for the Public Employment Relations Board, and a Judge *Pro Tem* for the Superior Court of Los Angeles. He has been an Arbitrator and Mediator for over forty years in labor management disputes, and is a member of a number of arbitration panels.

He received his B.A. from the University of California, Berkeley; J.D. from U.C. Berkeley's Boalt Law School; Ph.D. from U.C.L.A.; LLM from U.C.L.A. Law School; and did post-doctoral work at Yale University School of Law. He is a graduate of the National Judicial College and has taken graduate level courses in a variety of subjects.

Joan Goldsmith

Joan Goldsmith, M.A., H.L.D (Doctor of Humane Letters), has been an educator, coach, mediator, facilitator, and organizational consultant with higher education, government agencies, public and corporate sector organizations for over forty years, specializing in leadership development, diversity and organizational equity, organizational change, team building, strategic planning, organizational design and development, collaborative or win/win negotiation, and conflict resolution.

She was an administrator and faculty member at the Graduate School of Education at Harvard University, where she directed the Masters of Arts in Teaching program. She was founder of the Institute of Open Education at Newton College of the Sacred Heart and Director of the undergraduate and graduate school to lead it to become Cambridge College, for adult professionals. She taught high school in Boston and has been an adjunct professor and organizational consultant for UCLA, Cambridge College, USC, Antioch University, College of the Bahamas, and Southern Methodist University, and is currently teaching at Pepperdine University School of Law, Straus Institute on Dispute Resolution.

She has been a consultant to numerous corporate and educational clients in private practice and as a Principal and organizational consultant with the Index Group. In partnership with Sidney and Yulin Rittenberg, she was a founding Director of Index China, a consulting company dedicated to providing advice to U.S. corporations seeking to work in China.

She has been an executive coach and consultant on a variety of organizational issues to schools, health care organizations, universities, government agencies, and Fortune 100 companies in the United States and internationally. She has served on the Boards of Directors of Cambridge College, The Teachers Network, Deaf Self-help, Mar Vista Family Center, the Coro Foundation, and Theatre Comique.

She has coached executives and leaders at many corporations in fields including hospital and health care, aerospace, banks and financial institutions, entertainment companies, city and county governments, schools, universities and non-profits. She has advised on leadership development, collaborative negotiation and interest-based bargaining, mergers and acquisitions, strategic planning, change management, conflict resolution, and organizational development, among others.

She is a mediator and trainer in conflict resolution specializing in school, workplace and organizational conflicts.

In the international sector, she has worked in collaborative partnerships with indigenous leaders in the Southern Hemisphere, and has had numerous international professional engagements, including in Mexico, Brazil, Canada, Cuba, the Bahamas, Japan, China, India, Zimbabwe, the Netherlands, Belgium, Scotland and England.

INDEX

Index

A
abolish, 149, 181
abolished, 302
abolition, 301
abolitionism, 301
acceptance, 35, 49, 163, 215
accommodation, 27, 94, 163
accusation, 168, 174–175, 213, 215
accusations, 49
accustomed, 124
acquisitions, 339
adaptations, 151
addiction, 129, 217
addictive, 216
adjudicated, 291
adversarial, 26–27, 46, 49, 98, 118, 162, 166, 170, 173–174, 202–203, 215, 219, 257, 286–289, 291
aggression, 27, 93–94, 161, 163, 205
aggressively, 47
agreeable, 209, 213
allegations, 83
amygdala, 205
analysis, 91, 164, 247
analytically, 253

anarchy, 49, 87, 89, 91
antagonism, 44, 205, 258
antagonistic, 38, 46
apartheid, 284
apologies, 261
apology, 248, 263
appropriation, 159
arbitration, 213, 249, 337
arbitrator, 213, 336
asphyxiating, 290, 316
attitude, 31, 37, 43, 76, 88, 123, 125, 253, 303
attitudes, 25, 27, 116, 122, 128, 150
attorney, 250
authentic, 82, 93, 95, 111, 218, 223, 257
authenticity, 39, 82, 94, 290
authoritarian, 31, 53, 152, 161
authoritarianism, 31, 49
autocracies, 117, 257
autocracy, 26, 257, 283, 287, 303
autocratic, 127
avoidance, 27, 94, 161, 163

i

INDEX

B
bankruptcy, 120
barbarians, 286
barbarous, 290, 316
betrayal, 303
betrayed, 167, 191
betraying, 221
bilateral, 256
brainstorm, 208–209, 213, 256
brainstorming, 41, 208
bribery, 93
bureaucracies, 94–95, 115, 117, 291
bureaucracy, 85, 87, 89–90, 92–95, 111–112, 119, 257, 287, 291
bureaucrat, 95
bureaucratic, 46, 93–94, 97, 118, 290
bureaucrats, 203

C
capitalism, 27
capitalist, 27
caucus, 212
caucusing, 44, 212
censure, 291
CEO, 36, 87, 96
CFO, 29
chronic, 21, 23–27, 45, 85–86, 88, 91–92, 94, 96, 122, 206, 218, 247, 250–251, 254, 257, 259, 286–287, 302–303

CIA, 95
citizen, 25, 299, 302
citizens, 292–293, 297, 299
civility, 289, 315
classroom, 172, 258
climate, 26
clinic, 82
closedheartedness, 45
collaborate, 24, 166, 175
collaborating, 23, 259–260
collaboration, 28, 40, 88, 94, 118–119, 158–159, 162, 164, 166, 174, 178, 217, 258, 291
collaborative, 41, 47–49, 93–95, 97, 152, 159–163, 178, 205–206, 249, 255–256, 285, 290, 337–339
collaboratively, 83, 97–98, 207, 223, 254
collective, 255–256, 336
collegial, 161
combat, 202
communication, 39–41, 80, 83–86, 94, 116–117, 126–127, 151–153, 155, 162–164, 166, 176, 204, 220, 255, 257, 285, 296, 336
communications, 25, 34, 49, 86, 93, 95, 118, 150–151, 153, 215, 223, 225, 291, 304, 337
compassion, 24, 42, 88, 93, 170–171, 217

compensation, 85, 248, 259
competition, 27, 40, 124, 163, 177, 205, 322
complaint, 94
complaints, 248
compliance, 89, 91, 118, 222
confession, 168, 174–175
confidentiality, 44
conform, 125
conformity, 161
confrontation, 249
confronted, 23, 86, 251
Congress, 301
consensus, 49, 88, 94, 119, 152, 208–210, 216, 257–258, 289, 291, 296, 303
conservationists, 293
Constitution, 301
constitutionality, 302
consultant, 95, 122, 126, 154, 172, 221, 251, 336, 338–339
convene, 294
convened, 294
cooperation, 150
corporations, 22, 27–28, 76, 80, 93, 98, 286, 339
counseling, 97
counselor, 258
counterattack, 174–175
counterintuitive, 254
counterproductive, 28
courage, 88, 165, 175, 304, 335
covert, 163

coworkers, 36, 202
creativity, 74, 88, 94, 118, 149, 162, 335
crises, 89, 119
crisis, 89–90, 92, 166, 260, 294
crossroads, 46–47
curiosity, 88, 253–254, 260, 304, 335
customers, 78
cynical, 118
cynicism, 163

D

deceit, 118
decency, 289, 315
decentralization, 91
deceptively, 124
decisionmaking, 49, 286
deescalate, 40
defect, 92
defenders, 123, 137
dehumanizing, 171
democracies, 87, 117
Democracy, 95, 116, 300, 321–322
democracy, 82, 90, 95–96, 98, 114, 156–157, 257, 283, 286–289, 291, 322
democratic, 93, 96, 98, 113, 116, 127, 152, 161, 163, 291
demonization, 163, 170, 175, 178
dictatorial, 89

dictatorship, 49, 93
dignity, 76
dimensional, 49, 87
discrimination, 83, 219, 223, 337
diseases, 117
dishonesty, 217
disillusionment, 123
disintegration, 125, 139
disobey, 291
disorder, 119, 124–125, 139
disorganized, 37
disparities, 78
disparity, 26
disrespected, 175
disrespectful, 26
disruptive, 157
dissatisfaction, 225
dissent, 218, 291, 304, 321
diversity, 38, 74, 77, 91, 149–150, 152, 162, 164, 181, 218, 258, 289, 291, 304, 313, 338
divisive, 286–287
DNA, 297
dogmatism, 218
dominance, 27
dominate, 38, 206, 218
domination, 111–112, 205, 218, 286–287
dual, 166, 297
duality, 38
dysfunction, 27, 124
dysfunctional, 79, 158

E

earthquake, 89
ecological, 78
education, 76, 97, 130, 148, 172, 338
educational, 339
educator, 338
egalitarian, 178
ego, 173
Elections, 321
elections, 27, 287
elites, 92, 286–287
emergence, 50, 301
emergent, 73
emotion, 26, 43, 91, 297
emotional, 36, 39, 42–45, 47, 49–50, 152–153, 162, 167, 169–170, 173–174, 178, 201, 203–206, 218, 254
emotionally, 42–43, 49, 93
emotions, 42–43, 47, 49, 154, 162, 172, 202, 205–206, 254, 287
empathetic, 94, 218, 222, 295
empathetically, 223, 252
empathizing, 260
empathy, 39, 42, 76, 88, 93, 121, 170–171, 206, 215, 217–218, 220, 223, 288, 296–298, 300
empiricism, 313
employee, 90, 97, 222–223, 298
employees, 32, 85, 90, 165,

iv

222–223, 249, 252
enemies, 114, 123, 137, 170, 285, 290
enemy, 29, 46, 95, 202, 287, 321
engagement, 41, 118–119, 257, 285
entrepreneurs, 76
environmental, 26, 78, 96, 248
equalities, 78
equality, 291
equally, 30, 215, 223, 313
equity, 291, 338
ethics, 76, 96, 285, 287
ethos, 287
evaluators, 122
evildoer, 170
evolution, 25, 46, 75, 88, 117, 124, 176, 206, 291
evolutionary, 75, 91, 115–116, 297
exaggeration, 125

F

facilitation, 337
facilitator, 160, 255, 295, 336, 338
facilitators, 295, 300, 304, 335
Factfinder, 337
faculty, 31, 338
fairness, 222
fanatic, 284, 307
fanaticism, 313

farmers, 114
fascism, 31
fearbased, 205
feedback, 29–30, 75, 77, 85, 127, 152, 156, 160, 204, 208, 219, 221–222, 248, 251–252, 254, 295, 304, 335
finalized, 29
fiscal, 27
forgiveness, 45, 173
freedom, 48, 50, 91, 302, 322
fugitive, 301

G

gender, 150, 164, 177, 258, 304
genocide, 219, 249
gift, 38, 74, 162, 167, 191, 221
goal, 74, 90, 92, 94, 150, 160, 172, 216, 259, 291, 304, 312
goals, 22, 25, 40, 90, 94, 115, 155, 161, 163, 176, 209, 255, 287–288
government, 28, 80–82, 96, 111–112, 114, 155, 251, 294, 322, 338–339
grief, 42
grievance, 94, 205, 336
grievances, 248
grieving, 294
guilt, 42, 224

H

harassment, 86, 172–173, 204, 337
harmful, 126, 171
harmonious, 157
heartbased, 206
heartfelt, 50, 223, 288
helix, 297
hero, 129, 165, 169
heroes, 165
heterarchical, 161
heterarchy, 87
hierarchically, 84, 89
hierarchies, 87, 92, 94, 98, 116–117, 205
hierarchy, 44, 80, 84–87, 89–90, 92, 97, 111, 115–116, 118–119, 155, 162–163, 251, 257, 291, 304
historian, 31
holistic, 152
holistically, 253
Holocaust, 114
homeless, 82, 210
homelessness, 210
hostile, 42, 92, 95
hostility, 113, 171
humane, 113
humanity, 171
humanized, 163
humiliate, 218
humiliated, 173
humiliating, 203
humiliations, 172
hunger, 116
hypercompetition, 258
hypocrisy, 118

I

idealistic, 287
idealizations, 76
illness, 31, 53
imagination, 77
imbalance, 215
imbalances, 215
immigrant, 299
immigrants, 292–293, 297, 299
impasse, 49, 87, 113, 162, 204, 211–213
Impasses, 211
inclusion, 162, 258
inclusive, 152
indigenous, 151, 339
individualism, 91, 152
individualistic, 161
individuality, 94
individually, 48
individuated, 158
industrial, 286
inequalities, 177, 257
inequality, 26, 213, 257, 287, 289
inequities, 257
inequity, 26, 257, 287
inertia, 111
injustice, 284, 307
innate, 24
innovate, 201

INDEX

Innovation, 111
innovation, 27, 94, 97, 129, 161–162
innovative, 28, 74, 81, 97, 121, 166, 204, 216, 224
institution, 155, 159
institutional, 283, 285
institutionalize, 93
institutions, 287, 290–291, 339
integrate, 97, 293
integrated, 27, 90, 96, 139, 149, 181, 250
integration, 90, 139, 288
integrity, 36, 88, 94, 96, 121, 125, 127, 206, 223, 285
intellectual, 320–321
intelligence, 43, 47, 204, 206
interconnected, 96, 294
interconnections, 96
interestbased, 286, 339
internationally, 119, 165, 339
interpersonal, 74, 80, 300
interpretation, 38, 167, 172, 175, 177, 291
interpretations, 177, 291
interrelated, 293
interrelationship, 124, 139
intervention, 25, 41–42, 224–225
intimate, 38, 153, 300
intimidated, 120, 174, 214–215
intimidating, 28
intimidation, 31, 53, 205
intolerance, 44

introspection, 42, 205
intuition, 91, 223
intuitive, 254, 258
investigation, 127, 222
investment, 84
investments, 83
investors, 76
invitation, 175
irreconcilability, 313

J

JAMES, 321–322
janitor, 258
jointly, 176, 251, 255–256, 296, 304
judgment, 214, 223
judgments, 176
Judicial, 337
jurisdictional, 94
justice, 48, 170, 261, 322
justification, 171
justifications, 285, 313

K

kindness, 288, 335

L

Lastly, 257
Latino, 294
leader, 29–32, 91, 113–114, 118–122, 154, 156, 158, 163, 165, 173
leaders, 28–29, 32, 85, 111, 113–116, 119–122, 128, 158, 163, 248, 258–260,

293–294, 321, 337, 339
leadership, 25, 29, 32, 43,
    76, 84, 88, 90–91, 96,
    113–123, 127, 154–155,
    248, 288, 335, 337–339
learners, 122
litigation, 249, 252, 257

M

majority, 85, 286, 301–302
management, 27, 31, 43, 53,
    79, 88–90, 160, 221, 223,
    247, 249–250, 256, 258,
    260, 337, 339
managerial, 43, 88, 90
manipulate, 218, 291
marital, 336
marriage, 159, 255
mathematical, 35, 288
mechanics, 37
mechanism, 77, 92, 117,
    150, 248, 302
mediate, 81–82, 84,
    120–121, 207, 211, 216,
    218, 254, 301
mediated, 155, 218, 223, 301
mediating, 113, 201, 204,
    223, 303
mediation, 24, 32, 43, 77,
    81–84, 113, 115, 119–120,
    122, 149, 157, 163,
    172–173, 176–177, 201,
    204, 206, 211, 215–221,
    223–224, 248, 288,
    302–304, 337

mediations, 204, 300–301
mediative, 220
mediators, 29, 32, 42, 44,
    80, 113–114, 119–121,
    128, 151, 164, 174, 176,
    211–212, 215, 218–219,
    223, 248, 251, 285, 287,
    292–293, 300–301, 335
meditative, 82, 93, 204
mergers, 159, 339
merits, 313
Methodist, 337–338
methodologies, 35, 44–45,
    77, 252
methodology, 39–40, 44, 46,
    253, 257
methods, 23, 31, 53, 118,
    150, 161, 167, 171, 207,
    213, 215, 217–218, 285,
    289
microsurgery, 176
miscommunications, 26
misdemeanors, 251
misery, 50, 202
Mismanagement, 123
mission, 80, 83–84, 97, 155
MIT, 31–32
molecule, 99
monarchical, 290
monk, 123, 137
monologues, 257
morale, 250, 252
moralists, 290, 316
morality, 76, 285
motivation, 85, 94, 162, 252
mutuality, 293

viii

mutually, 209, 213
myth, 31
myths, 194

N

narcissism, 218
narrative, 166, 169, 174, 178
narratives, 178
negotiation, 27, 41, 49–50, 127, 159, 250, 255–257, 336–339
negotiations, 255–256, 336
neighborhood, 82, 98, 295, 299
neighbors, 82, 208
neutrality, 284, 307
newspapers, 290, 316
nonprofit, 82, 154
nonprofits, 22, 24, 80, 117
nonviolent, 204
normative, 156
norms, 151, 161

O

obedience, 49, 89, 91, 93, 118, 163, 291
observer, 128, 295
obstacle, 216–217
obstacles, 92–93, 163, 218
Officer, 81
officers, 85
ombudsperson, 83, 154
operative, 42
opponent, 47–48, 224–225
opponents, 34, 129, 149, 157, 181, 203, 288, 296
opposition, 38
oppressor, 215, 284, 307
oratory, 290, 316
organization, 21–22, 24–25, 27–28, 36–37, 44, 73–83, 85–91, 96–99, 115–122, 126–127, 151–152, 154–155, 157–158, 160–166, 172–173, 177–178, 210–211, 215, 217, 219, 222, 225, 247–252, 254–255, 258–260, 297–298, 300–301
organizational, 21, 23–25, 47, 77–80, 83–85, 87–88, 90–91, 95–96, 98, 113, 116, 118–119, 121–128, 151, 154, 156, 158–159, 164–165, 172, 177, 201–202, 204, 207–209, 216, 223–224, 247–249, 251, 255, 257–260, 283–285, 287–288, 296, 298, 303, 336–339
organizations, 21–23, 25–28, 31, 34, 36, 38–39, 43–48, 51, 73, 75–80, 85–93, 95–98, 113, 115–117, 119–124, 128–129, 150, 153, 155, 158, 160–163, 207–209, 215, 217–219, 221, 247–248, 250, 258–261, 283–285, 290–291, 296, 298,

INDEX

300–301, 337–339
outbreak, 149, 181
outcome, 41–42, 45, 49–50, 87, 116, 157, 159, 175, 225, 257, 285, 288
outcomes, 22, 34, 41, 91, 125, 127, 159, 161, 205, 221, 223, 285, 288
ownership, 85, 91, 118, 161–163

P

paradigm, 37, 124
paradox, 37–38, 91, 163, 252
paradoxical, 38, 91, 162, 253–254
paradoxically, 213
participants, 29, 294–296
participation, 82, 88–91, 119, 127, 257–258, 260, 291
participatory, 204
particle, 37
particles, 253
partnership, 258, 339
partnerships, 339
paternalism, 31, 53
pathos, 287
patriotism, 321
peacemakers, 321
peer, 44, 81, 177
performance, 222–223
perpetrator, 169–171
persecution, 292, 313
personalities, 219
personality, 26, 45, 219

persuasion, 287–288, 313
pluralism, 313
plurality, 288
polarity, 38
polarization, 125, 297
polarized, 216, 297
prejudice, 175, 304
President, 31, 113, 337
president, 119, 154, 165, 172–173, 289
presidents, 29, 83–85, 165
preventative, 21, 46, 129, 206, 247, 254, 337
prevention, 249
procedurally, 302
Propaganda, 320
propaganda, 291, 320–321
psychoanalyst, 30
psychology, 156
psychotherapy, 219

Q

quantum, 37, 253

R

racial, 177
rapid, 117, 122
rebellion, 91, 118
rebelliousness, 152
reciprocity, 159, 221
recognition, 31, 40, 53, 221–222
recommendations, 252, 295–296
reconcile, 48

reconciliation, 45
redesign, 248
redesigned, 259
redesigning, 155
reduction, 249, 257
reductionism, 126
reductionist, 253
refereeing, 204
reformer, 123, 137
reframe, 175, 178, 205
rehabilitated, 82
rehabilitation, 82
relationship, 22, 27, 37–39, 41, 47–48, 50, 73, 75, 78–79, 115–116, 120, 149, 152, 157, 164, 167, 178, 209–210, 212–214, 220, 253, 255, 283, 337
relationships, 27–28, 33–34, 73, 75, 78–79, 81, 94, 99, 113, 120, 127, 152, 156–157, 202, 206, 223, 225, 255, 258, 261, 288, 290, 292, 303–304
reparative, 48
repent, 305, 333
repercussions, 156
repetition, 26, 259
resent, 202, 227
resentment, 220
resistance, 28, 93, 125, 128–129, 289, 304
resistant, 26, 30
resolvable, 206
resolved, 25, 36, 42, 45, 121, 127, 150, 158, 217, 251, 283
resolving, 21, 25–26, 32, 77, 79, 83, 85, 155, 172, 205, 208, 213, 215, 252, 288, 336
respectful, 94, 176, 299, 303
respectfully, 115
responsibility, 27, 51, 76–77, 94, 96, 113–115, 118, 131, 157, 165, 169–170, 173, 177, 289, 315
responsive, 127
responsively, 252
restorative, 48, 170, 261
retributive, 48, 170
revengeful, 48
revolution, 93
revolutionaries, 290, 316
revolutionary, 123, 137
rhetoric, 205, 287, 290, 316
ritual, 165
rituals, 165
rivalry, 42
robotically, 210

S

sabotage, 95, 118
sabotaging, 95
salaries, 158
scaffolding, 248, 263
scary, 34
schizophrenic, 82
scientific, 35
scientist, 31
secrecy, 257, 287

secretarial, 80–81
security, 37, 91, 93, 156
selfcorrecting, 254
selfish, 216
selfishness, 163, 170
selfmanaging, 91, 97
Semitism, 303
Senate, 301
separation, 40, 94, 126, 160
separations, 93
siloed, 86
silos, 86–87, 90, 96, 151
sirens, 295
skills, 25, 28, 32, 34–35,
    43–44, 46–48, 81, 83–85,
    113, 120, 124, 126, 157,
    163, 177, 205–206,
    219–222, 285–286, 295
slavery, 301–302
sociologist, 93
soldier, 122
soldiers, 119
solution, 43, 49–50, 152,
    166, 174–175, 201, 208,
    212, 219, 254, 259, 288,
    313
solutions, 38, 41, 48, 74,
    152, 166, 204, 208,
    212–213, 253–257, 260,
    286, 289, 294, 296, 313
sovereignty, 287
spiritual, 44–45, 156
spirituality, 206
spokespeople, 122
spokesperson, 298, 301
spouses, 81

stagnation, 305, 333
statesman, 285
statistics, 39
status, 78, 85, 87, 92, 94,
    115, 122, 162, 215–216,
    257, 304
stereotype, 171, 175, 179
stereotyped, 172, 175
stereotypes, 172–173, 178,
    298
stereotyping, 125, 171, 214
storyteller, 170
storytelling, 169, 172, 199,
    255, 288
strategists, 122
structural, 92
subcomponents, 225
subcultures, 151
subdivide, 91, 212
subdivided, 85
subgroup, 178
subgroups, 178
subjugation, 159
subordination, 93, 205
substitute, 215, 257
substituting, 111
summarize, 77, 81, 174, 256
summarizing, 204
superficial, 38, 174, 297
supervising, 88
supervision, 90
supervisors, 85, 90
supplementing, 224
supporters, 122
suppress, 38, 43, 258, 304
suppression, 159

Supreme, 301–302
survival, 89, 116
symbols, 150
symmetrically, 297
symmetry, 215, 288
synchronously, 90
synergies, 258
synergistic, 152
Synergy, 288
synergy, 88, 118, 250
syntheses, 92, 288
synthesis, 91, 170, 297
systematize, 22
systemic, 23–24, 45–46, 91–92, 126, 251, 259, 287, 303

T

tactics, 253
teacher, 258
Teachers, 339
teachers, 80, 206
teamwork, 81–82, 90–91, 161, 260
Technology, 31, 119
technology, 27–28, 80–81, 83–84, 99, 116–117, 157–158
teenage, 49, 176
teenager, 49–50
tension, 25, 155, 293
termination, 118, 221–222
territory, 224
timekeeper, 295
timeline, 165

tolerance, 26, 161–162, 288–289, 313, 315
tolerate, 313
tradition, 34, 152
trainer, 336, 339
traitors, 287
transcendence, 24
transform, 45, 83, 93, 174, 284, 307
transformation, 24, 118, 251
transformational, 87, 91–92, 257
transformations, 258
transformative, 206
transformed, 29, 166
transforming, 167, 173
transforms, 36, 206
transitional, 119
transparency, 91, 204, 251
transpire, 87
transportation, 116
trauma, 218
triangle, 169
triangulates, 205
triplicate, 92
tyrannical, 111–112
tyranny, 111–112

U

unconditional, 223, 260, 303
unconditionally, 221
unconscious, 248, 263
unemployed, 114
unequal, 27, 117
unequally, 216

INDEX

unexpressed, 42
unfulfilled, 124
uniformity, 91
unimaginable, 166
unionized, 94
unity, 48, 77, 250
unjust, 170
unmitigated, 123
unpredictable, 33–34, 127
unresolved, 41, 43, 118, 126, 158
unsolvable, 166, 219
unspoken, 24, 51, 76, 154, 173, 177
unthinking, 291
unwilling, 26, 211, 214, 221
unworthy, 286
usefulness, 37
utmost, 149, 181

V

validate, 304
validity, 302
vengeance, 284, 307
venture, 31, 53
vice, 29, 83–85, 88, 165
victim, 169–170, 214, 221
victimization, 163, 170, 175, 178
victimize, 47, 174, 288
victory, 170, 206, 259, 292, 313
videotaping, 29, 335
villain, 165, 169–170
villains, 165

violation, 36
violence, 249, 284, 286
virtues, 288
vision, 80, 83–84, 90, 97, 120, 124, 127–128, 130, 148, 155, 161–162, 209–210, 255, 260
visionary, 90
visions, 120, 172
voluntarily, 294

W

wealth, 216, 257, 304, 322
wealthy, 286
weather, 24, 217
web, 96, 117
webs, 96–98, 116–119
willingly, 296
willingness, 123, 128, 170, 204, 217, 256, 261, 304
winner, 286, 290
winwin, 206
wisdom, 34, 206
workload, 178
workplace, 24, 27, 30, 35–36, 43–44, 50, 116, 204, 207, 299, 336, 339
workplaces, 23, 25, 76, 259
workshop, 155

Y

youth, 295

www.ingramcontent.com/pod-product-compliance
Lightning Source LLC
Chambersburg PA
CBHW021335230426
43666CB00006B/302